A RECIPE FOR DISASTER

Cooking Up a Big Italian Idea

THE COOKUCINA COOKS
Tam Courtenay and Lia Rocchiccioli

A RECIPE FOR DISASTER

Cooking Up a Big Italian Idea

by

Stephen Phelps

 I am a writer and former TV producer living in Le Marche, Italy. For the BBC and C4 in the United Kingdom, I produced *Rough Justice, Watchdog* and *Dispatches*. With an MA in Creative Writing from University of East Anglia I write both books and radio plays. I also work on occasional major documentary series for Al Jazeera TV in Qatar, London and DC.

Drayton Park Publishing
London, England

First Edition July 2017

ISBN: 978-1-9997776-0-9

stephenphelps@blueyonder.co.uk

Contents

A RECIPE FOR DISASTER

DIGESTIVO

ON THE NIGHT OF August 23rd 2016 the world described in these pages fell apart. At 3.30 in the morning we woke to find our seven hundred year old house shaking like a rag doll, a deep, dark roaring coming up from the depths of the earth below. Our little Italian hill town of Sarnano was being rattled by the earthquake that struck the nearby village of Amatrice. We survived (*grazie dio*) but our home did not. We had to move into "temporary" accommodation, where we now expect still to be living in 5 years' time. You won't have heard much about the series of earthquakes that have continued to rock this area because nobody has been killed in the ones that followed. Some of them have been bigger even than that first, shattering night-time blow that killed over 300 people in Amatrice, Accumoli, Arquata and Pescara del Tronto. There were two on one Wednesday night in October, followed by an even bigger one on the Sunday morning. No-one died because we were all "ready" for them. Not that you are ever really "ready" for your frying pan to jump off the cooker, or for the walls of your house to wobble like blancmange. But we *were* ready in the sense that we knew to run as soon as the tremors started. An earthquake, you see, is not a single event – it takes time, anything from a few seconds to several minutes depending on its magnitude. But if you are "ready" (and lucky) you'll be able to get out of the house before the collapsing starts. Trouble is, that first tremor can be anything from a minor, hardly perceptible shimmer to the beginnings of a major disaster – you just don't know. And here's the rub... we are living in a *swarm* of earthquakes. Since August the 23rd there have been (are you sitting down?) more than 60,000 quakes greater than magnitude 2.0. If you count *any* magnitude there have been well over 100,000. And remember, each time the shaking begins you have no idea how it will continue. Is this just a wobble, or is it the start of the one that can kill you, your dog, your family and reduce your life to rubble?

I called this Preface DIGESTIVO because it's the last act of the meal I am about to take you through. Here in Italy the *digestivo* is generally a *grappa* – a fiery slug of something to help the food go down. But in this case it's what we all turned to at four in the morning on that sunny August dawn when the whole town assembled in the main square and Basilio's bar opened up even earlier that usual. In the case of this book the *digestivo* comes first because it's what you need to know in order to see this book (and the accompanying videos) in its proper context. They are a window on a simple life in one of the most beautiful places you will ever see. A pleasant, uncomplicated world where small things assumed large proportions, little things that are still central to our lives but are now overshadowed by the continuing threat of devastation on an unimaginable scale.

Hopefully the swarm will have stopped by the time you read this, and life here in Le Marche will have begun the long journey back to normality. But for the moment, let me take you back to those innocent times and let's begin a meal which will take you on a culinary journey through life in a spectacularly beautiful part of rural Italy.

We'll start, as always, with an Antipasto.

ANTIPASTO

THIS IS THE STORY of an attempt to re-write the laws of physics. Or at least the laws of the world of television. It's about a crazy attempt to make a television series on no money and a lot of enthusiasm. Enthusiasm for a spectacularly beautiful part of Italy, the wonderful people of the region and their matchless food. It's a quixotic tale of trying to achieve something against all the odds, then ending up in a whole different place.

Ten years earlier I had given up my job in television. Well, strictly speaking I gave up making it, as a Director, and settled for the cozier option of becoming a part-time Executive Producer. I had been promoted. Which meant I had stopped doing anything really creative in favor of telling other people what to do (and what they had done wrong, of course). An Executive Producer is rather like a dentist - everybody has to have one, but you'd rather you could do without them. Working in television had stopped being fun and become more of a daily chore. But I missed the creativity. I can't paint, sing or play a musical instrument, and when I got a job directing TV films it was the first time I had tasted the joys of real creativity. So, like a moth to a flame, when the opportunity came to set up a small team to film an Italian cookery series in the medieval Italian hill town that I now call home, I just couldn't resist.

The original aim was to make a conventional TV series, exploiting the lovely region of Le Marche as a backdrop to some simple Italian recipes. Perhaps for the BBC, or Britain's Channel 4. The end product, the dish that finally emerged from the oven as it were, is this book, and the TV series that accompanies it, now available online.

You can find it on Amazon Video Direct, Google Play and, hippest of all, even iTunes.

http://amzn.eu/19rlEnz

http:/bit.ly/2sOlKme

http://apple.co/2s5RAgo

We have traveled a long way from the original conception. This book, the story of the making of the series we called *Cookucina,* is a vehicle for the highs and lows, the laughs and frustrations of living as an Englishman in rural Italy. Hopefully the book stands up on its own, but if you take the trouble to connect with the TV series you will be able to see many of the events for yourself, as they happened. You'll get to know the characters in even more depth than I can convey in these pages, you will see for yourself some of the beauty of Le Marche, you will learn how to cook some simple yet unusual recipes and you will get to know the joys and frustrations of life in Italy's rural hill-towns.

I hope you enjoy the strange journey that followed from our Big Italian Idea, an idea that grew out of nothing into... but no, I'm getting ahead of myself.

PRIMO

The Ideone

IT ALL STARTED at the dinner table. Of course. Lia had invited us. She had *un ideone* that she wanted to discuss with us - a big idea. Intriguing. But any kind of idea would have done really because Lia is a fabulous cook, and an evening spent in her delightful medieval house would mean a seemingly endless stream of delicious food emerging from the kitchen, washed down with a glass or two of *Rosso Piceno* and capped with a *caffè corretto* - an espresso fortified with a healthy dash of Sergio's home-made grappa. We were not disappointed. Highlight of that particular evening as I recall was a dish of slow-roasted tomatoes - seasoned with herbs and orange zest, drizzled with extra virgin olive oil and baked in the oven. It looked like it had come straight from the pages of a high-quality cookbook. "No, no - it's really simple" she told me. Here's how it's done.

SLOW ROASTED TOMATOES

- *500 g. Tomatoes*
- *salt*
- *1 clove garlic*
- *a sprig of thyme*
- *basil*
- *1 ½ tablespoons of sugar*
- *grated zest of 1 orange*
- *extra virgin olive oil*

Wash the tomatoes and cut them in half. Cover the bottom of a baking sheet with greaseproof paper. Place the tomatoes, squeezed tightly together with the cut side up, add salt and sprinkle with the chopped herbs and grated orange zest, sprinkle with sugar, drizzle with olive oil and bake at 100 degrees for two hours.

I can't remember much else about that evening, other than the *ideone*. Tam and I had met Lia some months earlier and we'd become firm friends. We'd eaten whenever we could in the little restaurant they ran in a nearby town. In London or New York *Piatto Ricco* would have been the perfect Italian restaurant. The little gem you discover tucked away in the back streets of Soho or Little Italy, run by a couple who speak barely any English but don't need to because their simple but delicious food does the talking for them. But in Le Marche, the little-known hilly region on the Adriatic side of Italy's Apennine mountains, *Piatto Ricco* was a worker's cafe. Or what passes for one in rural Italy. It was a delightful little place, dark woodladder-back chairs jostling for space among the bright gingham tablecloths. Old cooking implements (or were they instruments of torture?) hung from the oak beams as Sergio and Lia bustled in and out of the kitchen with today's home-made dishes - they're not big on menus in this part of the world.

Piatto Ricco was always full. It sat in the middle of what you would have to call an industrial estate (Italy is a country where they still make things), though in this land of style even industrial estates look classy. The surrounding warehouses and offices guaranteed *Piatto Ricco* a regular and hungry clientele. But there's only so much you can charge for lunch in what amounted to the works canteen of several local factories, so Lia and Sergio worked a fearsome day just to keep their heads above water. Sergio began the day with a trip to the *orto*, his allotment, to harvest today's vegetables, while Lia started on the bread she made fresh each morning. *Piatto Ricco* was a 45 minute drive from the little medieval hill-town of Sarnano where we all live, and they needed to get there early to set up for lunch and to get some of her slow-cooked dishes under way. With no air-conditioning in the kitchen, in the height of summer temperatures there in the engine-room reached into the high 50s. Paola came by each day to help with the waitressing, but apart from that Sergio and Lia did everything themselves. By the time the last customers had left and everything had been cleared, washed and stowed back in its proper place, it was late afternoon. On the drive back to Sarnano Lia would start to plan tomorrow's dishes - some of which would need advance preparation before the day's work was out. That's it - no evening opening, even though the Soho version of *Piatto Ricco* would have been packed out two or three times over, making someone a small fortune. But things are different here in Le Marche.

It was exhausting. And Lia had had enough. But what to do next? Lia has such a love of food and cooking that she'd probably just cook and hand it out to strangers if she wasn't doing it for a living. That was one of the joys of living just 20 meters from her front door. Tam and I were constantly being invited to eat with them *all'improvviso*. I'm a pretty good cook myself, but I'm always prepared to call time on whatever I'm preparing when one of Lia's invitations arrives. And somehow she seemed to be able to manage to rustle something up even when she'd been hard at it in the restaurant since breakfast time.

My partner Tam, on the other hand, does NOT cook. Cooking is something other people do. Her repertoire, painstakingly built up over several decades, is either red goop or green goop. "Goop" here is not meant as a pejorative term, merely a description of what happens when many different ingredients are thrown together in the same pan and mixed up over a slow heat for the best part of a hour. And the red and green versions are surprisingly different, dependent, I think, on the presence or not of tomatoes. Both are very tasty (as a rule), but the variations begin to run out after a while. On occasions when I've been sick in bed for a few days, or injured my chopping hand, we've had red, red, green. Or sometimes green, green, red. Lia, as you might imagine, was not too impressed, and when it was Tam sick in bed, and I was out of the country, there would be a ring at the doorbell and when Tam staggered to the door she would find a plastic bag containing a full three course meal, and Lia nowhere to be seen. That's what I mean by handing it out. She seemed to enjoy being Tam's personal soup kitchen. And yes, it has crossed my mind that maybe sometimes Tam was feigning illness. Not that Lia would care.

So anyway, that evening we had guessed that the *ideone* would be something to do with food - and we were right.

Smart Names and Ryanair

Tam and I had discovered Le Marche eight years earlier. We'd both been working in television in London. Tam had just finished researching a difficult documentary about the 2003 invasion of Iraq. She was mentally and physically exhausted and I could see she was in need of a bit of a break. And she had come home with an idea. The director of the program had apparently asked if we would like to come and stay in the house he had bought in the Italian countryside. Tuscany? I asked. Umbria, maybe? That, I'm sad to say, was about the limit of my understanding of the Italian countryside. A couple of decades earlier I had had two fabulous holidays in a Tuscan villa so perfect that it featured on the front cover of a Sunday newspaper's magazine special on "Chiantishire". That's it, I thought. I've done Italy. It'll never get any better than that. But I was wrong.

When Chris - the director - told us his new house was in Le Marche I was bemused. I'd never even heard of it. I knew about Calabria. And Puglia. And Basilicata. I even knew there were different types of Mafia depending on which of these regions you were in. So they would be bound to have their own Mafia in this place, wouldn't they? Probably extorting protection money from people trying to scratch a living running their small, old-fashioned family businesses. That's it. That's the image I conjured up for myself. Because it couldn't be at all like Tuscany could it? Otherwise we would have heard of it. And lots of lawyers and city types would be going there for their holidays. No, Le Marche was a sort of giant industrial estate. A dreary flat plain, a sort of endless industrial strip mall. With *mafiosi*. And it was raining. In my imagination that is. I was wrong. Again.

I guess we owe it all to Ryanair really. Back in the 1990s Irish entrepreneur Michael O'Leary came up with the bright idea of opening up new routes into Europe to places where they wanted to encourage tourism. There were plenty of small airports, sometimes ex-military but big enough to land a 737, dotted across the continent, where the landing fees would be small or non-existent and you might be able to pick up a subsidy from the regional authorities. One such place was the *Aeroporto Raffaello Sanzio* at Falconara just outside Ancona. There should have been a clue in there for me. *Raffaello Sanzio*, Raphael - among the greatest of all Renaissance painters. Because in Italy they have an enchanting habit of naming airports after local figures who made their mark in history. Genoa is the *Aeroporto Cristoforo Colombo*, Perugia is the *Aeroporto San Francesco d'Assisi*, both of whom left their mark (in rather different ways) on the world we now live in.

Ryanair had started flying into Ancona so that now (and remember I'm talking about before the global crash) you could get from London (London Stansted actually - 45 minutes from London by train) to Le Marche in a couple of hours. And the British began to do that, a few at a time. First discovering a wonderful place for a holiday or long weekend, but then, increasingly, looking to cash in the over-inflated values of their houses in South-East England and buying into the Italian dream. That's what Chris had done. And that, eventually, is what we did.

The Italian Dream

Like all dreams, the Italian dream is not quite what it seems. It was a lovely golden autumn when we first arrived. Warm sunshine lighting up trees in such a huge variety of colors they would not disgrace Vermont. A brisk nip in the air when you stepped into the shadows, and just cool enough in the evenings that the restaurants had their roaring wood fires lit (there's a lot of wood round here). Now, though, as I write in January, it is minus 11 outside and there's four inches of snow making the cobbles in the old town treacherous to walk on, let alone drive. In fact the old town, and by old I mean 13th century, is comparatively easy to get around in these conditions. But most people who buy into the dream do so during a holiday in the hot summer months when the temperatures are regularly in the mid to high 30s. They fall in love with an ancient stone-built farmhouse, tastefully renovated so as to preserve all the original features, and all they have to do is add a swimming-pool so they can cool off. Then they go back home to work, and soon decide that they've had enough of the rat-race, and "Hey, let's do it. Let's cash everything in and go and LIVE in Le Marche." Only to find that when it's minus 11 in the old town, it's minus 15 up in the hills. And these are serious hills.

Sarnano is in the foothills of the Sibillini mountains, about half way down the Apennine range which runs down the spine of Italy. The Italian "boot" is basically a fold in the earth's crust that juts up out of the Mediterranean, so the mountains are pretty dramatic, seeming to thrust up out of nowhere. There are something like thirty peaks over 2,000 meters in the Sibillini alone, and our little town itself sits right underneath them at 539 meters. That's eighteen hundred feet in old money, and it's quite a bit colder up here than at sea level. It can be hotter, too, in the summer. Not <u>actually</u> hotter, but the air is so clear that direct sunlight is really fierce, whatever the time of year. Minus 11 today, but just three days ago we were sitting outside *Bar Casciotti* in shirtsleeves. Until the shadows crept over.

My first full winter here came as a bit of a shock. I had never quite understood, when I was coming here in the summer, why Sarnano sold itself as a ski resort. Then, one particularly chilly February day, it started to snow. And it didn't stop for eleven days. The snow was up to two meters deep. *Bar Casciotti,* that's our favorite cafe in the *Piazza della Liberta,* had to cut trenches through the snow so you could get through to the rickety old chairs where we were used to sitting under the awning to escape a blistering sun.

BAR CASCIOTTI IN FEBRUARY

They're good with snow round here though. They understand it. As soon as it starts they'll have the snow-plows out clearing and gritting the main roads - especially the one up to Sassotetto and the ski-lifts. It's a strange place to ski. In the Alps or the Rockies you pretty much see snow-covered mountains everywhere you look. But here, you drive about 20 minutes out of town up to the slopes and when you get onto the chairlift the first thing you notice are the fantastic views away towards the Adriatic sea, across the foothills to a coastal plain where people might well be sitting outside cafes in a t-shirt. Though not that particular February, of course.

So if you're going to come and live here you had better be prepared for a climate that varies wildly from one extreme to the other. Maybe that's what most people are used to, but I come from the UK where the weather is pretty much fifty shades of grey - but much less exciting. Here in Le Marche we get all four seasons, and each of them has a lot to offer. In spring, for instance, the mountains suddenly sprout the most extraordinary range of wild flowers even while the snow still lies thick on protected, north-facing slopes. You can sign up for an orchid walk if you're that way inclined, with a specialist who will help you find some of almost forty varieties that flourish in the Sibillini.

Pian Grande

About an hour and half to the south of us there's an extraordinary place called the *Pian Grande* (the big plain). It's high in the mountains, something like 1,400 meters, so that you climb up through the tree-line into rugged, bare grassland before bursting through a narrow pass to find a huge plain, almost three miles long, spread out before you as flat as a pancake. In the winter it's a hostile environment - so much so that the one habitation, a tiny little town called Castelluccio perched on top of the one outcrop of rock, is pretty much abandoned in the winter. Go to Castelluccio out of season and you feel like you've stumbled onto the abandoned set of a spaghetti western (maybe this is where Sergio Leone made his western masterpieces? No, that was Spain, wasn't it...). But in the spring Castelluccio comes alive again because that's when the visitors start to come - in pursuit of the most spectacular display of wild-flowers you could imagine.

Castelluccio is famous in Italy for producing some of the country's most sought-after lentils. It's a crop they've been growing here since pre-Roman times, and it is clear that the strange topology of the plain produces the conditions for the perfect lentil. The *Pian Grande* is a karstic plain. Karst topography is a landscape formed in areas of soluble rocks like limestone, dolomite, and gypsum. The dissolving of these rocks over the millennia has produced a landscape of underground drainage systems with sinkholes, disappearing streams, underground caves and reappearing springs. And lentils. Lentils from Castelluccio and nearby Norcia can be found in good food shops all over Italy, and visitors to the town will always go home with a bag or two of slightly over-priced local lentils. But that's not, in the main, why they come.

PIAN GRANDE

For most of the year the pasture of this vast, billiard-table flat plain is a chromatic monotone of greeny-brown (lentils are delicious but not much to look at). But each year between late May and July this plain plain is transformed by what the locals call *La Fioritura*, which roughly translates as The Flowering. For a few short weeks, which will vary according to the precise climatic conditions of that particular year, the monotony is broken by a vibrant mosaic of wild-flowers in colors ranging from bright yellow to deep red ochre. Mosaic is maybe not quite the right word, because the local method of cultivating the lentils produces a sort of strip-farming effect, so that when viewed from Castelluccio, a hundred and fifty meters or so above the plain, you have the sensation of looking out on a patchwork quilt made of long strips of brightly colored material. Get down into the fields themselves and the feeling is quite different as you'll mostly find yourself standing in the middle of a sea of one particular flower. And as you walk, the color of the sea changes according to the dominant species - gentianellas, narcisi, purple violets, poppies, buttercups, daffodils, clover, shamrock - the variety is astounding. A real highlight of Spring in Le Marche.

LA FIORITURA

Food, wine and Italian time-keeping

The slow-cooked tomatoes came out of the kitchen on a huge baking tray. Great succulent tomato halves, topped with a crust of baked herbs, breadcrumbs and orange zest. Bigger by far than the regimented, uniform billiard balls you get offered back home even in the *best* supermarket (*Italian* according to the label on the vacuum-pack, but unrecognizable to someone like Lia). Bigger, and misshapen, these guys would have been rejected by the supermarkets, for sure. How could they possibly fit into the perfectly hemispherical indents in the plastic tray?

And what a feast these *Marchigiana* tomatoes turned out to be. An explosion of flavor, they simply melted in the mouth. Really, I mean it. It's not just a figure of speech. I got that for the first time that evening. And there was the *Rosso Piceno* - a deliciously robust red wine from the vineyards a little to the south of us, where the *Piceni* were making this wine in pre-Roman times. We often get asked about the local wines - which ones come from Le Marche? So that people can look out for them in their local vintners and surprise their friends at dinner parties with "this lovely little Italian red, so hard to find it's almost a secret". Well, yes they're very hard to find. That's because they're almost all drunk here, by the locals. These wines come from small family-owned vineyards, and they're not churning out industrial quantities for the export market - they're looking to make a decent wine and a decent living. That's the way of life here in Le Marche. It can be exasperating at times.

Take our *geometra* for example. A *geometra* is someone you have to have if you're going to buy and renovate an old house in Italy. He's a sort of cross between an architect and a project manager. And he's pretty much bound to be a "he". I've never met a female one - the Italians are a bit traditional like that - but that's another story. Meetings with Luigi (he's our *geometra*) almost always take place in a bar, over a *caffé* or an *aperitivo*. Even when you try to fix a meeting in his office because today is going to be really businesslike, it somehow always gets transferred to the bar, because his previous meeting (*aperitivo?*) has overrun, or he has to meet his cousin to collect something for his mother. By the way, these places are called bars, but they'd be known anywhere else as a cafe. They open at about 6 in the morning and pretty soon they'll be crowded out with workers getting their hearts started with an espresso and a slice of *ciambellone*. Sometimes the espresso will be "corrected" even at that time in the morning, especially if you're on your way to work in the sunflower fields. These bars don't close for lunch (as does everything else in Italy), and they keep on going right through the evening till two, three, four o'clock in the morning. For a long time I thought Basilio, who runs *Bar Casciotti,* must be some kind of medical miracle who could survive on two hours sleep a night, or had an identical twin, but in fact he's just the eldest of a family trio, sharing the load with his brother Alfredo and sister Donella. When I say sharing, though, this is rural Italy, and it always seems to be Donella who's rushing in and out with a tray of coffees or *prosecchi,* while one brother or other is holding court behind the bar.

Anyway, it was a Thursday, market day, when we were scheduled to meet Luigi the *geometra*. And on Thursday the main

Piazza, we knew, would be heaving with the wives of the local *contadini* who had come into town in search of a bargain. Which always strikes me as odd, because the stuff is exactly the same as it was last week. Reminds me of Dr. Johnson's observation on second marriages which, he said, represent "the triumph of hope over experience". But still, a lot of people do it, don't they? Marry for a second time, I mean. That particular Thursday was warm and sunny, and the business we had to transact with Luigi was pretty straightforward, so it was the perfect day for a meeting outside Basilio's bar in the sunshine, and that's what we'd agreed in a text exchange with Luigi over breakfast a couple of hours earlier. Eleven o'clock, he had suggested. Perfect for us, as it's just about the latest you can order a cappuccino without getting a funny look. Cappuccino is a breakfast drink to the Italians, and that's that. Why would you drink it after 11.30? In fact, we disgrace ourselves regularly in the eye of the locals - all the more so because Tam likes to drink *caffè latte,* and that's just a drink for children - whatever the time of day. That day we flew in to Ancona for the first time, our director friend Chris picked us up at the airport, and before we hit the road he suggested we get a drink. Tam ordered a *latte*, just as she would have done in London. And that's what she got - milk. Lesson number one, things are different here.

In fact breakfasts themselves are very different too. When we first started coming here my favorite hotel was a slightly shabby old villa at the edge of town. It was cheap - the price list seemed to have been printed in the 1950s and the prices must have been stuck there ever since. Mind you, the rest of the hotel hadn't changed much in the last sixty years either. At breakfast my first morning I asked for **caffè** *latte* (I had learned my lesson) and after about five minutes the *padrona* produced some of the most spectacular coffee I have ever drunk. A nice fresh *cornetto* (a croissant to you and me) to go with it, and I'd have had the perfect Italian breakfast. But no such thing was in evidence. Only some dry cakes in cellophane wrappers. I opened one. It more or less crumbled in my hands. The *padrona* arrived with more coffee, so I enquired after something fresh to eat - a *cornetto,* maybe? Sorry, she said, and she looked genuinely upset that I was underwhelmed by what all her Italian guests obviously expect to find on their breakfast table.

"Let me see" she said and disappeared back into the kitchen. Moments later I glanced out of the window to see her scuttling off down the drive, and in a few minutes she was back with no *cornetti*, but profuse apologies and a fresh-from-the-oven *ciambellone,* a kind of giant sponge doughnut. It was delicious, almost as good as the one Lia would make for us in Episode 4 of the TV series that would be the end product of the Big Italian Idea. We're getting ahead of ourselves a bit here, but it's as good a place as any to learn how to make a *ciambellone.*

GRANDMA IRMA'S CIAMBELLONE

- *5 eggs*
- *flour of the same weight as the eggs*
- *sugar of the same weight as the eggs*
- *a small glass of peanut oil*
- *a pinch of salt*
- *a teaspoon of baking powder*

Weigh the eggs, beat them well with the same weights of sugar and flour together with the baking powder. Add the oil and mix well. Butter a baking mold and lightly dust the buttered surface with flour. Transfer the mixture into the mold and bake at 160 degrees for about 40 mins.

But we're getting ahead of ourselves again here. We've still got to meet up with Luigi, the *geometra*. Tam and I arrived in the square fifteen minutes ahead of time so we could relax over our cappuccino and what we now know is a **caffé** *latte* by ourselves for half an hour. Yes, half an hour, because Luigi slots nicely into an Italian stereotype of never *quite* being on time. But 11.15 came and went, and no Luigi. Another fifteen minutes, still no sign. Half an hour. So we phoned. "Oh, so sorry," said Luigi, "I'm in the mountains". He had simply decided the day was too gorgeous to miss the chance to get up into the wildflowers, and whatever he had to discuss with us could probably wait. And he was right.

Return to the Ideone (Part 1)

Sat in Lia's house, the four of us round the big oak table, we were closing in on the end of the meal and she still hadn't got round to the big idea yet. Like I said, we'd worked out it it was going to be something to do with food, but so far she'd said nothing. I wasn't bothered, though, because I was too busy enjoying the meal. The slow-cooked tomatoes had been simply delicious. They really aren't difficult to make by the way - provided you've got a regular supply of tomatoes from Le Marche. We asked Sergio once what the secret was. How did he manage to grow them so huge yet still bursting with flavor. Reluctantly, and after much cajoling, he let us in on it. Water, he said, and sunshine. And the earth. That's it - water, sunshine and the earth. We know there's plenty of sunshine here - high in the mountains and well to the south of the French Riviera. But water? There's plenty of that too, an endless supply rushing down from the Sibillini mountains to ancient, elaborately decorated iron fountains dotted all round town. Some of them have push buttons, like some sort of medieval water cooler, but others just sit there pouring water all day long, winter or summer, rain or shine.

And the water's pretty special too. The stuff that comes out of the town's municipal water supply is so good I don't personally bother going to the fountains. But many of the locals have their favorite water supply - often out of town up in the foothills where the gushing fountains are fed directly from one of the many tumbling streams that cut deep gorges into the rolling countryside - all part of the local inhabitants' protection against outside invaders, as armies from ancient Rome to Hitler's Panzer divisions could testify. On a Saturday morning you'll find queues of cars at these roadside fountains as families load plastic *bidoni* of water into the trunk of the car until it can take no more. And that's just for water. They take this food and drink stuff seriously round here.

Everyone has their favorite source, but there's one that's really special, one that has left a big mark on the town. In the late 1920s Mussolini's government was trying to revitalise an economy that had been hit particularly hard by the Peace following the Great War. Despite fighting alongside the victorious Allies against the Central Powers, Italy had gained precious little from the Treaty of Versailles. And the huge losses she had sustained fighting the Austrians had taken a terrible toll on the workforce of what was still a largely agricultural country. The global slump that followed brought Italy to its knees. Fertile ground for Mussolini's strange brand of nationalism that grew from genuine socialist roots. In 1929 public works were a key to lifting Italy out of the doldrums. That's when the local government here in Le Marche decreed there should be a new road built to connect Sarnano with Gualdo, the nearest of the many small hill-towns that decorate the local countryside. Quite why, I am not sure, because to this day there's nothing much goes on in Gualdo. But this project produced a huge, and totally unexpected bonus.

The Spa

The biggest obstacle to getting from Sarnano to Gualdo is the *Rio Terra*. It is one of two rivers that run down from the mountains skirting either side of the old city walls before joining up on their way to the Adriatic Sea. With their characteristic deep gorges they formed a natural defense during the middle ages when Sarnano was built as a "castrum", a town constructed from the outset on principles designed for defense against armed attack. These are not big rivers, by any means. You might do better to think of them as large streams. But over thousands of years they have cut gorges, often forty or fifty feet deep, whose sheer sides make them virtually impossible to cross. So the new road would need a bridge, and in the process of building this bridge the workers discovered a natural spring, which they named after *San Giacomo della Marca* an important 15th century theologian from Le Marche.

OUR VERY OWN MINERAL WATER LABEL

This was a pretty welcome find, because bridge-building is thirsty work, especially in the height of summer. But it soon became apparent that this was no ordinary spring when the workers realised they were having to urinate much more often than before. The spring water was analysed and discovered to be a very powerful diuretic, rich in minerals that could be used to cure urinary tract and gastrointestinal diseases. It was the beginning of a whole new life for Sarnano. Further mineral springs were soon identified locally, also with healthy properties but crucially with a much greater rate of flow. Within a few years Sarnano boasted a brand new Spa complex built around the original source, and a major mineral water bottling plant which shipped Sarnano's water all across Italy. A wonderful old photograph from the 1930s shows a horse-drawn cart loading up with crates of *San Giacomo* water bound for Genoa and the transatlantic liners.

IMBOTTIGLIAMENTO ACQUE S.GIACOMO

TAKING WATER FROM SARNANO TO GENOA

The Spa is still there today, a wonderfully quaint old building with a hint of Art Deco about it and beautiful gardens reaching down to the gorge and the source itself. One of the benefits of living in Sarnano, or at least being a *registered* resident (they like you to register for things here), is that you are entitled to go to the Spa and collect two liters of water every day. The locals will tell you this is one of the things that contribute to the extraordinary longevity of the people round here.

One of my neighbors just celebrated her 80th birthday, and the guest of honor was her *mother*. The old lady herself had just hit 104. Although to be honest, I am not sure whether the health-giving properties of carrying my two liters of *San Giacomo* water back up the hill to town does more for my health, or the water itself. Maybe it becomes clearer as you get older.

Return to the ideone (Part 2)

The slow-cooked tomatoes (seasoned with herbs and orange zest, you'll remember) had come and gone, and they'd been followed by a rich *tagliata* of local beef with nuts and rosemary. The food here is mainly pretty straightforward, just wonderfully fresh local meat (they go in for lots of meat) cooked with fresh herbs and vegetables, and most importantly, as Lia will tell you, *con amore* - with love. When I say local beef, by the way, I am not just talking about locally pastured or slaughtered. It is that, both those things, for sure, but what I am talking about is the local breed of Marchigiana cattle. You see them in the summer months grazing up in the mountains in small herds. They're unusual beasts, pale colored, white even. And with strong horns and muscular-looking bodies. They look like cattle should. You could even imagine them fending for themselves like the ancient giant aurochs would have done in these very same mountains before they were domesticated by man many thousands of years ago. It is why the meat is so tasty, although it might need a bit more cooking than many of us are used to nowadays.

MARCHIGIANA CATTLE

We'd got through that, followed by some unspecified dark green vegetable, sautéed in olive oil and spiced with *peperoncino*. But we still hadn't got round to the big idea. For several months Lia had been making vague suggestions about a small business venture.

"You make TV programs," she had said, "and I cook. So why don't we make a TV cookery program?"

She always seemed conveniently to forget that we had come here to **avoid** making television programs. Each time we would gently remind her of that fact and move on.

"It would be lovely idea," I would say, "but TV is a complicated business, and you need money, equipment, people, a studio to shoot in... and a TV channel for it to run on".

I could see this wasn't putting her off.

"Yes," said Lia, "but we **have** people. We can shoot in my kitchen, and couldn't we sell it on the internet?"

Well, trying to explain the complexities of the 21st century broadcast environment, with its cartels, restrictive practices and almost total lack of moral compass, in my broken Italian, to a woman whose English was limited to asking after my health, was a bit beyond me. So I would just smile and nod and treat the whole thing as an amusing but ill-conceived idea. And then change the subject.

So I was pleased when she had invited us round to dinner to talk about an *ideone*. This was clearly going to be something different. A business proposition. Import-export? Shipping local produce to high-class shops in London, maybe. A restaurant, perhaps - but where? I would quite like to run a restaurant, as long as I don't have to work after about six o'clock in the evening. Although I am not very good with *people*. And I drop things.

Anyway, Tam and I had agreed in advance that we should just listen to whatever it was and remain non-committal until we had had a chance to discuss it on our own. So tonight would be straightforward - just listen and nod encouragingly with perhaps a little tilt of the head to suggest the idea that this wouldn't be as simple as it sounded. (You see how we improve our non-verbal communication by living in a foreign country? I am even beginning to make gestures as I speak now. Like a proper Italian. After a while you can't help it[1]). But in the event we were taken by surprise.

A Script

After the *tagliata*, and the green vegetable, when we might have expected the flow of food to run out, there was a *dolce*, a rich chocolate

---

[1] The great, and quintessentially English, Beachcomber, once wrote that the word "gesticulation" means "any movement made by a foreigner"

tart made (somewhat improbably) with no butter or sugar. I can't say I was looking forward to it when this was pointed out, but it was (of course) delicious. And (of course) I opted to have a second slice on the grounds that this must be some kind of health food - a view not shared by Tam, who clearly saw it, rightly or wrongly, as heart attack material. I could certainly feel the effect after the second slice, but I take that sensation of the heart beating just a little bit faster as a positive thing - a sign that the blood is being pumped round the body in a vigorous fashion designed to make sure it gets to all points where it's needed. A bit like taking exercise really. Yes, yes, I know that's rubbish, but it seems very persuasive to me when I am confronted with chocolate.

It's amazing what you can convince yourself of when there is a wonderful taste sensation in the offing. And it happened again right there, because alongside the chocolate tart, Sergio appeared from the kitchen with a double espresso, laced this time with *mistrà,* a local *anise* that's roughly 50% proof. Chocolate, coffee, *mistrà...* yes, this was going to be the one night when these things WEREN'T going to keep me awake. Turned out, though, that they were firing me up for a lively discussion.

Mistrà is very much a local speciality of the Marche region, though it has an interesting history. It starts with the Venetians conquering the Greek city of Mistra near Sparta in a campaign that lasted for almost thirty years from 1687 to 1715. The Venetian armies, clearly in need of a restorative, took to drinking the local *ouzo* and brought the drink back to Venice with them when the war was over. Over the years it fell out of fashion until the late nineteenth century when Girolamo Varnelli, an enterprising chap from Le Marche, rediscovered it and started to sell it to local shepherds as a protection against Malaria (I feel I ought to add at this point that I have not contracted a single dose of malaria since I started to drink *mistrà*). Varnelli built a big business out of it, and you can buy Varnelli's *mistrà* in the shops, but the locals started to make their own, and now most *marchigiana* families have got a granddad or an uncle who's an expert producer of home-made *mistrà*. And when these are good, they are very, very good. They still like to drink it in Venice by the way in the Greek way, mixed with water, like *ouzo.*

We had been eating for a good couple of hours now. Talking

about this and that - mostly food itself and everyone's health - the things that Italians just *love* talking about. Along with football, of course. They love their *calcio*. The only time I've seen anyone in Sarnano come close to having a fight was over football. Two guys who were fanatical *tifosi* of different Serie A teams - one Roma, one Inter Milan. They were "discussing" the merits (and morals) of Jose Mourinho, then the manager of Inter Milan. The "discussion" involved a lot of arm-waving and finger-wagging, which eventually metamorphosed into finger-stabbing until finally they were pulled apart by their respective mates. The impetuosity of youth you might think, except these guys were both well into their 80s. Like I say, they *love* their *calcio*. In fact you could be forgiven for thinking it's the ONLY sport as far as Italians are concerned. One of the many daily sport-only newspapers here is called *TuttoSport*, but I think it would be more accurate to call it *TuttoCalcio* because you have to get all the way through to the bottom of page 37 before you'll find anything else. Crazy really, because the Italians are quite good at lots of other sports - MotoGP, Alpine skiing, tennis. And just up the road from us in Jesi (where they make that wonderful crisp white wine *Verdicchio dei Castelli di Jesi*) is a fencing academy that has turned out a whole string of world and Olympic champions in recent years. Perhaps that's what the locals do with their spare aggression.

By the end of the meal we seemed to have covered the full range of health/food/football issues, so I thought it was time to bite the bullet and find out exactly what the *ideone* was. So I asked.

"Well..." Lia said, with a warm smile on her face, "you make TV programs, and I cook. So I've been thinking... why don't we get together and make a TV cookery program?"

"It would be lovely idea," I said, after a nervous glance at Tam, whose face was an impenetrable mask offering no hint of how she thought I should handle the situation.

"But TV is a complicated business, and you need money, equipment, people..." The words were drying up in my mouth. They didn't seem to be having any effect. Lia just smiled her encouraging smile, and Sergio was looking rather intense, with a sort of offer-you-can't-refuse sort of look (the Mafia came unaccountably into my mind at this point). And a quick look at Tam produced what I swore afterwards was an encouraging nod of agreement. So I cracked.

"Why not? If we can film in your beautiful house, and with food like this - well, we can't go wrong", I said hopefully. And this time everyone smiled and nodded. The die was cast.

But how would we start. I am a producer/director, so we would need to find a cameraman (or woman). Preferably one with a camera. And there's the editing to think about, and music. Not to mention finding someone to broadcast it. Suddenly the programs I had been making for years at the BBC and for Channel 4 looked about as complex and difficult as putting together a mission to Mars. The big difference of course was money. In those days there was plenty of it - always somebody else's - and now we had none. This cookery show was looking a bit like a mission to Mars without a rocket.

"When do we start?" said Lia

"Not sure about when," I replied, "but *where* we start is with a script."

"Good idea," said Tam, "and Steve is just the man to write it. That's what he's been doing since he moved out of TV... writing scripts!".

Well that was true - up to a point. I had taken myself back to college to do a Master's in Creative Writing, and I had spent much of the last couple of years writing three or four full length movie scripts. (Don't ask which, you won't have heard of any of them, because they're all still stashed in a drawer in my study - I never did quite get the hang of how to get them on the right desk). I'm not sure that it would be enough to see me returning to my *alma mater* in a blaze of glory, but I guess scripting a cookery show is still Creative Writing. Isn't it?

Then it dawned on me - maybe this scripting was going to be the way out of trouble. If I agreed to kick the project off by taking a week or so to draft a script, maybe the heat would go out of the situation and I could come back and say, "Hey, I tried it, but I just can't seem to make it work." That's the standard response of a writer who has failed, but maybe they wouldn't know that. So that's what I agreed to do. I would go away and script (for the first time in my life) a cookery show. Little did I know that by the time we next sat down together I would have written six!

Reasons to be cautious - one, two, three

Next day, I sat down at my computer with a heavy heart. I had lain awake most of the night thinking about the problems - all the reasons why this was NOT going to possible. To start with, there was the language issue. All the dinner-party conversation recorded on the last few pages was not quite as reported, because everything that we had said to each other had been in Italian. Neither Lia nor Sergio spoke a word of English, beyond "ow are you?" and "I very well thank you", all with a comedy Italian accent. And there was no chance of them learning English. Most people round these parts see very little need to speak anything other than Italian and, notwithstanding the fact that Tam teaches English for a living, we only had a few weeks to get the whole thing together. Lia and Sergio were full-time employed at *Piatto Ricco* and I had made it clear to them that making TV was a long, slow business - we would need a good couple of weeks just to get the shooting done. I thought at first that that might put a damper on the whole thing (in the event they were equal to every impediment I put in their way), but Sergio pointed out that the restaurant closed (like just about everything else in Italy) for the entire month of August for *Ferragosto,* a sort of month-long public party. So now we had the bones of a schedule. We were planning to shoot a cookery program in the often blistering heat of August.

Language. Well, obviously Lia was going to have to speak Italian, but there was no way we would get anywhere trying to make an Italian TV program. None of us had any contacts in Italian TV, and anyway we would be up against people making television the *ordinary* way, i.e. with an actual *commission* from a channel and with plenty of money to make it. I didn't fancy my chances of hawking round a semiprofessional product to total strangers who spoke a different language to me. And anyway, surely nowadays the future was the internet? Who needs TV now there's Youtube and Vimeo, Netflix and Amazon, and even good old-fashioned websites? And the *lingua franca* of all that stuff is English.

Then there's the issue of directing. How on earth would I know what to tell Lia to do? What was the Italian for "Stop! Don't cut the head off that rabbit until I've re-positioned the camera"? And how would I know that "*Sto per separare le uova*" meant "Next I'm going to separate the eggs"? No, trying to do it all in Italian looked like a recipe for disaster. In fact it struck me then that that might be an appropriate name for the show - *A Recipe for Disaster*. At that point I really couldn't see my way through it at all. My biggest problem was going to be persuading the others that the whole thing was a non-starter. Until suddenly I had a brainwave.

Tam can't cook

I had been sat at my computer for most of the morning ("slaving away" would be putting it too strongly) and it was closing in on lunchtime. It was a Monday, so Tam was teaching at home instead of her regular trips every other day of the week to the nearby metropolis of Tolentino (pop. 20,381). She had volunteered to "get some lunch together" which generally means taking some salami and cheese out of the fridge and popping into town to pick up the ingredients for a salad. (Goop, in case you're wondering, is an evening meal.) But this time she was pushing the boat out - galvanized by all this talk of cookery programs she had decided to have a go herself. And it had not gone well.

"I thought you said it was *three* minutes for a hard-boiled egg," she said as she poked a thunderous face round the door of my study, "It's run all over the place."

"That's a soft-boiled egg," I said (helpfully, I thought).

"Well, it's all gone wrong. I'm off out, and if I can get down into town in the next five minutes before the *pizzeria* shuts you'll have pizza for lunch - otherwise it's a sort of raw omelette."

And with that she stomped off towards the front door (you can always tell Tam's mood from the way she walks), and just before she slammed the door (or shut it firmly as she later claimed) she yelled back down the corridor, "...and don't forget, my first student will be here in less than an hour."

And that's when it struck me. This should be a show presented by BOTH women. Tam and Lia would make a wonderful front-of-camera pairing. They had all the ingredients - they get on like a house on fire, they're both good-looking women, both strong characters (to put it mildly!). Lia's a fabulous cook, Tam doesn't know what the inside of an oven looks like. Lia speaks no English but is desperate to learn, and Tam teaches English for a living. So let's do everything two-for-the-price-of-one... Lia can teach Tam to cook "simple Italian", while Tam teaches Lia some kitchen English. And you, the viewer at home, get to pick up some kitchen Italian along the way as Lia shows you how to cook *alla Marchigiana*. Brilliant, I thought! I've even got the first chunk of script down...

```
In kitchen        TAM OOV
                  I'm Tam Courtenay. I've lived here for
                  three years now, and I teach English

IN VIS            TAM/LIA I/V
                  This is my friend Lia. She's got an
                  unpronounceable surname...

                  LIA I/V
                  Rocchiccioli

                  TAM I/V
                  She's a fabulous cook, but she doesn't
                  speak very much English

                  LIA I/V
                  I speak English very well

                  TAM I/V
                  I speak pretty good English...

                  LIA I/V
                  (WHISPER TO CAMERA) But she can't cook

                  TAM I/V
                  ...It's true I'm afraid, so as Lia
                  teaches me how to cook, I'm aiming to
                  pick up a few words and phrases of
                  kitchen Italian that will help all of
                  us understand what's going in those
                  Italian menus[2]
```

Maybe this *could* work after all. It's amazing how persuasive your own ideas can seem - at least until you try them out on other people. But, for now I had the bit between my teeth, and I settled down to write the opening of a program that was beginning to take real shape. As I did so, and as my words revealed acres of empty space on the left hand of the page (that's where the pictures go in a TV script) I realized I was going to have to find a cameraman pretty fast. And there were two other things nagging away at me as I wrote - what were we going to cook, and how on earth were we going to make a program in two different languages?

---

[2] OOV, by the way, means Out Of Vision, and I/V means In Vision

The Checklist and Peter

I didn't get too far that first day. The simple fact of sitting down to write a script is far and away the best way to find out what you're going to need, and what you'll have to do if you are going to deliver this far-off dream. That's actually the principal function of a shooting script. The first time I quit the BBC was shortly after they'd appointed a new Director General who wanted those of us working in Current Affairs to write a shooting script before we left the office - one that we would be expected to stick to. He wanted us to actually come back with a film we had written before we went out into the field to find out what the real story was - out there, on the ground. Something that I always thought was the fundamental purpose of journalism - talking to people on the spot, in the heat of the action. How on earth could we understand the real stories of something like the Miners' Strike sitting behind our comfortable desks in BBC HQ? No, shooting scripts are just a way of scoping out needs and possibilities - but the fun of the thing is making it up as you go along when you are out there with the camera. So I didn't panic when I hit what would be the first of many sets of buffers. Instead I fell back on an old lifeline in times of difficulty - make a list!

Daunting. It took me, what, two minutes? to make, but suddenly my list seemed to add up to an insuperable set of hurdles. I mean most of this is easily solved by the application of money, but that's the one thing we didn't have. This project was really going to test the new democratization of TV, the principle that everyone can do everything. But if people can make money out of shooting cat videos on their mobile phones for YouTube, surely we, as TV professionals, could pull it off. As it happens it would turn out that our professional training was a disadvantage as often as not. And one of the clues was in the last item on my list, finding a Distributor - someone who sells TV programs around the world. But that was still a long way down the line

- for now the best I could hope for was that we might get some short videos made for the Internet, and that maybe, contrary to expectations, some backwoods TV channel somewhere would buy them as "interstitial material" - that's their posh name for the short (and inexpensive) pieces they use to fill in the gaps left at the end of programs bought in from America, where because of all the ads, an hour-long program is in fact only just over 45 minutes.

COOKERY VIDEO
CHECKLIST

What	Who
Camera	
Cameraman	
Lighting	
Audio Equipment	
Sound Recordist	
Make-Up	
Costumes	
Continuity	
Edit Equipment	
Editor	
Local Fixer (Italian speaking)	
Translator	
Subtitles	
Music	
Website	
Recipes	
Distributor	

The next job was to address the right hand side of the list... WHO. **Who** was going to either DO this job, or be responsible for solving the problem. And in another couple of minutes I had reached this point...

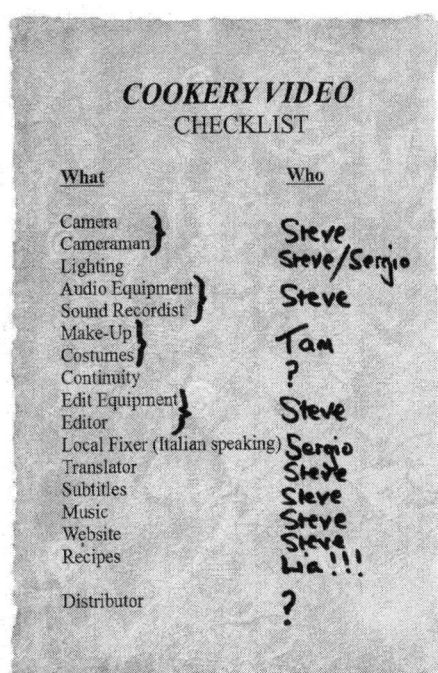

COOKERY VIDEO
CHECKLIST

What	Who
Camera	
Cameraman	Steve
Lighting	Steve/Sergio
Audio Equipment	
Sound Recordist	Steve
Make-Up	
Costumes	Tam
Continuity	?
Edit Equipment	
Editor	Steve
Local Fixer (Italian speaking)	Sergio
Translator	Steve
Subtitles	Steve
Music	Steve
Website	Steve
Recipes	Lia !!!
Distributor	?

Now things seemed to have gone from bad to worse. Lots for me to do, most of which I was totally unqualified for. And there were those few gaping holes - make-up, costumes... a cameraman. That was a biggie. And it was Lia who solved the problem. With Tam's help.

The three of us met for coffee the following morning. As ever. Not at Basilio's though, but across the square at the grandly-titled *Gran caffè Italia*. This is a cut above Basilio's. The chairs are upholstered, and mostly in one piece. And in the winter it catches the morning sun on the terrace outside. So we're in the habit of wrapping up warm and sitting out in the sun whenever we can. And this was just one of those mornings - clear blue sky and not a cloud in sight. The sun caught the snow on the mountains like a many-faceted mirror, somehow seeming to magnify its watery brilliance. This would pass for summer back in the UK.

I shared my list with my would-be stars. I pretty soon took to referring to them in the American way as "the talent", which Tam took as some sort of insult, though I meant it sincerely (most of the time). I was sure it would put them off, convince them that the whole thing was a non-starter. But no, Lia was confident we'd find an answer to most of our "little" problems.

"But what about the big one," I asked, "where are we going to get a cameraman capable of shooting this thing? And a camera?"

"Your friend Peter" said Lia. Peter was a director of many award-winning documentaries who had worked for just about every channel in the UK, and some across the Atlantic. Lia had met him when he'd come to spend a few days with us the previous summer.

"He's a director," I told Lia, "He's not a cameraman."

"Yes he is," said Tam, "he's bought himself a brand new Sony something or other. I spoke with him last week - he wants to shoot his own stuff from here on. Says he's fed up with young cameramen who know less than he does."

"He will come." said Lia, ever the optimist. "He will come over and help us."

"I think he might" I replied, "As long as you're happy to feed him while he's here." Peter had been invited round to eat at Lia's a couple of times during his visit.

"*Ma certo*", said Lia, and inside 24 hours Peter had agreed to join our let's-do-the-show-right-here-in-the-barn project, which so far remained nameless. A Title! Another problem to be added to the list - just as we had ticked one off.

Scoping the work

Two days later Peter flew into Ancona for a lightning visit to discuss the project. That evening we sat down in Lia's to scope out some ideas. Or rather to eat a delicious *pollo alla birra* (chicken in beer) which she wanted to include as one of the recipes. It's a simple enough dish but, made with chickens who have spent their lives running around farmyards, and beer from a local *birrificio artigianale,* it was just bursting with flavor. The beer incidentally is called Route 77, named after the SS77, the main road running through southern Le Marche from coast to mountains, and on to Rome. Apparently the guy who runs the *birrificio* is a big Rolling Stones fan, so it's something of an *omaggio.* So far I don't think Mick and the boys are aware of its existence, but I have a feeling they would be quite flattered. If you fancy having a go at this recipe for yourself, you'll want to try to find a blond beer that's quite strong and very hoppy, but then the beauty of cooking with alcohol is that more or less any variety will work - even though the end products might all be quite different.

It was important that Peter should enjoy the next couple of weeks. A happy cameraman is a hard-working cameraman. Peter likes chicken, beer and the Rolling Stones (he even made a documentary with them once), and I could see he was beginning to understand that the meals might be one of the side benefits of this thing. He likes chocolate too, so I knew he'd enjoy the dessert Lia had lined up for us that night. I had asked her to make one of those chocolate tarts she had used to soften me up that first night:

SOFT CHOCOLATE CAKE AND ICE CREAM

- *250g. dark chocolate*
- *4 large eggs*
- *a pinch of salt*
- *a glass of brandy*
- *8 tablespoons of sugar*
- *icing sugar*
- *vanilla ice cream*

Melt the chocolate in a bain marie or in the microwave. Separate the egg yolks from the whites. Put the whites into a blender, add a pinch of salt and 5 tablespoons of sugar then whisk them until stiff. Beat the egg yolks with 3 tablespoons of sugar, then add the brandy. Mix the melted chocolate into the egg yolk mixture, then add the egg whites and gently fold them in lifting the chocolate mixture from the bottom upwards. Pour the final mixture into a 24 cm. diameter pan lined with parchment paper. Bake at 160 degrees for 20 mins.

We had struck lucky with Peter. As Tam had said, he had indeed just bought himself a new camera, and he'd been scouting around for a project to try his hand on as a cameraman. As Sergio cleared away the dishes, Peter seemed to have a bit of a warm glow about him. He settled back into his chair with a broad smile (Peter smiles a lot!). He likes a glass of wine too, so we had plied him with a favorite local red called *Lacrima di Morro d'Alba*. I thought that a few glasses of that coupled with my own powers of persuasion would bring him on board, that we could do a deal which would get him to do the job for a pittance as he was untried in this particular role. But Peter holds his drink rather better than I do, and when we woke the following morning I suddenly remembered that, in a fit of *bonhomie,* in the afterglow of a delicious meal, good wine and a couple of grappas I had offered Peter a slice of the action.

So there were now five of us - me, Tam, Lia, Sergio and Peter. The not-so-famous five, with a plan to conquer the (cookery) world. In fact the idea had taken on quite a bit more shape during that evening's dinner. The five of us were working well together, and feeding off each others' ideas to put more flesh on the bone. So far the plan had been to make a series of short segments, maybe 8 to 10 minutes each. But someone (exactly **who** was lost in a *grappa* mist) had suggested that we stick them together, three at a time, to make TV-length programs of half an hour. The next bright idea (and this one was mine, I'm sure) was to make each set of three add up to a full meal - one starter, one main course and a dessert. It took a while to persuade Lia that this made sense because that's not the way they eat round here. You normally kick off with an *antipasto* of some sort - mixed salamis, cheese, cold roasted vegetables, that sort of thing - which can sometimes be big enough in itself, so that you want to go straight to the *tiramisu*. Next there will be a choice of *primi*, and this is where all those wonderful variations on pasta and sauce come in. *Secondi* are meat or fish dishes. If you want vegetables (*contorni*) they will come separately, and generally after the meat. It can be the devil's own job for the English to persuade the *cameriera* that you want your chips **with** the meat. And finally, but only sometimes, you can get a *dolce*. More often that not a *marchigiano* will go straight to an espresso, which, if you are lucky, will come with a selection of home made spirits (my favorite so far was a chocolate liqueur served up at a restaurant in San Severino Marche - and I mean this was not just chocolate flavored, it was like liquid chocolate).

It was good to have Peter on board, but his availability actually put us under even more time pressure. Lia and Sergio were free for the whole of August. I didn't tell them (none of us quite knew) that by the end of that period we would all be absolutely exhausted. It doesn't matter what you say, how much you try to explain, but people always think that making television is just a matter of pointing a camera, shouting "Action" and away you go. An old enemy of mine always used to say that in TV most of the time was spent waiting. Waiting for someone to do something, or adjust something, or arrive with something. Then, as soon as you're ready to start, something goes wrong. The battery on the camera runs out, a light bulb blows, or someone has to take an "absolutely vital" phone call.

And then there's the fact that you have to do everything at least three times, so that you've got the same piece of action covered from different angles, and in different sizes of shot. That's how you make TV action into an apparently seamless timeline, cutting from the wide shot to a reverse angle to a tight shot (a Close Up) of the same action. And this stuff is especially difficult (as we were to discover) with cookery. Either you prepare and cook the same dish three times over (by which time you are thoroughly sick of the sight of it), or you suddenly stop the action while you zoom in and re-position the camera (a straightforward zoom in hardly ever works). Try cooking in that way for yourself some time. You're about to crack eggs into a bowl when your partner shouts "STOP! Hold it right there" and you have to hold the egg in the brace position while he/she repositions themselves before shouting "OK. No, wait, WAIT! The battery's gone flat". And once you get the hang of it, try it again in a language you only barely understand.

Anyway, our window for shooting had narrowed to only three weeks because Peter had been invited to spend the last week of August on a luxury yacht cruising off the French Riviera. And when I say "luxury", I mean this yacht had a permanent crew of twelve and a grand piano. I tried to persuade Peter he'd rather spend that week cooped up in a blistering hot kitchen under arc lights, but he wasn't budging. So three weeks it was - we'd have to be a well-oiled machine, and that was my job as Producer. It's all in the planning...

We had plenty to do. We had convinced ourselves that by

stitching all the constituent parts together we could make proper TV programs. But these days, and with this kind of stuff, no-one can use a single program. TV channels use cookery to eat up great swathes of airtime. It's cheap and endlessly repeatable. We had decided we could manage six programs, which is only just about enough. These days they like runs of thirteen if they can get them. Nothing between six and thirteen seems to work, though I've never understood why. One of the many mysteries of TV scheduling. Yes, six was the bare minimum, thirteen would have been preferable, presumably 480 would have been ideal. Never mind the quality, feel the width.

Six half-hour episodes was all we could manage in the time. Had we been shooting *just* the cooking we could, no doubt, have managed more. But by now, fuelled by red wine and uncontrolled ambition, our plans had become much grander.

Out in the countryside

Lia, you see, had ideas that extended beyond the kitchen. It's the quality of the ingredients that are the hallmark of *Marchigiana* cooking. So we decided that each show would be much more than just a recipe and the method of delivering it. The programs would be an opportunity to get out into the countryside of Le Marche in search of the genuine local produce Lia used in *Piatto Ricco* and in her own kitchen. She and Sergio are a mine of information about where to find proper *ricotta dalla montagna*, or *ciabuscolo*, an absolutely divine soft salami that they swear to you cannot be found even 25 kilometers away, because it's the exact climatic conditions of the foothills of the Sibillini that make it so special.

So alongside making the dishes for each program, we would get out of the kitchen and into the countryside, or a nearby farm, or a local butcher's to round up the ingredients. And in the process we would meet some fascinating people, and most importantly of all, get to know the area. What had started as a cookery program had grown like Topsy. Now it would be not just a regional cookery course and an Italian language primer, but also a travelogue and a history lesson. And believe me, there's plenty of history round here.

When we first arrived in town some ten years ago there was a small exhibition on in the *Palazzo del Popolo* in the Piazza Alta at the top of the town. It's a beautiful building, part of the medieval political structure, which had a degree of socialism about it way back when. The exhibition was about the history of Sarnano itself, with lots of old artefacts, and pictures of churches, convents and ruined castles. The town itself is a historical monument, of course, but it didn't figure much in the history exhibition because it's still inhabited - even if the old defensive walls have lost their battlements over the years. At the time my Italian was not even the stumbling, semi-incoherent version I speak today. Back then it was virtually non-existent. So I opted for the foreigner's friend, those ugly wand things you see clamped to the ears of tourists in the *Uffizi* in Florence or St Peter's in Rome. I started in Room One (I find it's the best way, generally) and listened to an account of pre-historic settlements in the region. Then, as I gradually moved through the exhibition over what seemed like about half an hour, the broken English account went on to explain the impact of various occupations of Sranano and its surrounding territory by the Florentines, the Franks, and assorted powerful families from the North. Finally, my guide got round to bringing me (I thought) bang up to date when she said "eventually all this came to an end when, in the year....." And at this point I was convinced, absolutely convinced, that she was going to say something like 1848. Instead, though, it was "eventually all this came to an end when, in the year 1265, Sarnano was established as an independent commune". And that's when I realised that in this country they really DO have a lot of history.

No place for learning

By now the thing was beginning to take real shape. Six episodes, eighteen recipes, three segments/recipes in each show. Lia teaching Tam to cook, with a little bit of language learning thrown in. And a good 40-50% of each program would be filming out and about Le Marche as we picked up the ingredients and got to learn something of the area's rich heritage. Meeting, as we did so, some of the local *Marchigiani*, a breed of people, who like to do things *their* way, and see no reason to change. The original idea had been to shoot short segments, one recipe at a time, and post them on the Internet - everyone, it seemed at the time, was talking about how this was the future for projects like ours. If Jamie Oliver and Anthony Bourdain could do it....

Trouble was, none of had a clue how you make money from the Internet, so we had fallen back into old habits and decided to make it as a TV series. When you looked at the idea on paper it seemed to have a lot going for it as a TV program. But we would still have to find a way t *sell* the thing. So I called an ex-colleague who had gone on to work in the mysterious world of TV sales. She gave me the name of a Distributor who she could not (she said) recommend more highly. I am not talking to my friend any more, but that's jumping ahead with the story. Enough to say that I now use the word "Distributor" as a term of abuse. On the phone he sounded very encouraging. Talked about being in it for the long-term. A ten-year relationship. Said he'd like to see a sample as soon as we had got anything recorded. He wanted to take the series with him to MIPCOM, a huge TV market that happens every autumn in Cannes in the South of France. It sounds fabulous, doesn't it, but in reality you spend all day every day in a giant aircraft hangar crammed with hundreds of stands flogging an unimaginable variety of television programs, from multi-million dollar drama series with Hollywood stars and budgets to match, down to 128 episodes of

Ultimate Cage Fighting Girls. And the occasional home-made cookery series too, of course. Probably *Cage Fighting Cooks* for all I know.

But David the Distributor had already spotted a problem. Filming in August wasn't ideal, he said, because he would need to be sending out a trailer in September. Our timescale just got tighter. Normally you would make a trailer after you had edited the series - now we would have to do one before we had any idea how it would come together. And he had two more *"really important points"* to make...

"Forget about the language learning," he said, "I can't get enough cookery, but no-one wants language lessons - smacks of education TV!" Television, I thought, has changed a bit from the days when the BBC was run by Lord Reith. His mantra was that the television's job was to "educate, entertain and inform", something the BBC did quite well for most of its life although it seems recently to have forgotten that programs are supposed to do all three at the same time!

And second, David the Distributor said, "You've got to come up with a catchy name for the series, and quickly." He was about to send the proofs for this year's catalogue off to the printer, and if we wanted to be in it, we'd need to give him some blurb, some photos and a NAME.

I got off the phone and passed on the good news. Sure we'd have to give up one of our unique selling points, the language primer, but this guy must know what he's talking about. And he seems keen, so let's go for it. We all agreed. We'd sign up with this "Distributor" and our home-made series would be straight into the number one international marketplace. Only.... two tricky issues still remained. We had about 24 hours to come up with a Title that we'd be stuck with for ever, something that said 'food' and 'Italy' and preferably 'Sarnano' too. And we still had nothing on paper, let alone on tape.

Naming the Thing

I soon realised there was a third issue - Tam. Now we had been told that language learning was a thing of the past, Tam's role from now on would be restricted to being an idiot in the kitchen. I wasn't sure how that would go down - she may not cook, but she's a proud woman. But for now that was the least of our worries - the most pressing issue was that we had to come up with a series title. Well, this was still, inevitably, going to be a series in two languages - the target audience was anglophone, but the cook spoke only Italian. So we settled on a plan; in the kitchen Tam would be in the driving seat, she'd be the main Presenter (was I just appeasing a proud woman?). Lia would explain to Tam what she was doing - method, ingredients, tips and so on - and Tam would interpret it all to the camera in English. This had the added bonus of simplifying things, which worked well as we were targeting a non-expert audience.

But away from the kitchen Lia would take over as the lead presenter, speaking Italian to anyone we came across while we were rounding up the ingredients. Tam's Italian is good, but not up to dealing with the heavy accents and many dialects in use in the region. This way, with Lia in the lead, these "documentary" segments would feel natural, local, and truly Italian. These bits of course would need subtitling. We decided to ignore, for the moment, what would happen when the program was sold somewhere like the Balkans, when we might end up with Serbo-Croat translations of English subtitles of Italian dialect. There's a fine line between "international appeal" and the Tower of Babel. In the event, though, this was no major problem, as TV viewers in Croatia can attest.

Our title then, we felt, ought to reflect this bilingual approach, so we started to play with cookery terms in both languages. Now, I have never been very good at program titles - it's a difficult art, trying to condense three or four hours of TV into a couple of words. One past success was a series I had made for several years about miscarriages of justice. I had spent a couple of years as the producer of a BBC series called "Rough Justice". Great title that (NOT one of mine!), and when I and some of the production team wanted to defect to Channel 4 (we thought the BBC were losing patience with a program that ruffled official feathers) we had to come up with a new title for what was, essentially, the same show. You couldn't really improve on "Rough Justice", which has that does-what-it-says-on-the-tin feel about it, but we were very pleased when we landed on "Trial and Error", which did very well for us for the better part of a decade.

To be honest, though, that's the only time I've had any role at all in coming up with a decent title. I'm not going to put you through the misery of all the lousy ones - except perhaps for the true nadir of a program in which a modern writer retraced the steps of Laurie Lee when he set out to walk across Spain in the 1930s and bumped into the Revolution, a journey chronicled so lyrically in *As I Walked Out One Midsummer Morning*. I am pleased to say that my proposed title of *In Laurie's Boots* was rejected flat out by the rest of the production team.

We wanted our title to say "cookery". But also to say the program was about *Italian* cooking. And that we're talking real Italian home-cooking, not flashy restaurant recipes. This series would be shot in the kitchen, the *cucina*. And so, and I can't remember whose idea it was (certainly not mine!), we decided to run the two words "cook" and "cucina" together to make our series title *Cookucina*. You will notice that the 'c' at the beginning of "cucina" has disappeared. Nothing in television is simple, and whether that 'c' should stay or go probably involved a grand total of about 24 (wo)man-hours of discussion - and a liter or so of *Rosso Piceno*. But in the end it went. For better or worse we were on our way to making a series (A website? A YouTube channel? A book? An Internet phenomenon?) called *Cookucina*.

Sadly there had been no room in the title for Sarnano, but we were a bit equivocal about that anyway. The BBC once had a big, and long-running, hit called *Last of the Summer Wine*. It was a gentle comedy about three elderly men who lived in a sleepy West Yorkshire village. It was shot in a delightful (and sleepy) little place called Holmfirth. Sleepy no more. Such was the success of the program that people started flocking to Holmfirth to see for themselves the rustic cottages and cobbled streets they'd seen on TV. They came by the busload. Still do, I think. No doubt some people did well out of it, but Holmfirth has been changed for ever. Fame for Sarnano (should we ever get that far) would be a two-edged sword. Best we keep quiet about its attractions.

Sanpietrini

Sarnano is, to my mind, unique. To start with, it is built of pink brick. Even the floors of most of the old houses are pink. But underfoot the pink is richer, darker. And the material is tile, not brick. They're called cotto tiles and they are typical of the region. There is a history to this (there is a history to everything in this part of the world). The local stone is not suitable for cutting by stonemasons, so the men who built this town were forced to find another route. They began to take on specialist workers, originally from Lombardy in the north of Italy. In the centuries following the end of the first millennium these skilled artisans had begun to travel south to export their skills to provinces in central Italy. Here they had established workshops where they were able to pass on those skills to local apprentices. If you had happened across this area in the middle of the 13th century, during the building of Sarnano, you would have been presented with a startling sight. The top of this steep-sided hill is a hive of activity. Men shout, hammers ring on metal and stone. Donkeys bray as they haul heavy carts up steep tracks. And as the buildings of the new town begin to rise, their foundations, and the men laying them, are shrouded in thick smoke pouring from dozens of furnaces turning out the bricks and cotto tiles for the houses rising on the hill above them.

SARNANO, LE MARCHE

There is a uniformity about Sarnano that gives it a special charm. A sense of consistency derived from the use of the same bricks, the same roof and floor tiles for houses, churches and *palazzi* constructed over several centuries as the town grew. Yet this is also a fundamentally organic place, where each building has its own individual character and nothing was built to a proscribed pattern. The pattern, the order, derives from the street plan itself, the gently curving terraces of tall houses shading the narrow streets below just as they form a defensive wall to protect the town against hostile invaders. This uniformity of materials has survived more or less intact for seven hundred and fifty years. We recently had the roof on our house rebuilt. Not that you would know it, though, because the visible roof tiles (the *coppi*) are all decades, if not hundreds, of years old. A *coppo* is like an elongated floor tile which has been shaped into something like a half-pipe. It's about an inch thick and tapers slightly so it is thinner at one end than the other. A tiled roof in this part of the world consists of a double layer of *coppi*. The bottom, invisible, layer is laid with its outer edges curving upwards so it acts as a gutter, and this is capped with rows of *coppi* laid the other way up so they act as a run-off, into the gutter *coppo*. Repairing a roof means salvaging all the intact ancient ones for the top layer, while replacing the bottom layer with new ones. When the roof goes back together it looks just the same as it has done for the last few centuries. It is one of the ways the Italians have learned how to retain the patina of age while making their towns livable in the modern age. I guess in a couple more centuries my new tiles on the bottom layer will eventually become a piece of architectural heritage themselves and gradually migrate to the top.

ROOFS AS OLD AS THE HILLS (NEARLY)

And my new tiles, by the way, will be made to exactly the same dimensions as those of seven hundred years ago. They made sure of that because they built a "yardstick" into the fabric of the town so that the size of building materials could always be checked. If you go to the church of *Santa Maria Assunta*, in the *Piazza Alta* at the top of town, and if you know exactly where to look, you can find inscribed into the outer wall of the church two shapes, one perfectly rectangular, the other tapering slightly at one end. These are the prescribed dimensions for a *cotto* floor tile and a *coppo*. So if I thought my builder was trying to get away with using smaller *coppi* I could always ask him to take one up to the church to check - just as any earlier owner of my house could have done at any time during the previous seven hundred and fifty years.

Outside the houses, in the narrow, gently curving streets of Sarnano there is another pleasing uniformity underfoot. Just like Holmfirth, the streets here are cobbled. The shaped stones used here are called *Sanpietrini* because they are similar to the stones used to pave St Peter's Square in the Vatican in Rome. The story goes that the first *Sanpietrini* were laid in the late 16th century on the orders of Pope

Sixtus V, after he was flung against the side of his carriage when one of its wheels got caught in a rut. The artisans and tradesmen who worked in and around the Vatican who got landed with the job were known as *sampietrini,* or *sanpietrini* (little Saint Peters). They were seen as the children of Saint Peter who looked after his church and his legacy. They employed the ancient guild of stonecutters, the *selciaroli,* to cover St. Peter's Square with cobblestones. Legend has it that every stone laid around the Vatican represented a soul saved by Saint Peter. Over time the stones themselves, like the caretakers of the church, came to be known as *sanpietrini,* the children of St Peter. In Sarnano, as in Rome, we call these stones *sanpietrini.* Elsewhere they have different names - in Bologna they are *bolognini,* in Venice *salizzade* and in other Italian cities they are generally referred to as *selciati.* But here in Le Marche they are *sanpietrini,* perhaps because Sixtus V was himself a *Marchigiano.*

Whatever you call them, the stones are about the size of the palm of a man's hand and sort of rectangular, but narrower at one end than the other. I think my maths teacher would have called them *trapezoid.* This unusual shape allows them to be laid in interesting patterns, but they also have the virtue of being practically indestructible. Look, I didn't really want to get dragged into this geometry thing (it was never exactly my strong point), but these *trapezoids* are not flat stones, they are solid bits of rock. Think of a fist instead of the palm of a hand. They are in fact a three-dimensional *trapezoid.* Strictly-speaking they are called *trapezoid prisms.* I know that because looked it up.

Anyway the point is cobbles last forever, or for hundreds of years at least. It always struck me as bizarre when you see tarmac road surfaces in London being torn up and re-laid every few years, and as they take them up they reveal the old cobbles underneath then cover them up again with another layer of tarmac which will start developing cracks and potholes in no time at all. They have even (is nothing sacred?) started doing the same in Rome in recent years. Yes, I know the argument is that people expect the smooth ride of a tarmac surface nowadays, but then all the big cities are putting in speed bumps and other clever contrivances to slow people down. Maybe rattling over the old cobbles would do the job just as well.

A few days ago they started to lay some new *sanpietrini* just outside our house. It was gravel before, but they are about to open up a new lower level to the town's museum and our gravel parking spot is destined to become the new entrance to the museum, so we needed smartening up a bit. Actually, calling it a gravel parking spot is selling it a bit short because it's a little *piazzetta* with the most spectacular view in Sarnano, out across *cotto*-tiled roofs, and the fields and woods beyond, towards the Sibillini mountains looming over the whole vista. In fact it's the view you've just been looking at a few minutes ago, of the roofs. It's a delightful spot and has been criminally disregarded up to now, except by the young *Sarnanese* who came here to do their courting under the lime trees. The work began one day when, with a mighty roar, a truck unloaded several tonnes of *sanpietrini,* forming a miniature mountain on our doorstep. The following day the work began, and as I stepped out of my door it felt as though I had been whisked back to the middle ages in a time machine. You see no-one has yet figured out a way of laying *Sanpietrini* mechanically - this is work that has to be done by hand, just as it was five hundred years ago. It was about 11.30 in the morning and the sun was high in the sky. It was hot. The terrain had been flattened and marked out carefully with little wooden stakes and lines of string. Two or three men wearing only rough cloth shorts, their backs heavily bronzed by the sun, were laying the *sanpietrini* in an intricate clamshell pattern where each shell somehow melded into the next like an Escher drawing. Their hammers, measures, stakes and string could easily have been handed down through the years by their predecessors, the *selciaroli,* and as they sat working on tiny one-legged stools, just six inches or so off the ground, they could have come straight from a Brueghel painting.

This looked like the quintessential family-trade, skills, tools and techniques passed from one generation to the next. This, after all, was the basis of the powerful medieval guilds. But it turned out the most of the men doing the work outside our house were not Italian at all, but immigrant workers from the Balkans on the other side of the Adriatic Sea. Here then was a microcosm of a key issue facing Europe today. Laying *sanpietrini* is back-breaking physical labor, and despite job shortages there's not much of an appetite for that sort of thing in modern Europe where the young have grown up accustomed to an easier life. Instead it's immigrant labor which is prepared to pick up this kind of work, which brings outsiders into the community and stokes suspicion and resentment which is in turn capitalized on by right-wing politicians and press. So the Catch 22 is that preserving the heritage requires hard physical labor which brings in immigrants which fosters a xenophobia latent in much of Europe. And heritage is a lifeline for Italy in the modern economic client - it's often referred to here as "Italy's oil" - so maybe it's time to wake up to the fact that immigrant labor and cultural tourists are two sides of the same coin - a coin that could be extremely valuable for a country so blessed with its past.

Our museums, by the way, are four. There's the *pinacoteca*, the art gallery, which has one or two quite sublime religious paintings, a museum of the flora and fauna (stuffed birds and small animals, in short), and a collection of small arms (many of them suitable for killing the birds and small animals that then get stuffed). But my favorite, and I am pretty sure it is unique, is our museum of hammers. Don't ask me *why* we have such a thing, but it's very useful when you want to see how much the hammers used to lay *sanpietrini* have changed over the centuries. The answer is not at all.

Recipes

By now there were just a couple of weeks to go before Peter turned up with the camera and all I had written was the opening of the first program. We also had no recipes yet - no list of the meals we would actually be making. This was entirely down to Lia, but she didn't seem fazed at all, despite the fact that she and Sergio were still flat out in the restaurant. Lia's a very calm and confident person (so unlike the insecure and panicky, though sometimes brilliant, people who work in television). She just kept saying,

"*Non ti preoccupare,* don't worry about that."

Coming up with recipes and planning the meals, she said, was the easy bit. And maybe for her it was. But I was finding it hard to write scripts for programs built around non-existent food. I just couldn't think what to say. And, like a good TV professional, I was starting to panic. Then, one Sunday morning my phone rang. It was Lia.

"I have for you recipes," she said, using that twisted English that I could only assume was her way of getting back at me for what I did to Italian. She had done all eighteen. Chosen six complete meals, and written out lists of ingredients together with the method, the instructions on how to do it. Trouble was, it was all in Italian. This was a job for Tam, and she duly sat down and turned them all into English. Just about. I have come to realise that one of the joys of living in another country is the constant reminders of what you DON'T know about the language. Every time you think you're on top of it something crops up that reveals some gaping hole in your understanding. Often it's to do with specialized areas (like cooking, and building works, and taxes) that have their own vocabulary that seems designed to keep the uninitiated out. After ten years of coming and going to Italy, I get by on a day to day basis, but I am acutely aware that I begin to flounder once the conversation starts to go beyond the commonplace and the practical - health, football, that sort of thing. It's the *nuances* that escape you - like maybe when you want to say you're feeling a bit down in the dumps, without giving the impression that you are suicidal.

Political opinions are particularly difficult too. Perhaps that's an underlying, unacknowledged reason why people go and live in a country where they don't speak the language. You are *forced* into a simpler sort of existence. You can't be drawn into complex political discussions beyond a general sense of whether you're vaguely left-wing, or vaguely right-wing. A bit like American politics I guess. And you only have one word to describe your varying degrees of existential angst - you're either depressed or not. I am sure that linguistic philosophers would say that such limitations will define one's actual ability to *feel* these things. But that's not a conversation I could have with an Italian. Fortunately, though, what they want to talk about 99% of the time is health or football. Oh, and food, of course.

Scripting Ep 1

Now there was no excuse. I had to sit down and knock out the scripts. My bluff was being called. Because every time Lia had assured me that I needn't worry about her ability to produce the recipes, she had told me that she couldn't see how I could possibly write six scripts for three hours of TV.

"Nothing to it," I had said, "It's what I do. No problem at all."

Most of which had been about convincing myself, but now it had to be done. In fact the cooking part turned out to be the easy bit - you can't really script that, it's more of a "live" operation, just filming things as they happen. With quite a bit of the "STOP! Hold it there for a second while I move the camera" going on. That turned out to be quite a big issue, as it happens, because moving the camera almost always entailed adjusting the lighting. Which meant, "Hold it there for a second" was more like "Hold it there for three minutes". And while Tam and Lia were quite capable of freezing the action while we moved the camera (and lights), it was a bit more difficult to "hold" what was going on in the saucepan. More than once the "Hold for a second" meant binning the previous half hour's hard work and starting all over again.

So scripting the actual cooking was simple - just write:

```
TAM/LIA I/V        LIA I/V

in Lia's           (in Italian)
kitchen
                   Oggi facciamo prima Labneh
                   con Pepperoni Grigliati

                   AND THAT'S WHAT WE DO, (3.30)
```

That's it, three and a half minutes allowed. We simply film whatever Lia does, with Tam translating to camera on the fly and get it down to the assigned three and a half minutes later, in the edit. All in the great tradition of putting off the difficult bits till later. At some stage during production a Director will inevitably say the (in)famous words "We'll fix it in the edit". For now though the task was to navigate through the basic structure of a show.

The three recipes Lia had chosen for the first program were Labneh with Grilled Peppers, then a main course of Fresh Trout Oven-Baked With Vegetables, and finally *Pere al Vino Rosso,* pears cooked in (local) red wine. So the basic structure of the program would look something like this:

TITLE SEQUENCE

INTRODUCTION TO THE SERIES

THE 'TALENT' INTRODUCE THEMSELVES

WHERE/WHAT IS LE MARCHE?

WHAT ARE WE COOKING TODAY?

WE GO TO SERGIO'S *ORTO* FOR FRESH PEPPERS

IN THE KITCHEN - MAKE THE LABNEH

ROAD TRIP INTO MOUNTAINS TO A TROUT   FARM

IN THE KITCHEN - MAKE THE TROUT

GO TO NEARBY VINEYARD FOR TOP RED WINE

IN THE KITCHEN - MAKE PEARS IN RED WINE

IT ALL GETS SERVED UP AS A MEAL

TEASE THE NEXT EPISODE

CLOSING CREDITS

Looks pretty simple doesn't it, but actually it's tricky trying to get it all done quickly and naturally in a way that leads nicely from one thing to the next. It's got to do the job, yet still feel like it's just two people chatting while they cook. But, hey, why don't *you* try making "Let's just pop over the mountains for some trout" sound natural. In the end, and in the edit, you can. It's the magic of television. Here's the script I ended up with for the first episode (the column on the right shows how far through the show we are):

```
TITLES                                          0.00


                 TAM OOV                        0.20

                 Le Marche. Italy's hidden
                 gem. A region of rolling
                 hills, majestic mountains,
                 and most important of all
                 fabulous food. This is
                 where Italians come for
                 real food..

                 ...And this is the little
                 medieval town of Sarnano.


TAM/LIA I/V      TAM OOV                        0.35

In kitchen or    I'm Tam Courtenay. I've
Coffee bar       lived here for three years
                 now, and I teach English.


TAM/LIA I/V      TAM/LIA I/V

                 This is my friend Lia.
                 She's got an
                 unpronounceable surname...
```

LIA I/V   0.40

Rocchiccioli

[Tam tries to say it]

LIA I/V

Bravo

TAM I/V   0.45

She's a fabulous cook, but
she doesn't speak very
much English

LIA I/V

I speak English very well

TAM I/V

I speak pretty good
English

LIA I/V

But she can't cook

TAM I/V

It's true, I'm afraid. And
how can you live in a
region like this without

being able to cook...

AGRICULTURE/FOOD MONTAGE   0.55
(30 secs)

[Wide shots farming -Hay
making, Sheep, Marchigiana
Cattle, Porchetta stall,
Monterotti's counter,
Cheese shop, Family
outside butcher's shop]

TAM/LIA I/V	LIA I/V	1.25

In kitchen   *So I am going to teach Tam*
to cook alla Marchigiana

TAM I/V

And I'm going to help Lia
improve her English

And along the way we're
going to let you in on
some of the food secrets
of Le Marche

LIA I/V [in Italian]

[and I'll take you to some
very special places to see
how they make things round
here]

TAM TRANSLATES THE ABOVE
(adding...)

...and I'm hoping Lia will
show us some of the
spectacular scenery and
history around the little
town of Sarnano, where we
both live

LIA I/V

*of course. And I will show
you how we eat here in Le
Marche - simple food
beautifully cooked*

SARNANO MONTAGE	SARNANO MONTAGE (introducing the idea of the women popping up in the alleys - which will later be used as stings) (20 secs)	1.55
TEASER SHOTS FROM PART TWO	TAM OOV Later in the show, we'll be going over the mountains to meet a woman who gets her trout straight from the mountain stream. ACTUALITY And visiting the Cantina di Saputi to find a special wine for one of Lia's recipes. It's a wine	2.15

you'll find hard to get
anywhere else because the
Marchigiani like to keep
it to themselves.

STING   2.35

TAM/LIA I/V   TAM/LIA I/V   2.40

in kitchen   Now Lia, what's on the
                 menu today?

                 LIA TELLS US TWO THINGS
                 (In Italian)...

                 Labneh fatto a mano con
                 peperoncini grigliati

                 Trota al forno con verdure

                 TAM TRANSLATES, adding...

                 ...and as Lia teaches me
                 how to make these dishes
                 I'm aiming to pick up a
                 few words and phrases of
                 kitchen Italian - like "al
                 forno" (in the oven) and
                 "fatto a mano" (hand-
                 made). Words that will
                 help all of us understand
                 what's going in those
                 Italian menus
                 (*conspiratorially* -
                 because they don't really
                 DO translations in this
                 part of Italy).

                 LIA I/V   3.20

And I have a *dolce* for you
as well - Pere al Vino
Rosso

TAM I/V

I know what that is –
pears in red wine.

LIA I/V

*Si, ma e un vino rosso
molto particolare*

TAM I/V

She says it's a very
special red wine.

So... let's get started
shall we

TAM/LIA I/V   3.30

in Lia's   LIA I/V
kitchen
                  (in Italian)

                  *Oggi facciamo prima Labneh
                  con Pepperoni Grigliati*

                  AND THAT'S WHAT WE DO, (3.30)

                  TAM AND LIA I/V (with TAM

OOV as necessary)

until...

TAM I/V   7.00

Well let's put that on one
side now, because we've
got two more courses to
make. And didn't you
promise me a trip into the
mountains?

LIA/I/V

*Si, andiamo a Visso, dall
altro lato della montagne
per comprare una trota*

TAM TRANSLATES (adding...)

...and this will be a
first chance to see the
spectacular mountain
scenery round here!

Andiamo!

MOUNTAIN TRIP   MOUNTAIN TRIP MONTAGE +   7.20
MONTAGE   MUSIC

                       [Start in piazza, Getting
                       in car, Along via Giacomo
                       Leopardi, Under Brunforte
                       Arch, Up in the Mountains
                       x 5]

TAM OOV: 7.45

Coming up shortly, we'll
find out what makes this
woman's trout so special

ACTUALITY CLIP +
TRANSLATION

And trying today's recipes
out on friends and family
in the family *orto* –
that's an allotment, but
it's not the sort of
allotment I'm used to

NICE SHOT + ACTUALITY CLIP
+ TRANSLATION

.

BREAK

STING + Prog Title

Mountains   TAM OOV   8.15
montage recap

We've come over the
Mountains to Visso to pick
up a rather special fish
for Lia's Trota alle
Verdure – (Trout with
green vegetables)

ACTUALITY SEGMENT WITH   8.30

TROUTMAN (1.45)

TAM/LIA I/V	TAM I/V	10.15
LIA'S KITCHEN	So this is *trota alle verdure*. What are *verdure*,	
Trout on slab	Lia?	

LIA EXPLAINS AND
INTRODUCES US TO THE
GREENS

TAM AND LIA I/V (with TAM   10.30
OOV as necessary)

**LIA MAKES TROTA ALLE
VERDURE (3.30)**

TAM I/V   14.00

So you've got one more
course for us today, Lia,
is that right

LIA I/V

Pere al vino rosso – Pears
in red wine. *Ma prima
dobbiamo fare la spesa.*

TAM I/V

We're going shopping.

LIA I/V

*Pere e un vino rosso molto
particolare*

TAM I/V

For some pears and a very
special red wine

ACTUALITY AT GINO'S	ACTUALITY SEGMENT SHOPPING AT GINO'S FOR PEARS (1.15) Ending on Tam trying to buy the wine there, but...	14.15

LIA I/V

*Rosso Piceno e molto
buono, ma oggi voglio
andare a una cantina qui
vicino.*

	ANOTHER UP AND PAST CAR SHOT, THEN TURNING INTO CANTINA DI SAPUTI	15.15
ACTUALITY AT CANTINA	ACTUALITY SEGMENT WITH CANTINA MAN (1.45)	15.20
TAM AND LIA I/V	TAM AND LIA I/V	17.05

In kitchen	**THEY MAKE PEARS IN RED WINE (2.00)**

TAM I/V   19.05

So that's it. I've learned
how to cook a three course
meal *alla Marchigiana*

LIA I/V

And I have learned to say
in English ......
And ....

TAM I/V

But the most important
thing, as always here in
Le Marche, is the food.
Well it's lovely summer
evening here, so we're
going to do what we do
whenever we can and get
down to the órto for *la
cena*. And tonight Lia's
got some family in from
Toscana, that's Tuscany of
course, who are going to
see if the meal I've
cooked with Lia comes up
to her usual standard

ACTUALITY IN ORTO	ACTUALITY SEGMENT WITH FAMILY IN ORTO (ALLOTMENT)	19.40

(0.45)

SHOTS OF ORTO   TAM OOV   20.25
MEAL CONTINUE

Not a bad start, and in
the next edition, I'll be
hoping to pick up some
more tips on how to cook
the Marchigiana way –
simple food, beautifully
cooked.

TAM I/V   20.35

And, as always, we'll
round the meal off in the
usual way, isn't that
right, Lia?

LIA I/V (WITH COFFEE
PERCOLATOR)

Si facciamo un bel caffé!

CREDITS OVER EATING   20.45

THE END   21.00

That, then, was our first Shooting Script. It's called a "Shooting Script" because that's what you set out to shoot. When it all actually happens things are likely to change substantially as you will see. Sometimes for the better - but not always.

Sarnano

There was one problem nagging away at the back of my mind. We were going to need to find someone who could edit this series. An editor takes all your "rushes" (the shots we were planning in the script), digitises them into a computer, and cuts them together into the polished final program. That's the theory, but the difference that's made to the final program by a good editor or an average one is massive. We would need to find one of the best and persuade him or her to come and "play" with us for no money, or at least for payment "on deferral" (this is the TV equivalent of "your cheque is in the post"). All we had to offer was the chance to come and stay for a few weeks in our exquisite little medieval town of Sarnano, and then to blend shots of town and surrounding hills, lakes, and mountains into a cookery show (editors generally like a challenge).

My first thought was a genius editor who had come to visit a couple of years back and fallen in love with the place. As I walked with him through the narrow, winding alleys on the way to the bar for a sunset *aperitivo,* he mumbled,

"Great place to make a film." At the time the thought had never even occurred to me, so I said,

"What kind of film?"

"Any kind of film." Which gives you some idea of how an editor's mind works - they think they can do *anything*, and often have to.

I could see what he meant. There is no such thing as a straight line in Sarnano. And absolutely nothing is flat. The curving alleys (or *vicoli*) are always offering up a new vista as you walk, opening up into delightful little piazzas, or *trompe l'oeil* staircases that climb to another level but get narrower or wider as they do so, so that it's hard to figure out how long or steep they are. And every *vicolo* is lined with a new and subtly different terrace of buildings, but each one is made out of the ubiquitous ancient pink brick that is the hallmark of this town. I sometimes think of it as a miniature pink Siena. We don't, unfortunately, have a paint color named after us, but Burnt Sienna started life as *terra rossa* since it was derived from the particular red earth mined near Grossetto in the middle ages. Sarnano brick could well be called *terra rosa* but maybe not enough of those Renaissance artists who put the *terra rossa* to work made it down here to Le Marche. We do have one spectacular painting in the *Pinacoteca*, the art gallery just round the corner from Lia's place, which by now had come to be known as the Cookucina house. It's a sublime *Madonna col Bambino* by Vittore Crivelli, brother of the more famous Carlo (try Room 59 of London's National Gallery). Nearby Monte San Martino, incidentally, has a church that is stuffed with Carlo's work. As well as some triptychs he and Vittore worked on together. It's a secret treat for fans of Pre-Raphaelite painting - provided you can find the man with the key to the church.

Sarnano was definitely going to be a "character" in our films. And it would be a perfect setting for the publicity photographs we (rather optimistically) decided to shoot well before we had the series in the bag. But you can see why...

PUBLICITY PIC No. 1

It was clear that the town was a key part of our USP, so we wanted to get it into every episode. Several times. Shopping was an obvious place to start because our local recipes called for local ingredients, and that gave us an opportunity to meet some of the local characters. Like Gino, our number one *fruttivendolo*. Actually you met him a while ago, in the script for Episode One. Gino's was where we went for our pears for *Pere al Vino Rosso*. And it's where we get most of our fruit and veg - which means pretty much whatever Sergio doesn't grow in his *orto*. Gino is a big cuddly bear of a man. With a small, but equally cuddly wife, Luciana. They have a daughter, Cinzia, who works with them in the shop. Cinzia is only *quite* cuddly, and a little bit taller than her mother, which is not difficult. Altogether they're a very cuddly family, but their shop, built into the city wall just outside the Brunforte gate, the only survivor of four ancient entry gates to the walled town, is tiny. I am not 100% certain, but I am pretty sure that I have never seen all three of them in there at the same time. Probably impossible, come to think about it.

Gino doesn't have much competition in Sarnano - there are only two other fruit and veg shops. That's because most people round here grow their own. Meat is another matter, though. This little town, population three and half thousand, has no less than seven butchers. They all sell animals that are slaughtered either in the local *mattatoio* or in their own backyard. They're pretty unsentimental about meat. A couple of doors down from Gino's there's a butcher's with a life-size picture of a lamb on the door under the legend "We slaughter our own". Three doors further along there's Monterotti's, specialising in pork. On Saturdays you can buy freshly sliced *porchetta,* which is a spit-roasted piglet stuffed with mixed herbs. Sig. Monterotti has not only reared the pig himself but that morning he was out in the woods and pastures behind his farm collecting the wild herbs for the stuffing. You should add Monterotti's *porchetta* to your list things of things to do and eat when you next come to Italy. But do remember to ask for some *crepitio,* that's the crackling! We have our favorite butcher's, it's called Germano's, and we get pretty much everything there. Which only goes to show that we are not yet proper Italians, because they'll have a favorite butcher for each different type of meat, sausage or salami.

We have seven butchers, but we also have seven churches, and that's in the *centro storico* alone. Only two of them are in full-time operation now, which is probably just as well, otherwise the *Sarnanese* would obviously have a favorite church for each type of service, or confession or whatever (you can tell I am one of the godless minority in Italy). In fact, just recently there *have* been signs of a specialty growing up. The nearest church to our house is *San Pietro o Santa Chiara* (quite why it has two names I have not yet worked out). It was originally built in the 14th century, like our house just across the steps, but it was refurbished in the 17th century, so on the rare occasions it is open you step through a pink brick medieval exterior into an exquisite little Baroque masterpiece. Until recently the only time it was opened up was for delightfully intimate concerts laid on by a local opera singer, but about a year ago it seemed to become popular overnight as a place where bodies are brought to lie in an open coffin for the 24 hours or so before the funeral. Strange getting used to glimpsing a coffin festooned with flowers through the ornately-carved dark wood doors every now again on the way down into town for coffee, but the Italians are very matter-of-fact about death and, as in Levantine cultures, funerals happen very quickly after death, and then suddenly everything is back to normal.

Small towns like Sarnano in rural Italy are places where the sense of community that has so noticeably vanished from the big cities of the western world still survives. One of the regular rituals, that fuels many a conversation over morning coffee or an *aperitivo,* is to stop off to read the death notices. There are several noticeboards round town where the local practice is to post a large and elaborate poster informing friends and neighbors of a recent death. And when I say recent I mean within a matter of hours. It is all part of getting the funerary rites over and done with inside about 72 hours - a practical tradition handed down from the days before refrigeration in a country where summer temperatures can reach 40 degs C. Personally I am all for it, because it means funerals remain simple affairs. Funeral directors in Italy seem like a much more down to earth bunch than their gruesomely obsequious counterparts in Anglophone societies, who seem to regard their job as finding ever-more expensive things to do with a dead body. Here, there's just a short lying-in period in *San Pietro o Santa Chiara* followed by a simple but moving religious service that's open to all and then a procession to the cemetery when anyone who had ever known the departed has a chance to walk behind the hearse.

The English often think Italian death rituals are a bit perfunctory, but, simple as they are, they are only the beginning of a regular connection with your ancestors. November 1 is a big public holiday here. 'Holiday' might perhaps not be quite the right word, though, because November 1 is the Day of the Dead, and the local florists (there are three of them, by the way) do a roaring trade as everyone makes their way to the cemetery to remember their father, mother, uncles, aunts, friends and family. Here in Le Marche it's a thriving social custom, only slightly tarnished by the creeping adoption of American style Trick or Treating on the night before.

One startling thing that study of the death notices reveals straight away is factual confirmation of the claim that people round here live a very very long time. There are always the occasional but heart-breakingly sad accounts of the death of young people, mostly in road accidents (all those stereotypes about Italian drivers are, sadly, fairly accurate - I was once overtaken by a hearse travelling at 90mph), but in general you are hard pushed to find anyone dying under about

85. That 104 year old mother we came across earlier can expect her daughter to live until *at least* 85. Although she will have to hang on until she's 109 to go to *that* birthday party.

Partly I think it's because they breed them tough round here. I once fell into conversation in a cafe with an elderly man with only one leg. He was pretty much retired by now (his son having taken over the farm), but he had carried on working for several years after his accident.

"How did it happen?" I asked. And he told me. At some length.

Paraphrasing somewhat, the story was that he had been out shortly after dawn ploughing one of his more difficult fields. It was on a steep hillside and full of wild undulations. He made a mistake. A big one. He was thrown out as his tractor turned on its side and ran him over, practically severing his leg in the process. He was alone, in the middle of nowhere at the crack of dawn. And bleeding heavily. No mobile phones in those days, so he did what he had to do and dragged himself across the field to a nearby road where he could flag down a passing car for help. It saved his life but not his leg. But at least he lived on to be able to play "guess my age" with *stranieri* like myself. (The answer was 92).

This longevity is not limited to Sarnano. It seems to be a region-wide thing. Just recently there was a news story that Le Marche was the longest-lived region in Europe - average life-expectancy, 84. Drive south from us, through Amandola and on towards Ascoli Piceno and after 20 kilometres or so you come to a little town called Comunanza, where a banner across the main street proudly proclaims that there are more centenarians in Comunanza than in any other part of Italy. Maybe it will be a good idea to move gradually south as I get older. Or perhaps I would just stuff up their statistics.

The Schedule

Sarnano, then, was a gem at our disposal. But how to make sure we made the most of it? Getting Tam and Lia out shopping was good, but most of the shops were actually in the new part of town. Sarnano has a unique atmosphere because of the "new" town that has grown up alongside the *centro storico* over the last 150 years or so. While the old town remains pretty much as it was several centuries ago, the new town has grown so that the population is big enough to make it a busy, lively place (particularly in the summer) while still being small enough to be an intimate community. Le Marche has many other ancient hill-top towns, but few of them have been left alone like Sarnano's *centro storico* and many feel somewhat mummified instead of being a living, breathing, functional town like Sarnano.

So how to use the "talent" to showcase this unique old town? I had a brainwave. Magazine-style television programs sometimes make use of a device called a "sting". They're those irritating little musical jingles lasting only a couple of seconds that get popped in between items that have nothing to do with each other. They're a kind of visual alternative to the "And now for something completely different..." bit of script. Mostly the visual will be some kind of graphic device like the Title of the series magically building itself up out of a pile of lego-type bricks (not a bad idea come to think of it). How about a sting, I thought, but instead of graphics we would just show a beautiful shot of Sarnano? About 3 to 4 seconds of music, and a beautiful, picture-postcard shot of the old town. We should try to shoot them all at "golden hour", that magical time of the late afternoon, early evening when the shadows began to grow and the light has that rich golden hue captured so wonderfully by the artists of the Renaissance. One remarkable thing that happened to me when we found Le Marche, by the way, was the realization that their impossibly beautiful backgrounds of rolling hills, castles and rows of cypresses bathed in honey-colored light were not figments of their imagination, but real. I look at one from my kitchen window every day.

I tried the Sting idea out on Peter the cameraman during one of my regular phone calls briefing him on what to expect when he flew in. I was pleased with the idea, and I expected him to bounce around on the other end of the phone when I pitched it at him. Instead there was silence. For a moment or two, and then...

"But you'll get fed up with shots like that in no time at all," he said. "Six programs, three items, a title sequence, a coming-up tease, in and out of the half time break, and an up-next-week trailer before the close - that's about 8 or 10 in each show, times six, is 50 or 60. That's an awful lot of postcards." I could see what he meant, so we talked it over and decided that we had to use them sparingly. But crucially he said, "there's got to be something *happening* in them. We *are* making moving pictures, after all."

After five minutes of brainstorming we had the answer, and it came from a rather macabre place. Back in the 1970s the great cinematographer and director Nicholas Roeg made one of the scariest films of all time. It's called *Don't Look Now*, and it starred Julie Christie and Donald Sutherland as a married couple struggling to come to terms with the tragic drowning of their little daughter. It's set in Venice, and without giving too much of the plot away, Julie Christie keeps thinking she catches a glimpse of the girl flitting across the end of the long dark alleys of back street Venice - just a flash of red mac in the distance.

We decided that the alleys and staircases of old Sarnano lent themselves beautifully to this same sort of approach - only instead of being dark and threatening, it would all be bright, sunny and positive. And the sinister figure in the red mac (for that is what it turns out to be) will be replaced with our two women stepping lightly in and out of view, brightly dressed and maybe even waving to the audience. Here's a still from a test shoot...

STING TEST 1

So we started to build a shooting schedule with these little stings built in. Not 50 or 60 though, because anyway Peter had pointed out that making these look good would take a lot of time, and time was not something we would *have* a lot of. But certainly we would need a dozen or more, and each one would need a costume change. These shooting schedules are complex things. When you shoot a film you don't shoot it in order. Far from it. You break the whole thing down into scenes and set-ups. Each set-up is a single location where you might want to shoot two or three scenes that happen at different times in the film, but in that same place. Let's say they are Scenes 15, 19 and 34. Well instead of shooting 15, then going on to 16, 17, 18, then back for 19 to the original place where you shot 15, you build a schedule so that you shoot 15, 19 and 34 all at the same time. That's because most of the pain in filming on location is lugging all the kit from one place to the next, then setting up the camera and lighting, along with dressing the scene and maybe even crowd control. This can all take hours, and it may be that Scene 15 is only a single shot, lasting a couple of seconds. This is Time And Motion at work, but with a series like ours it can get even more complicated, because Scenes 15, 19 and 34 might be from 3 different programs, and that means three different outfits for the "talent". And when I say outfits, it quickly became apparent that this means hairstyles, earrings, make-up, the lot.

The girls had seen this coming, and when I shared the emerging Schedule with them their first question was, "Who's looking after Continuity?" This is another one of those jobs whose importance you only discover when you're close to the wire. And it was one thing that had dropped off my early list of problems to solve. Someone has to make sure that (for example) Presenter Number One is wearing the same earrings in Shot 115 and she was in Shot 114, even if they were shot on different days. A properly financed film will have a specialist Continuity Girl (sorry, but I haven't yet come across a Continuity Man) watching all these important points, as well as making sure that wine glasses don't magically disappear from one shot to the next in the finished film. Continuity is a genuine skill and an honorable profession, but we have poor Continuity to thank for all those internet sites pointing out that Robert de Niro changed his trousers between getting out of the car and walking into the bar in Oliver Eastwood's 70s classic *Godmother IX, The Return*. So who was going to be doing Continuity for Cookucina?

"I am." I said. "I'm looking after Continuity."

"And Wardrobe?"

"Yes, that's me."

"Hair?"

"I have a brush."

"Oh and Make-up too, I suppose?"

"Ah, you're on your own there, I'm afraid."

There was a rather threatening clicking of the lips as Tam and Lia turned and walked away enveloped in a dark cloud. It was beginning to come home to all of us that this do-it-yourself TV might be a little more difficult than we thought. By and large I managed these jobs quite well. Although there *was* the nasty incident of the hurried retake with Tam wearing jeans with an orange dress hanging round her ankles - but, as usual, I am getting ahead of myself here.

The Schedule Completed

Within a week or so we seemed to have all the ingredients. Eighteen recipes, six different outfits for each of our "stars", half a dozen Stings (we had decided we could use them in more than one episode), six scripts and twelve "outings" to places where we were going to buy really special produce to take home and cook. For Episode One we had already decided to go up into the mountains to Visso to buy trout fresh from the mountain stream, and to Urbisaglia to visit the *Cantina di Saputi* for some of their delicious red wine for the pears. Trouble is, Visso and Urbisaglia are in totally different directions. It would have been madness to try to do them in one afternoon (we had cooking to do in the morning) - even if they had both agreed to see us on the same day.

In fact you have to organize your travel in much the same way as your shooting schedule. It made sense to shoot the Visso trout farm on the same day as we went to *Picciolo di Rame* an extraordinary little restaurant in a ruined village in the hills outside nearby Caldarola. It's special because Silvano cooks all his food the way they used to do it in bygone years. Fitting those two visits into the same day made sense, notwithstanding the fact that Visso was in Episode One and *Picciolo di Rame* was intended for Episode Two. Now this throws up a couple of issues. One, how much time do you have to allow for getting from one to the other, traveling over the mountains. Two, there would have to be a costume change, and three, how much time should we build in for the (very likely here in Italy) possibility that one of our interviewees wasn't there when we turned up.

We also had to factor in all the time necessary for PTCs. These are the "Pieces To Camera" that we planned to do to introduce some of the segments. Next door to Urbisaglia, for instance, are the remains of the Roman town of *Urbs Salvia*, complete with an only partially ruined amphitheater. The Romans would be pleased to know that it still gets used every summer for open air opera and theater performance. I had written a PTC for Tam to record here. It should have been simple, but it took about three times as long as we thought, largely because the light was going by the time we got there. Or at least that's my excuse. Tam would tell you it was because I had written a piece of script she found particularly difficult to say.

And then there were the "beauty shots". These are the GVs of mountains, lakes, hilltop villages and Sarnano from as many different angles as possible, with which we wanted to pepper the series. Getting the beauty shots of Sarnano was a particular logistical challenge because it's all a matter of where the sun is at any particular time of day, and we wanted some of them to be at dawn and others at dusk, and so on. I had worked in television for about two years, by the way, before I discovered that GV meant "General View".

The limited availability of Peter and his camera was a key variable that had to be taken into account. He only had a little more than two weeks with us before he had to leave for his trip on that luxury yacht. So here was another challenge - devising a schedule in which we could accomplish all this away-from-base shooting in the most efficient manner. In the fifteen days available. We needed a chart. A spreadsheet, no less. I gave each program a letter (A to F), and each little segment of each script got a number. And then I allocated the segments to a particular day depending on where we were going to be. And there was the cooking to take into account too. That all had to be built in, and it had its own problems too - the traveling Fish Salesman Lia wanted us to include, for instance, is only in town on Tuesdays and Fridays. Here's my first Shooting Schedule for the whole series (the cooking is in **bold** by the way):

SCHEDULE

COSTUME	NOTES	A	B	C	D	E	F	Daily
		tba	tba	tba	tba	tba	tba	
Tuesday	Collect Peter							
Wednesday						8-9-10-11 / 17-18-19 / 21-22-23		10
Thursday	Frantoio/Orto today		19-21-22-23-24-25-26-27-28			(5)-6-7		12
Friday	Fish Pirate		3-4-5-6-7-8-10-13-14-16-17-18	8-9				14
Saturday	Orto Meal + family	10-11 / 15-16-17-18 - 30-31 / 32-33-34						11
Sunday	TITLES SEQ?			15-16-17 / 18				4
Monday	Picciolo di Rame? + Orto meal friends?		29-30-31-32-33	10-11 / 19-20-21-22 / 24-25-26-27-28			(5)!	17
Tuesday	NO KITCHEN Visso + Mountains + Circolo + Gino	2 / 3-4-5-6-7-8 / 9 / 12 / 19-20-22-23 / 27	2-9 / 15	5	2-3-4	(5)		22
Weds	FESTA!	24-25-26				2-3-4 / 12!		7
Thursday	Circolo + Truffles + Gelateria + Market Day			2-3-4 / 6-7 / 23			(3)-4-21	9
Friday	NO KITCHEN Monterotti / Forno a legna + Urbisaglia + Cantina di Saputi	24-29			5 / 6-7-8-9-10 / 15-16-17-18			12
Saturday	Dinner at Donella's				11-12 / 19-20-21-22-23-24-25 / 26-27-28-29-30-31			15
Sunday	OFF	OFF	OFF	OFF	OFF	OFF	OFF	
Monday	Aurelio after here? Fiastra + Aurelio					OFF	2-4 / 6-7-8-9-10 / 12 / 16-17-18-19-20	12
Tuesday	Ricotta man + English in orto					(5)-15-16	22-23-24-25 / 26	9
Weds	Family in Orto + Sagra!					20! / 24-25		3
Thursday		RESERVE DAY	RESERVE DAY	RESERVE DAY	RESERVE DAY	RESERVE DAY	RESERVE DAY	
Friday	Peter to Airport							

It probably won't surprise you to learn that by the end of the first day of shooting it was... well, I can't quite say it was in tatters, but it was certainly badly damaged. One of the jobs I didn't see coming in this whole exhausting exercise was that I had to sit down every night and re-draw the schedule for the following day. The good news, though, was that we always had a delicious meal available from that day's shooting in the kitchen!

Titles and Lighting

We were just a couple of days away from the first day of shooting now. I called Peter in the UK, just to check that everything was OK and he was still on target to fly in the next day.

"Fine," he said, "Everything packed - camera, tripod (he called it 'the sticks' because he's a professional), memory cards, microphone, all cables present and correct. Everything booked in for the flight. What are we doing about lights?"

LIGHTS! I hadn't thought of lights. I had spent so much time planning all the exterior shooting that I had completely forgotten that we'd need to light Lia's kitchen. Cookery programs need to be bright, colorful and attractive, not shot in a stygian gloom.

"All taken care of" I lied. No point in worrying him now. I had the rest of the day to fix it. About twelve hours to find a TV lighting kit in a small country town in rural Italy - and everyone was about to shut down for their afternoon's *riposo*.

Sergio had the answer. Sergio has the answer for everything. He knew a man who knew a man who had a portable lighting kit. I tried to make it clear that we needed something special for television, but it's difficult to explain the arcane language of TV in another tongue. TV lights are called things like 2Ks and Dadoes, and even Redheads and

Blondes, so it was pointless trying to fish them out of a dictionary. And anyway, right now we needed any kind of lights at all - something, anything, would be better than nothing.

That evening we went along at the appointed time to meet Stefano in his studio. That sounded good - a studio! As it turned out, a studio is a workshop, and Stefano was a *marmista*, a marble cutter, who fashioned extraordinary things out of local marble in a huge sort of underground cavern lit by sets of four adjustable lights on portable rigs. One of these was earmarked for us. An important bit of the regular television lighting kit is the "barn door". All of the lights can be directed or shaped by adjusting a square of four flaps surrounding the reflector of each light. It's how they get those strips of light across the background of an emotional interview with the survivor of some disaster or other. Just by almost completely closing down two of the barn doors opposite each other. The magic of TV. Our lights - four of them on a sort of portable T bar, 500 Watts each - were pretty close to what we wanted except for the total absence of barn doors. Subtle lighting was clearly not going to be part of our style. Which was probably just as well because our Lighting Director (me) didn't really know much about it.

I broke the news on the phone to Peter last thing at night, as he would be up and on his way to the airport at the crack of dawn. He was not pleased. I sensed that what-have-I-got-myself-into tone in his voice. Don't worry, I told him, it's going to be loads of fun. He didn't sound convinced, and to be frank neither was I. I was beginning to feel it might be difficult to keep him happy - and a happy cameraman is vital to an enjoyable shoot, something I learned in my early days with the BBC when I became convinced that the simple act of picking up a video camera could plunge even the sunniest of individuals into a deep depression. Or maybe it was their pay scale.

Fortunately, Peter *is* one of those people whose sunny disposition shines through whatever the circumstances he finds himself in. Which was just as well because we got off to a bad start. He was flying into Pescara airport, about 2 hours to the south of Sarnano. It's number three on our list of most convenient airports and so I am not very familiar with the route. To make matters worse, I discovered they had opened a new road since I last drove down there and, Italian road-signage being what it is, I got lost. I had gone a good half-hour in the wrong direction before I discovered my mistake and by the time I got to Pescara Peter had been waiting nearly an hour. He was standing outside the airport with his camera bag and his sticks and a weary look on his face. This was not what he needed after a 3 a.m. start.

This journey was not my finest hour. We were now late for Peter's first meeting with Lia and Sergio and I picked up a speeding ticket on the way back. I put my foot down after we got past an Ape we had been stuck behind as we wound through the mountains. Apes are those funny little three wheeler scooters with a tiny cab and a miniature flatbed on the back. They're driven by fourteen-year-olds, often with their girlfriend sat on their lap, or old men, and no-one in between. Which is to say the drivers are either 14, or they're old men; not that the laps of the fourteen-year-olds are occupied by either girlfriends or old men. (Tricky stuff, this writing lark). An Ape sounds like an aggravated hornet (*ape* means "bee" in Italian), and they go uphill at about five miles an hour. Not a good enough excuse for speeding though, according to the *Polizia Stradale*. Was it ALL going to be like this, I began to wonder? You're probably asking yourself why I wasn't using a Satnav in this day and age, which might have saved all this trouble. The answer is, I would have been, but Tam had stamped it to death a few days earlier when it couldn't cope with the one-way system in the nearby medieval town of Fermo. But that's another story altogether.

Top of the list at the team meeting back in Sarnano was the Title Sequence. As you can imagine the first 20 or 30 seconds of any TV program are really important. The job of that half minute or so is to stop the viewer getting to the remote control. You have to assume that someone who watched the previous program is not going to be interested in yours - unless you can hook them in with your Title Sequence. We had already decided it was going to feature Tam and Lia, our two stars, walking through the streets of Sarnano smiling and carrying baskets of local produce - all ending up in the Cookucina Kitchen at Lia's house. Peter had been thinking about it on the plane (and presumably in the hour he spent standing outside the airport on his own).

"We need some shots out in the countryside round Sarnano,"

he said, "something where we can feature the whole town in the background. Against the backdrop of the mountains."

No problem.

"But there's got to be something interesting going on in the foreground. They can't just be randomly walking through the countryside with bags of vegetables. What about putting them in one of those angry hornet things?"

Lia and Tam protested that they couldn't drive an Ape. In fact they put it a little more strongly, or at least Tam did. Something about not being seen dead in one of those things. But duty calls, and we decided in the end that Sergio would borrow an Ape from Gino, the cuddly *fruttivendolo*. Sergio would drive (even though, as he protested, he was nowhere near old enough), and the two women would sit on the back of the flatbed, smiling and holding baskets of fruit and veg. Once again it sounded like A Recipe For Disaster.

SECONDO

The Shoot - Day One

"IT'S A BIT SMALL." It was our first day of shooting and Peter was seeing Lia's kitchen for the first time. He was right. And we were going to be spending much of the next fortnight in here.

"Yes, but it's a *real* Italian kitchen. We're after authenticity here."

"Authenticity!" He spat the word out like a swear word. "This is *television*. Since when has authenticity got anything to do with it?"

"That's the point," I said, "Cookucina's going to be different."

"It's going to be cramped." said Peter, "And quite possibly unwatchable. Unless I can find some way of lighting the cooker without taking that wall down. And we're all going to melt once we get these lights on and the cooker going. I presume there's AC?"

"Air Conditioning? In the *centro storico?* I don't think they had it in the fourteenth century when they built this place. Did I tell you that this kitchen we're standing in now used to be the guardhouse in the Barbican protecting one of the entry gates?"

"Well it certainly wasn't built as a TV studio, that's for sure."

"But we want *authenticity* not a studio."

"A studio is where they *create* authenticity" said Peter. He was right, of course.

"*Facciamo un bel caffè!*" Lia had walked in to the kitchen, looking

91

splendid in hair and make-up that would not have disgraced the Oscars. Clearly I would have to gently explain that she'd need to look a bit more casual in the kitchen, a bit more like a *casalingha,* but glamorous. A glamorous housewife. Peter was looking ever more exasperated. But for the time being Lia's offer of a proper Italian *caffè* took the heat out of the situation. It was a remedy she would fall back on many times over the next two weeks, and it worked every time.

Let me just describe the kitchen at this point. It's small - there's no getting away from that. On the left as you go in is a work surface, and alongside that there's a hob, and between them is a sink. There are cupboards and shelves along one wall with just about every spice and condiment you can imagine. Low beams, two small windows looking out over the countryside. Windows are all small here - they help keep the place warm in the winter and cool in the summer. Think of them as a sort of medieval air-conditioning. Walls that can be as much as two feet thick help too. That's it, pretty much, except for a small table and four ladder back chairs that just about take up all the rest of the space.

Into that space we now have to insert the following. Peter, his camera bag, his sticks, the lighting rig (plus cables), a sound recorder and microphone, along with me, Tam and Lia, Sergio and Tinker. I didn't mention Tinker yet? No, I didn't. Tinker is the Cookucina dog. A little black Patterdale terrier. Go back a few pages and you can see her on the right in Publicity Pic No. 1. She's perfect for life here in Italy, because she loves to get out hunting in the countryside, yet she is small enough and docile enough to be an indoor dog too for much of the time. Actually she is Tam's dog, they are inseparable, and Tam was sure she would be no trouble!

Enter the Cookucina Dog

After our *bel caffè* we managed to get the place tidied up a bit. Peter positioned the lighting so that the lights were bounced off the ceiling, and pretty soon he had created a really nice soft effect which somehow gave Lia's country kitchen a sort of warm glow. Tam and Lia started rehearsing and soon found a nice way of communicating with the audience - Lia explaining what she was doing to Tam, which Tam then translated on the fly into English for the camera. This was all very well until we started running into technical cookery terms. It's not so much that Tam's kitchen Italian is lacking (though it is, and we had to have a dictionary handy at all times), but more that, as you know, she doesn't cook. At all.

I know I've mentioned this before, but I do think I need to drive home the point. She is way out of her comfort zone in the kitchen. Food is something she expects to arrive on her table in its finished form. I think she feels it's a bit like not wanting to see Michelangelo knocking chunks off a knobbly bit of marble - better to wait till he's finished. She is, as a result of this, somewhat unfamiliar with the things you expect to find in the kitchen. Many years ago, when we still lived in London, I was planning to cook a meal at her flat one evening. When we left my house that morning I slipped a piece of ginger into her handbag as I would need it for the spicy beef I was planning to cook. Several hours later I got a hysterical phone call from Tam. She had dropped her handbag shortly after arriving home, and a brown cocoon had tumbled out on to the floor. It was huge, and there was clearly a massive insect about to emerge. She was calling me from her mobile while standing on a table to get away from the bug, which was lying on the floor between her and the door. What, she wanted to know, was I going to do about it?

I wasn't entirely sure at this point. I was, after all, in a different post code. But I tried to keep calm, and, more to the point, keep her calm too. I realized I needed to keep her busy while I tried to figure out what to do.

"Describe it to me," I said. "I'll try to look it up on the Internet, see if it's dangerous"

"It's brown. With sort of bulging bits."

"How big?

"I dunno. BIG! For an insect."

"But *how* big?"

"Dunno. Maybe two inches long and an inch fat. It's FAT! And there's a flat, lighter colored bit at the end. That must be where it's going to come out."

"What color is the lighter bit?" I asked.

"Sort of yellowy, darkish, orangey yellow"

"Would you call it a kind of *ginger* color." I suggested.

"You could say that, yes. Yes, it's kind of ginger."

"Tam, it IS ginger." And it was. She had been standing on top of the table for about ten minutes being utterly terrified by a piece of ginger. Like I said, Tam is a stranger to the kitchen.

The first recipe was called *Sformatini di Zucchini*. They're little individual cakes of courgettes (*zucchini* if we're going to be authentic) baked in the oven. Zucchini, eggs, parsley, a bit of cinnamon, some local cheese - preferably an aged sheep's cheese, a *pecorino stagionato* - and a bechamel sauce. Lia said it was nice and simple to kick off with. Well, it should have been. But television can make even the simplest things complicated. To start with there was the audio. Funnily enough, the sound is often the most difficult bit of making TV. We were recording audio directly into the camera, so we had to run a cable from the camera to the microphone. And once Peter had sorted out the lights and the camera position so that he could see everyone's faces, as well as the food, we discovered you couldn't actually hear anything anyone was saying. They all looked round for someone to blame. Me. That morning I had acquired another job - sound recordist. Peter had fixed me up with a gun mike - not as scary as it sounds, just something with a pistol grip you can point at people. Trouble was, I couldn't point it at either of them without getting in the shot.

"You'll have to go over the top," said Peter. Not the first time I've been accused of that, I thought.

"Sorry?"

"You'll have to get the mike in over the top of the shot, so you can point it back at them from above. We need a boom."

Now here's something else you can't get in a small country town in Italy at a moment's notice - a boom. Professional sound recordists use a specially designed telescopic arm that allows them to get their microphone into the best possible position without getting in the shot. Sometimes they can be twelve or fifteen feet away and still get a microphone close enough to pick up a whisper. And somehow, by magic, they seem to know just exactly how close they can get without their fluffy grey windsock peeking into shot. Sometimes they over-do it, of course, and every now and again it gets missed in the edit. That's when you see a second or so of furry grey mouse on the edge of frame - even in big-budget movies. Try *Nightmare on Elm Street Part 2: Freddy's Revenge,* when one of the characters falls asleep in biology class. When the teacher removes the snake from him, the boom mike is momentarily visible at the top of the screen.

"And a sock," said Peter, "we need a windsock - I'm getting popping". Popping is another audio hazard in TV - when all the 'p's and 'b's sort of explode with a big pop. It's very disconcerting. We didn't have a windsock (of course), nor did we have a "specially designed telescopic arm". So we had to improvise.

Fifteen minutes later we were ready. The arc lights were switched on and I swung my "boom" into position. The microphone was now attached to the end of a broom handle with a red and white striped towel wrapped around it to act as a windsock. This was the Dunkirk spirit in action. Lia and Tam were relaxed and ready to go.

Lia's ingredients were laid out and, I have to say, beautifully lit. Peter looked every inch the professional cameraman as he lined up the first shot in the viewfinder. I stood next to him, standing in a heap of cables piled up at my feet. One cable ran down the broom handle into a coil on the floor, then up over my arm and into the camera, my left hand holding it steady. Another came back out of the camera, to another big coil on the floor and up to my headphones. This one was draped round my shoulders to take up any slack when we moved. In my right hand I held the broomstick microphone. I must have looked a bit like an accident in a hardware store. I'll bet Stanley Kubrick never had to work under these conditions.

But now my moment had come. As Director of the series, my role was to set it all going.

"Standby," I said firmly, then opened my mouth to shout "ACTION" - just like Stanley Kubrick. But before I could, Tam shouted

"CUT! Where's the dog?"

"She's shut outside."

"No, that'll never work, she'll be whining to come in as soon as she hears me speak," said Tam, "if she can't get in."

"But she can't..."

"She'll be OK, let her in. She'll be quiet as a mouse and just sit under the table. She just doesn't want to be left out."

"But what if she wanders into shot?"

"OK, keep her on a lead then - just in case."

Well you have to keep the talent happy at a time like this, so in came Tinker, and yes, she sat down quietly under the table. But not for long. Because Tinker like eggs and five minutes after we got going with our first take, Tinker was on the move.

"Sit down," I mimed. "Sit down!" It's difficult to be firm with a dog when you can't make a noise because there's an active take going on. At first, though, it was successful. She gave me a puzzled look and sat back down to try and work out why I had been struck dumb. Then Peter spoiled it all by deciding he had to move to follow the shot.

"Don't pull me," he barked/whispered. "You're pulling my cable."

"It's not me," I whispered/barked, aware that I should be telling myself to shush at the same time. "It's not me, it's the dog".

Somehow the spaghetti of audio cable that I had not yet learned how to master had become tangled up with the dog's lead, while the dog had set off in the other direction hopeful of getting at the eggs. Suddenly I had become much more appreciative of the multi-tasking capabilities of the modern media studies graduate.

It was an inauspicious start, but somehow we got through it, and an hour later we had our first recipe in the can (that's TV-speak, not a statement about food production). *Sformatini di Zucchini* emerged from the oven looking like something out of a food-porn magazine. I had always known that Lia was a superb cook, but I was seriously impressed that she could produce beautiful stuff under circumstances like this. Tam had done terrifically well, too, translating on the fly in a really natural way and making sure there were none of those empty audio vacuums that television abhors. But then Tam is a class act when it comes to filling a silence, I'd always known that. Tinker had settled down nicely once Sergio had fished a bone out of the fridge for her. Sergio is clearly a smart man, and had seen this coming. Even I had performed reasonably well. Wearing my Director's hat I had shouted "Action" and "Cut" at all the right times, and in my role as sound recordist I had managed to keep the red and white striped mouse out of shot. Mostly. Peter, however, turned out to have a major flaw as a cameraman. But before we get into that, here's how you make *Sformatini di Zucchini*.

INDIVIDUAL ZUCCHINI CAKES

- *8 large zucchini*
- *a medium onion*
- *a sprig of parsley*
- *a few basil leaves*
- *salt and pepper*
- *olive oil*
- *2 eggs*
- *70g. Butter*
- *½ liter milk*
- *50g. Flour*
- *nutmeg*
- *50g. grated Parmesan or Pecorino cheese*
- *30g. bread crumbs*

Slice the zucchini and onion thinly, sauté them gently in a pan with olive oil and chopped parsley and basil. Season with salt and pepper. Meanwhile, make a bechamel sauce using 50g. of the butter, 50g. of flour and 500g. of milk. Season to taste with with salt and freshly grated nutmeg. Add the eggs and grated cheese to the sautéed zucchini along with the bechamel sauce. Coat the ramekins with the remaining butter, sprinkle them with breadcrumbs and fill them generously with the zucchini mixture. Sprinkle with a little more breadcrumbs and bake at 190 degrees for 25mins.

Watching the Rushes

That evening we all sat down to a meal of guess what? Yes, *Sformatini di Zucchini*, and they were absolutely delicious. I could see that this cookery TV might have its perks. Next on the agenda was one of the most enjoyable bits of the shooting phase - watching the rushes. In the movie business this process is called watching the "dailies", because they used to rush each day's shots off to the processing bath to get an early print back to make sure they'd got the shots they wanted. In those days of shooting on celluloid you had to process the film in order to see what you had. Only then could you see if the film was fogged, or if you had that mysterious invader "a hair in the gate", which wasn't a hair at all but a tiny sliver of film which got trapped in the "gate" where each frame of film stopped momentarily to be exposed. Now, in this digital age, you can see what you're getting as you shoot - simply by cabling the camera into a monitor. We had decided not to do that because it makes the whole crew that little bit more cumbersome and we were going to need to move quickly once we were out on the road. That was my excuse, anyway. The real reason was that it meant yet another pile of cable round my feet.

The film camera (even the digital ones we use today) has a magical quality about it. I have always found it extraordinary that you can spend all day in a perfectly ordinary location, then when you get the chance to watch the rushes back on a monitor, that otherwise mundane place will suddenly look beautiful. Who said the camera cannot lie! In my early days at the BBC I worked briefly with Selina Scott. She was the presenter of BBC's breakfast show, imaginatively titled *Breakfast Time*. Actually, that turned out to be not too bad, because several years later, and presumably after much high-level discussion and many focus groups, some big wig took the decision to "re-brand" the program. From now on it would be called *Breakfast*. Genius! Obviously I am not the only one who has a problem with Titles.

Not long after that I left the BBC to work on the early days of satellite broadcasting. The company I went to work for, British Satellite Broadcasting (another flash of naming inspiration) wanted their advertising to reflect the fact that, for the first time, the technology would allow them to respond directly, and individually, to the viewers. So they hired a branding consultant called something like Martle, Vogel, Rafferty (just name the company after the people) to come up with a slogan. Along with half a dozen others who were making programs for the broadcaster I was invited to take part in a brainstorming session with MVR's brightest young account executives. Everyone round the table got a chance to say what interactivity meant to *them*, and finally Mr Martle (or was it Vogel) thanked us most sincerely and promised a ground-breaking slogan within the month. Three weeks, and many thousands of dollars later, they delivered the results of all that hard work and brainpower. From now on BSB would be marketed as "British Satellite Broadcasting - Television with Ears". And amazingly everyone loved it. Just like the emperor's new clothes.

The point about Selina Scott, by the way was this... Selina was a very beautiful woman. Still is. At the time she was the most celebrated young woman in the country after Princess Diana. On the day in question I was directing a shoot with her out on the road. We were going to interview Barbara Cartland, the ancient and prolific author of a million romantic novels. I picked Selina up from her home. She looked drop-dead gorgeous, and I felt very lucky to be spending the day with such a famously good-looking woman. At the end of the day I got back to the office and loaded the tape to look at the rushes. The first reverse shot of Selina took my breath away. The woman on the screen was yet more beautiful than the one I had spent the day with. The camera is very kind to some people. Tam and Lia, fortunately, are two of them.

The only trouble was, on our rushes they were blurred. Peter, I had forgotten, was not a professional cameraman. He had read his new camera's manual all right, but he had fallen into an amateur's trap. In the old days, and still in the movies today, a cameraman would have an assistant called a focus-puller. His job was to change the focus on the camera as the shot developed, as required by the cameraman. We, of course, could not afford the luxury of a focus-puller, and Peter was quite happy without one because his camera had a feature called auto-focus, and that's what he had been using all day. Watching the rushes, to start with everything was OK. The shots were either on Lia, or on the food. But suddenly, when the shot changed to a 2-shot of Lia and Tam together, they were both blurred. Blurred is maybe an exaggeration - the positive way of looking at is that they were soft-focus. Of course you can get away with soft-focus in a certain type of film. But this was not one of those. And anyway, while the talent was "soft" the cupboard behind them was crisp and crystal clear. Auto-focus adjusts itself to whatever is in the middle of the shot, and with a nice 2-shot the middle of the shot is looking straight down the gap between them. It looked like some of Day One was going to have to be repeated.

The Frantoio lets us down

Day One had not ended well. Day Two began with a disaster. They're big on olive oil in these parts, but not just any old olive oil. It has to be cold-pressed extra virgin olive oil. Though frankly this is something of a hot potato. Shooting in the kitchen on Day Two, Tam asked why Lia was using extra virgin...

"*Sempre extra vergine*", was the reply. Always extra virgin. Now Tam's aunt is Italian, near as dammit. She's English by birth but way back in the mists of time (and other mists created in Chelsea in the 1960s) she fell in love with an Italian waiter. Much to the disgust of her family Plinny ran off with him to Italy, where she brought up five children with Ferando. As you can imagine, cooking runs in her blood too, and she takes the view that extra virgin should be saved for salads and you should use a lighter oil for cooking. Cookery is a broad church, even in Italy, it seems. I feel a very long conversation coming on if they ever sit down in the same room.

It's not that Lia will only use extra virgin. In fact she uses a variety of different types of oil - peanut, corn, vegetable and so on. But with the oil of the olive it has to be cold-pressed and first off the press. And today we were due to go off to buy five liters of the stuff, hot (or rather cold) off the press. Sergio had a favorite *frantoio* and he had taken me there a couple of weeks earlier when I needed some oil myself. Sergio would simply not entertain the idea that I might try to buy some from a supermarket, so he carted me off on a 90 minute round trip in search of the real thing. The *frantoio* was under a large house, and rather difficult to get to. We had to park some distance away to find a bit of shade under a tree, then walk down a long slope to get to the entrance. It was a hot day and I was feeling a little irritable by the time we got there. There was no-one else around, no cars and no visible customers - or even workers. It was the middle of the afternoon and quite possible that everyone was on *riposo*, which would mean an entirely wasted journey. By the time we reached the frosted glass door I was convinced we were wasting our time, and that we would have been much better off staying at home in *riposo* ourselves. But I could not have been more wrong.

I don't know if you've ever had that feeling as you approach a public toilet from some distance and you *know*, absolutely *know,* that it must be empty. You've been approaching it for a couple of minutes and a public toilet is one of those places where you get in and out fairly quickly. But when you step inside you discover there are five men already in there. And amazingly, they are still there when it's all over and you're on the way out. What on earth can be taking them so long, you ask yourself, and then maybe decide you'd rather not know. Well, opening the door to the *frantoio* was a bit like that. Not exactly, of course, but instead of the empty workshop I was convinced we would find even if the door was not locked, the place was heaving with old men sitting around the walls while a giant press, which pretty much filled the room from floor to ceiling, rotated slowly, oozing a murky brown liquid from what looked like stacks of giant olive-colored pancakes.

Inside the *frantoio* the atmosphere was dark and brooding. The air was heavy with the scent of olives, and the old men seemed to be watching each drip to make sure everything was just so. They hardly seemed to notice us coming into their space. The place felt a bit like a library, as though we would be breaking the rules if we so much as opened our mouths to speak. Sergio was not put off though. He wanted to know where the *capo* was - the boss. Out of the country, we were told, which was not strictly true as he had gone to Milan, to a trade fair. But to these guys, who looked as though they had never in their lives been more than about a hundred meters away from the olive press, the *capo* might just as well have been abroad.

Don't get me wrong, the atmosphere might have been one of quiet contemplation (I had moved on from the library analogy to abbeys and Benedictine monks) but it was by no means unfriendly. In fact when we told them that we had come for a couple of five-liter cans, they made it clear they were not going to sell anything to us until we'd had a tasting. One old guy disappeared into an ante-room (or maybe a small side chapel) and came back with a metal ladle and a small glass. A couple of minutes later I was drinking neat olive oil, drawn directly from the run-off of this giant press. It was delicious. It had never occurred to me that you might *enjoy* swallowing neat oil. My grandmother used to drink a tablespoon of olive oil every day and she lived to be 96. She got hers from the local supermarket. If she had been drinking this stuff maybe she would have lived to 130. Perhaps that's their secret down in Comunanza - they're all drinking extra virgin olive oil till they pass the 100 year mark. My grandmother swore by the stuff. She said it kept your brain and your joints in good working order. She was *compos mentis* to the end, and while she wasn't quite up to the standard of the Indian centenarian who runs the London Marathon each year, she could certainly get about under her own steam. Maybe there's something in all this, but for the time being I think I'll stick to drizzling mine on something edible before I ingest it.

Ten minutes later we were on our way back to Sarnano with a couple of five-liter cans in the car and a loose arrangement to come back to shoot the *frantoio* for Cookucina. I say "loose" because the old guys said they would be very happy to be filmed, but it was all up to the boss. They were sure he'd be fine with it, but it was best for us to check. He wasn't reachable right now (he had meetings all day), but Sergio said he would ring him to firm the arrangement up. Which he did.

In all the shooting we did for Cookucina, all the different companies, houses, farms and shops we filmed, nobody asked for money. Except the man with the *frantoio*. Sergio patiently explained that we were doing this on our own nickel, and that maybe he would like to think of it as free publicity. He didn't seem convinced but reluctantly agreed to be there on the relevant morning to give us a tour of the place and explain how the press worked and what was so special about his oil. I have to say that Sergio warned me that he sounded a bit unreliable, but I had been so entranced by this cathedral to the olive that I insisted we should give it a go. To be honest, I thought Sergio was just making a bit of a meal of it, that he had taken against the guy on the phone. Sergio can be a bit like that. If you are a friend, you are a friend for life, but there aren't many of them, and there are a lot more people who give Sergio a *mal di pancia*, a stomach ache. I was pretty sure that Mr Olive Oil was giving Sergio a stomach ache.

I should have listened. When we arrived at the *frantoio* on the morning of Day Two everything looked just as it had before. We parked under the trees, we had two cars this time, with five of us and all the filming gear, and walked down the slope. This time, though, the frosted glass door was locked, and there was no-one around. Not a soul. We banged on the door. Looked around for any sign of life. We were there for a good half-hour while we tried to sort things out, and I am not sure, but I think there is a very good chance that the old guys were still sitting there inside silently watching the oil drip slowly from the press. It seemed an essential part of the process. *Il capo* was not answering his phone, but eventually, by digging out one of the neighbors, we managed to get in touch with the man who had served us our glass of olive oil. The *capo* was away, he explained, and maybe we could come back some other time. I tried to explain the difficulties of filming schedules, and how the next two weeks were fully-booked, but there was nothing he could do. So I agreed to try to find a slot, but we would need to fix something absolutely definite next time. "Yes, yes." he said. No problem.

Sergio was having none of it. This was a betrayal. The *capo* had agreed, and when you give your word in this part of the world, you stick to it. Now Sergio definitely had a *mal di pancia*. So much so that I soon realised we had the start of a vendetta here. Sergio said he would move heaven and earth to find us another *frantoio* nearer home, and nobody would ever buy oil from this man again, he would make sure of that. At one point I was afraid he was going to make me pour my five liters down the drain, but I got away with that. Sergio did find us another *frantoio*, and every time we drive past the one that let us down we have to make that particularly expressive Italian gesture where you hit your left bicep with your right hand while your left arm is held up in a clenched fist. Sergio does it even when he is driving.

It gets hot in the Kitchen

Forty-five minutes later we were back in Sarnano. Hanging around outside the *frantoio* had not been much fun because the temperature was on the rise. August was the only time we could film Cookucina and we knew it would be warm, but the forecast for the next few weeks was now predicting record temperatures. All the way back from the *frantoio* the AC had been blowing a gale in the car. Outside it must have been well into the upper 30s, while inside Sergio's quiet fuming was adding a couple of extra degrees. It wasn't even midday yet and it was going to continue to get hotter. Ideal conditions for a whole afternoon in the kitchen. Tam wasn't keen. She feels the heat rather badly and suggested we might re-arrange.

"Out of the question." I was as firm as I could be without sounding rude. At least that's what I thought. Tam told me in no uncertain terms that I had overstepped that mark.

"Look, the schedule is as tight as a drum," I insisted. "We've already lost one thing today. If we don't stick to the schedule the whole thing will fall apart. Unpick one stitch and everything will start to unravel."

"It's a shooting schedule," said Tam helpfully, "not the bloody bible."

I thought that was a bit over the top, and I told her so. Peter stepped in to diffuse the situation (not for the last time).

"Let's stick with the current schedule for the time being Tam. I'm sure we'll need a Revised Version before we're done, but the poor man's only just finished the thing."

Frankly it had taken me so many hours and so many headaches to figure out a schedule that worked that I was terrified of the prospect of having to start all over again. I was convinced that if one thing moved, then so must everything else, and right now we simply didn't have the time for it. Not in MY schedule anyway. Peter was right, before we were done there would be more than ten Revised Versions, the latest one always at the front of my green Director's folder where I carried all the scripts, notes, and so on. Whenever I got separated from it (which was often), a cold shiver went down my spine. This was an important document, and from Day Two onward the rest of them always referred to it as The Bible.

This afternoon's recipe was *Vellutata di Zucchini*, a creamy courgette soup light enough for summer, hot or cold. As soon as we arrived Sergio went straight off to the *orto* for the zucchini. It's where he always goes when he's in a bad mood, and we knew that's where he would stay until our need for zucchini became urgent. Thirty minutes later we were set up in the kitchen and ready to go. The auspices for the afternoon were not good though. Every time Peter turned on the lights the room began to heat up like a sauna, and after fifteen minutes we had to power down while Tam and Lia went out to cool off. I know what you're thinking - kitchens are hot places... they're meant to be. Trouble is, women who front TV cookery shows all have to look springtime-fresh. Nobody sweats in a TV kitchen! And this was just rehearsal.

Finally everything was ready to go and we summoned Sergio. He arrived bearing an enormous basket overflowing with zucchini. There must have been thirty of them - big, succulent and an impossible glossy dark green. These looked like zucchini after the food stylist had been at them with hairspray or washing up liquid or whatever it is they use. It seemed a shame to slice them up, but that was the job Lia gave Tam, and one she pulled off admirably. Here's the recipe they conjured up over the next hour or so (with a few cooling-off breaks)...

CREAM of ZUCCHINI SOUP with GREEK YOGURT

- *8 zucchini*
- *1 onion*
- *vegetable stock*
- *curry powder*
- *4 slices of white bread*
- *salt, white pepper*
- *4 tablespoons of greek yogurt*
- *extra virgin olive oil*

Thinly slice the zucchini. Put the finely chopped onion in a pan with the oil. When it is slightly browned, add the zucchini, curry powder to taste, salt and pepper. Cover with vegetable stock, and when the zucchini are cooked, blend everything in a food mixer. Return to the hob to heat gently. Add a spoonful of Greek yogurt to each serving and serve with toast.

Toast. Sounds straightforward enough, doesn't it? But bread is another matter of heated debate here in Le Marche. Restaurants here have one big plus - no-one tips. Leaving a gratuity at the end of a meal would be seen as rather rude - most restaurants are family-run and it would be a bit like tipping your grandma. But there's one thing that **does** get added to your bill that personally I would rather wasn't. Bread. It works as a cover charge, you get it whether you want it or not. And plenty of it. But as far as I am concerned most of the time it's well-nigh inedible. Even in the best restaurants. There's a thing they have in Italy that dates back, I believe, to the days of Mussolini and the inter-war depression. *Il Duce's* very particular brand of socialism decreed that everyone should have access to bread, and all bakers would be obliged to make a simple, cheap loaf available at all times. It's called *pane comune,* it's cheap, unsalted, and uninspiring. Oh, and it seems to go stale in about three and half minutes. But it's the first thing that arrives on your restaurant table after you sit down. And as far as I am concerned it stays there until the dishes are cleared away at the end.

This is all a bit odd because you can buy the most wonderful bread in Sarnano - as good as you will find anywhere in France, or in upmarket eateries in New York or Vienna. Of course, there are several bakeries in Sarnano, four at the last reckoning. And that's not counting all the bars who make their own cakes. Then, out in the countryside there seem to be innumerable farms with a *forno a legna*, a wood-fired oven, where they bake and sell their own bread. I don't go out there much, because my own personal favorite baker on the main square does four varieties of bread each of which would win the Golden Slice at the annual Berlin Breadfair (if there was such a thing). I can't tell you what this particular *panificio* is called I am afraid. It's known to us as Gina Lollobrigida's because when we first discovered it the woman behind the counter was a dead ringer for Sophia Loren (...only kidding!). It turned out, in fact, that she wasn't Italian at all, but Cuban. And how she washed up in Sarnano is another story altogether.

Mind you, you have to know what day of the week it is because the different types of loaf are all baked on different days, and if you've got your heart set on a *Siciliano* and you go in to Gina Lollobrigida's on a Wednesday you will have to make do with a *Pugliese*. Or is it *Arabo* on Wednesday? I can never remember. It's all much too complicated really, especially as you have to remember when they take their day off.

If I get that wrong, then it's down the road to the Jolly Baker where I'll buy a *ciabatta*. Not because I **want** a *ciabatta*, but because he's always sold out of *Pugliese*. Which is completely different from Gina's *Pugliese*, by the way. Strange place, Italy.

The Fire-Blanket

Vellutata di Zucchini was our second cookery shoot in the kitchen, and by now we were beginning to feel like veterans. We had solved most of the teething problems from Day One. Tinker, for instance was now tucked up in her basket next door with a bone, instead of dragging me and the broom-handle boom all over the place. Watching yesterday's rushes Lia had noticed my microphone dropping into shot every now and again - a little red and white furry thing showing its face for a second and then disappearing just as quickly as it had arrived. Then five minutes later it would pop up somewhere totally different. Lia said it looked like a little *scoiattolo*, a squirrel, so that's what it became. For the next three weeks the microphone was always referred to as "the squirrel", and my job (or at least one of them) was being the squirrel-master.

The *Vellutata* went remarkably smoothly, though the squirrel-master was called on to handle something quite out of the ordinary for the first time when Tam decided to ad lib. I had warned her against this, knowing full well that she would ignore me sooner or later. It had come sooner than I thought. When you watch Nigella Lawson or Jamie Oliver talking to the camera over a plate of chopped shallots or whatever, you probably don't stop to think that they are not alone. In fact they are surrounded by a crew, each operating their own bit of equipment and standing, at least in our case, in a spaghetti of cables. And each of them is in a very precise position which has been worked out in advance as the director set up the shot. Jamie and Nigella are NOT expected to suddenly set off across the kitchen under their own steam. Which would, of course, mean everyone else has to move with them. Without getting in the shot, or tripping over each other. Yet that is precisely what Tam did half way through the *Vellutata*. Lia had asked

Tam to transfer the chopped *zucchini* to a large saucepan waiting on the hob. There was a little awkward moment when Tam correctly identified that Lia didn't quite trust her to get them all into the pan without spilling some. She ticked Lia off, confiding to the camera that she thought Lia was afraid she would start a fire.

"Which reminds me, just take a look at this..." at which point Tam set off across the kitchen.

Unbelievably, we pulled it off. I managed to duck down out of shot as Peter panned the camera round to follow Tam. I swung the broom handle round in a wide arc bringing the squirrel up underneath as Tam grabbed a fire-blanket from the wall.

"Look at what Lia's done, she's brought a fire-blanket into the kitchen for when I cook. She has so little confidence in me that this is just in case it goes horribly wrong."

Lia smiled a little uneasily, knowing she'd been caught out. But Tam thought it was hilarious, and suddenly both women dissolved in spontaneous laughter. Peter gave me the thumbs up - he'd got the shot - and I shouted "Cut". Tam's ad lib had worked a treat, injecting a little bit of the unplanned magic that really lifts a show. You can take a look for yourself if you want. It happens about 12½ minutes into Program Two. We were pleased as punch. But what we didn't know was that we had not quite seen the last of the fire-blanket for the day.

Crema di Nonna Giudi

We planned to shoot two recipes in the kitchen that day. By lunchtime we'd completed the *Vellutata* recording, except for the glossy "packshot" we had to do for each completed recipe. These can be surprisingly difficult, not just because of the problem of presenting the food in the best possible light, and preferably while it's still piping hot, but also (and this is not a problem on most other photographic assignments) because the subject matter is edible. And it was almost lunchtime. It was Peter's job to set up the food and grab that award-winning cover shot. But the rest of us were done for the session, and hungry. So it was very difficult to avoid the temptation to pick at the food. Peter eventually had to build an exclusion zone round the food till the photos were done.

Lunch that day was, of course, *Vellutata di Zucchini.* Followed by *Crostini with Ciabuscolo* and *Stracchino,* slices of bread toasted with salami and cheese. Which sounds fairly ordinary, but wasn't. *Stracchino* is a sort of soft spreadable cheese, halfway between *mascarpone* and *mozzarella.* This dish was a good example of the difficulty of transposing Italian recipes into English. There are only three ingredients - toast, s*tracchino* and *ciabuscolo.* The only one of the three that exists outside Italy is toast (though finding a good *Siciliano* won't be easy), so we had to scratch around for something that was a good approximation. For the *stracchino* we went for Philadelphia cheese, but the *ciabuscolo* was a real problem. It's that soft salami that you can only get the authentically in the foothills of the Sibillini Mountains, never mind in Manchester or Ohio. Anyway the Crostini were so good that Peter and Tam insisted we had to get them into the series. This was a change to the schedule that I could cope with - just a different dish to fit into an already-existing kitchen slot. I think I put it in program 4, so you'll have to wait for the full recipe, and the lowdown on the secret ingredient that goes into a top-dollar *Ciabuscolo.*

Lunch was done, the coffees were over and the kitchen cleared. Time to get back to work. This afternoon we were making our first *dolce* - it's called *Crema di Nonna Giudi* - Grandma Giudi's Cream Pudding. And things were about to get tricky. Lia was going to get Tam to do all the work on this one. The recipe was fairly simple on the face of it - just milk, eggs and sugar, but it involved a bit of multi-tasking. First Tam had to put a liter of milk on the stove to warm. A liter of milk means eight eggs. Four of them went into the food mixer whole, but the others had to be separated - yolks straight into the mixer, holding back the whites. But separating eggs was not (yet) among Tam's limited range of kitchen skills - so Lia gave her a crash course. Somewhat literally. In TV, as we know, you have to be prepared to shoot everything two or three times, so we had made sure we had plenty of eggs on hand. Which was just as well because we got through the better part of a dozen before we had four clean unbroken yolks ready for the mixer. I'm not sure what happened to the whites, but someone, somewhere, must have been eating a very large meringue the following day.

And while all this was going on, you will recall, the milk was warming gently on the hob. Alongside there was another pan in which Lia had got Tam to start on the caramel. This involved five big spoonsful of sugar and a squeeze of lemon being brought up to the temperature at which it would caramelize and start to turn that lovely nutty brown, with a taste to match. The trick here is NOT to interfere with it while it is coming up to heat. Absolutely no stirring allowed, but you have to keep a close eye on it because there's a very fine line between caramelized and burnt. As we were about to discover. The eggs of course were taking longer than usual, what with Tam's ineptitude and Peter's demands for re-takes. So much so that everyone had taken their eye off the ball. Suddenly, in mid egg, Lia, whose nose is finely attuned to the changing smells of the kitchen, yelled,

"Stop, STOP! *Il caramello!"*

But it was too late. We all turned to look at the pan, out of which were coming the first billows of grey smoke. In an instant the room felt extra hot. Lia lunged for the fire-blanket. Peter, with a cameraman's true instincts in time of disaster, kept rolling, and Tam made the best of a bad job by explaining the whole thing to camera and reminding the viewers that this was just the sort of thing she had told Lia would *never* happen when she first spotted the fire-blanket. Within seconds the pan was smothered and the emergency was over before it had begun. What's more we had another nice bit of impromptu stuff for the program. Things were looking good. Everyone had dealt with the situation in a proper professional fashion and we'd got a great little sequence in the can. Me? What was I doing during all this? Well the squirrel never made it into the frame, and you can hear what everyone is saying, so I can't have done too badly. But the truth is I think my part on the day was to panic. Well *somebody's* got to, haven't they?

Fifteen minutes later the second lot of caramelized sugar (carefully watched this time) arrived at the point of perfection and was poured gently into a waiting oven-proof dish where Lia expertly moved it around until it had finely coated the bottom. Next the milk and eggs mixture was poured on top and the whole thing set into a *bain marie*. Into the oven at 170°C, and 40 minutes later Tam had made her first *dolce - Crema di Nonna Giudi*. Here's how she did it. Sort of.

GRANDMA GIUDI'S CREAM PUDDING

- *1 liter of milk*
- *8 eggs*
- *5 heaped tablespoons of sugar (for the cream pudding)*
- *2 tablespoons of sugar (for the caramel)*

Separate four of the eggs. Beat four full eggs and four yolks with the sugar. Add the warm milk and stir gently together till smooth. Put 2 spoonsful of sugar into a heavy-bottomed pan with a squeeze of lemon. Heat gently until it has caramelized. Pour the caramel into a mold, pour the cream into the mold and bake in a bain marie for 40 minutes at 170°/180°.

The Fish Pirate

Sometimes the world just works. Two shoots in the kitchen and a fire was enough for the time being. But all was OK, because when we woke up the next day the sky was bright and clear, the temperature was already climbing and a glance at "The Bible" told us that today we were on the road. In the afternoon we were travelling up into the mountains to find a herd of the local cattle in their natural pastures. Tam and Lia were due to record a couple of PTCs. On paper it was a short and simple shoot. It should have been a pleasant afternoon out. But then, there is that old adage "never work with children or animals", so I suppose we should have been warned.

But for the moment we were starting in town, with a shoot in the main square. Every Tuesday and Friday a little van rolls into town and a very large man tumbles out of it. He's come to sell fish. He wears a big ground length apron that carries (at least in my mind) the scars and blood-staining of successful fish-dissection dating back at least a decade. And a bandanna. He must *have* a name, but I don't know it. We know him simply as The Fish Pirate.

The Fish Pirate is very popular, so there is always a crowd round his van. His fish must be good, though, because the crowds always turn up even though he sometimes doesn't. There are dark rumors that sometimes he doesn't come because he's hit the bottle. Rum probably. And he likely gets his parrot drunk on it too. Actually that's almost certainly just small-town gossip. My guess is he doesn't come because he's got some other piracy going on somewhere else. But today, as expected, he is here. Surrounded by *casalinghe* shopping for the family lunch. As usual there's lots of haggling and lots of waving of fish. And sometimes fish that wave about by themselves. Personally, I am a wimp who likes their food to be properly dead before it comes into my sight. The things that are alive on a fishmonger's stall tend to have far too many legs. For the next hour or so we'd have to try to bring all this under control so we could buy fish for two of Lia's recipes. But... big man, small van, lots of people, live crustaceans - I could see this might be a tricky shoot.

We were shopping for two dishes, *Acciughe Al Verde* and *Mousse di Scorfano. Acciughe* are anchovies, though there is another word for an anchovy that I find easier to remember. It's *alice,* which is my daughter's name. Alice was not impressed when I pointed this out, so I always have to call them *acciughe* when she's around. She won't even let me get away with the proper Italian pronunciation (AL-EE-CHAY). I am not a great fish fan, but Lia's *Acciughe Al Verde,* which is fresh-cooked anchovies sprinkled with oodles of chopped parsley and drenched with olive oil (*extra vergine*, of course) is to die for. *Mousse di Scorfano,* though, is another thing altogether, as I was about to discover.

Film cameras don't cut much ice round here. Especially not when they're getting in the way of the really important things in life. Like food. So Peter had the devil of a job getting the camera in amongst the customers and into a position where he could see Lia, Tam, the Fish Pirate and his fish. Fortunately Peter is quite tall and the *Marchigiani* are, by and large, quite short, and fairly quickly Peter gave me the thumbs up that he was able to shoot across the heads of a couple of elderly ladies discussing the merits of about a million types of fish. Lia and Tam had edged their way to the front and caught the eye of the Pirate (who does not, sadly, have an eye patch, which would have been a nice touch), I called "Action", and we were recording.

I hope you've got the picture that this was a bit of a scrum, because that's my excuse for the fact that I had become separated from my headphones, and even though I could get the squirrel in over the top so I was sure we were picking up the key voices, I couldn't quite hear what was being said. This is tricky, because the squirrel (or to be more exact the microphone inside) is very directional, which means you have to know who's talking, so you can swivel the squirrel to point directly at them. I was having to do it visually. Just point the thing at anyone with their mouth open. It generally works - but not always. Which is just as well because none of us could understand a word of what was being said.

I mean the English members of the crew, of course. Lia could understand perfectly well, but as soon as I shouted "Action", she and the Pirate had begun to talk in dialect. It's a funny thing about Italian that there's still a lot of discussion about what "proper" Italian is. It is a function of the complex history of this country. It has only actually been a single, united country for a little over 150 years. For most of the post-Roman period Italy was divided into many different kingdoms and dukedoms. And of course for hundreds of years a great swathe of it, including Le Marche and Sarnano, belonged directly to the Pope, and became known as The Papal Lands. Most of the rest of the country was under the constant dominion of foreign powers like France, Spain or Austro-Hungary, which has contributed much to the extraordinary richness of the Italian heritage. But, out of the respect for the Pontiff, the Papal Lands were largely left alone, which is why towns like Sarnano still retain their medieval character. In fact there was hardly any development in the Papal Lands for many hundred of years, while a procession of Popes lined the coffers of the Vatican with taxes drawn on the people. There's an old saying locally that it's better to have a dead body in your house than a *Marchigiano* at the door, because a stranger knocking at your door was generally the taxman.

"Proper" Italian, which is to say the language most commonly and widely spoken, originated in Florence, and just about everyone in the country can speak it. But that is not necessarily how they choose to communicate with one another, because Italy is still rich with thousands of local dialects. And when I say local, I mean very local. Sarnano has one. So much so that if I am having coffee with Luigi, our *geometra*, we will be having a perfectly serviceable conversation in regular Italian. I will understand 90% of what he says straight off, and if I don't I can ask him to repeat it slowly, *piu' lento*, or to say it another way. In short, we get by in Italian. But then we'll be joined by an old schoolfriend of his, and suddenly I cannot understand a word of what is being said. There's a heavy accent round here, for sure, which Luigi will fall into at the drop of a hat. That alone makes quite a difference. "T"s for instance, become "D"s. And "P"s become "B"s. I learned this last one at an early stage, and in somewhat unfortunate circumstances. Not long after we moved here our neighbors Walter and Bianca invited me to dinner one evening while Tam was back in England. I didn't know it at the time, but Bianca's accent is one of the heaviest around. They started to tell me that they were going on holiday soon. Where to,

I inquired? To the South they said, we'll be touring around. Now, I *thought* they said they were touring the south of *Italy* until Bianca started talking about how she had always wanted to visit Bombay. Ah... so they were going to Southern India. I hadn't realized that. So we embarked on a long conversation about the climate, the clothing, the temperature, the spicy food, during which Walter and Bianca were looking more and more puzzled. I couldn't figure out what was going wrong, until eventually we somehow re-wound the conversation and I discovered that the place Bianca had always wanted to visit was not Bombay but Pompeii. Or *Bombay*, as it is in the local *Sarnanese* accent.

The accent alone would be bad enough, but it's the dialects that make things really incomprehensible. And there are lots of them. The language of Italy still reflects its fractured history. The country is divided into twenty regions whose boundaries were largely drawn by the competing external powers. The regions are sub-divided into over a hundred provinces (we are in Macerata) and the provinces into *comuni* (like Sarnano) of which there are over eight thousand. And I wouldn't mind betting that most of those *comuni* have their own dialect. From my kitchen window I look out across rolling hills to the east, as the land falls away from the mountains towards the Adriatic Sea and Croatia. On top of one of the nearby hills I can see the little town of Gualdo. It's the nearest *comune* to Sarnano, about a fifteen minute drive away. And it has a totally different dialect to Sarnano. You don't quite need your passport to go there, but it must have felt like that 70 or 80 years ago, before they opened the new road and built a bridge across the *Rio Terra* river, which, as you no doubt remember, is how they came to discover the *San Giacomo* spring which led to the opening of the Spa.

Some years ago, Tam's Aunt Plinny came to visit us here, along with her husband Ferando (the Italian waiter she had met and married in Chelsea in the 1950s). We took them to see a delightful little house that was for sale in a hamlet up in the hills on the way to Gualdo. I was always a bit nervous of going up there by myself because of the old boy who lived in the house next door. He would always come out for a chat after his dogs had woken him up barking at the first sign of intruders from the outside world. And of course, the problem was that I couldn't understand a word he was saying to me - either because it was in dialect or heavily-accented Italian or both. So our conversations were short and a bit unrewarding, to say the least. Not that he seemed to mind. Except sometimes they were prolonged slightly by his daughter appearing with coffee and a home-made cake. This time I was looking forward to a more substantial conversation - with Ferando acting as translator. Unfortunately, even though we got coffee and cake, the conversation never really got off the ground. It turned out that Ferando couldn't understand a word he was saying either.

Buying the *alici* (sorry, Alice) went smoothly enough. The Fish Pirate was even bold enough to start telling Lia how she might cook them. Then it was time for the *Scorfano*. Now when I tell you that less politically correct Italians will sometimes describe a woman they don't like as *un scorfano,* you might begin to conjure up a mental image of this fish. It is not pretty. It's a species of rockfish, sort of orange and craggy - like a rock I suppose. It has a big head and an enormous mouth. The body is relatively insignificant, tapering away from the giant mouth towards the tail. My initial thought that they weren't going to be value for money as there couldn't be much meat on them was compounded somewhat when the Fish Pirate told us the price - 90 Euros for two of them. Now I understood why we called him a Pirate. I pointed out to Lia that this would make a big dent in our almost invisible budget and questioned the wisdom of cooking Fish Mousse. But she wasn't having any of it and insisted that their delicate flavor was just right for this light and delicious summer dish. But we were going to have wait to find out if the flavor justified the outlay. These guys were going in the freezer, because it was time to head for the hills.

Cattle, Sheep and Maremmas

There's nothing fancy about the way they eat meat round here. A lot of restaurants have a big sign outside saying *Tutto alla Braccia,* meaning "everything cooked on the grill". The *Marchigiana,* a nice hotel and restaurant just outside Sarnano, is one of them. The dining room is built round a central feature of a giant wood-fired grill so you can watch your meat cook while you're getting through your *antipasto* (which is to die for, by the way). You're hard pushed to find meat being served with a sauce anywhere, but then why would you do *anything* to obscure the taste of flame-grilled meat? Especially when the meat has lived its life in mountain pastures instead of in a shed.

Today's "Bible" reading called for a trip up into the mountains above Sarnano. Our job was to find a grazing herd of Marchigiana cows, the distinctive local breed of cattle, and a flock of sheep. We wanted to film a couple of PTCs and some "actuality" sequences of Lia explaining to Tam something of the local ways with rearing animals for food. But before we set off Sergio had a warning to impart. The cattle, he said, *look* dangerous, with their long horns, but it's the flock of sheep that you'll need to be careful of.

I laughed. I shouldn't have done, I know. But I honestly thought he was joking. He was not amused, and told me to listen carefully. It's not the sheep who are dangerous, but the dogs who look after them. And he began to explain something that had puzzled me for years. Driving through the mountains here, you'll often see a flock of sheep on an open bit of hillside with clear views for miles around and no shepherd anywhere to be seen. There are wolves in these mountains, and there's nothing they would like better than to pick off sheep from an unguarded herd. But it turns out they are not unguarded at all, because in amongst these flocks you will always find a pair of sheepdogs. And they are dogs of a very special breed. They're called Maremmas or *Maremmano*. They are large (think Pyrennean Mountain Dog) and white, with a coat that looks much like a sheep's fleece from a distance, so they're very hard to spot in a flock. And they are fierce! Their job is to protect the flock from wolf-attack. They're very popular with environmentalists, especially in areas like the Monti Sibillini National Park, because they work by deterring wolves rather than attacking them. So using Maremmas is a way of safeguarding the wolf population. As well as the sheep. They train the dogs by introducing the puppies (sometimes as young as 3 or 4 weeks) into the flocks so they bond with the sheep. Occasionally they are trained to look after cattle in this same way. And a few years back in Australia a Maremma puppy was trained this way so it could safeguard an endangered breed of penguin.

But though their main job is deterrence, you do not want to mix it with one of these guys. Even though they rarely find themselves in mortal combat with a predator, working dogs are often fitted with a *roccale*, a spiked iron collar which protects their neck in the event they get into a dogfight with a wolf. Sergio, of course, is familiar with the ways of the Maremma, and he wanted to point out that they very rarely attack human beings, and are much happier if they can make sure you stay away from their flock. But, he said, the one thing that really gets them going is dogs, and we of course, were going to have Tinker the Cookucina dog with us that afternoon. So he wanted us all to be fully aware of what Maremmas were and how they worked. And at all times to make sure Tinker stayed in the car when we were filming close to sheep. We all nodded in assent. He had made the dangers very clear, and with our first Health and Safety talk over, we jumped into our two cars and headed off up the mountain.

But after an hour or so of driving around we had seen not the faintest sign of a sheep, let alone a Maremma. I was in the front car, and when we rounded a bend and came across a farmhouse, I decided to take executive action. We needed a bit of local advice. I pulled over at the entrance to the farm and started to walk down the track to the house. It wasn't very far, maybe 50 yards, but when I got half-way down it I heard muffled shouting coming from Sergio's Fiat Panda, parked up behind my car. I stopped. Tam, in the passenger seat, wound down her window. She was mouthing something at me and pointing towards the corner of the farmhouse. What she had seen was a big Maremma coming along the side of the house to investigate. I looked towards where she was pointing. Just in time to see him come round the corner. He was gigantic. More like a small polar bear than a big dog. And as I saw him, so did Tinker. She started to bark.

So did the Maremma, who let out one blood-curdling deep roar, and began to move menacingly towards me. I was about ten yards from the car now, with the Maremma about another ten yards behind me. Sergio was gesticulating from the car - making sort of keep calm movements - both hands outstretched and gently moving up and down. Good advice, but then I also wanted to be back in the car with the door locked as soon as possible. So I did my best to keep calm and run at the same time. It came out as a sort of Michael Jackson moonwalk, only going forwards. And the dog was going exactly twice as fast as I was. Net result? We both arrived at the car at the same time, and suddenly the dog stopped, just inches away from me. We froze. The dog had me pinned up against the car. I was terrified. But I needn't have been. Hearing the dog bark, the owner, a little old lady wearing the ubiquitous old ladies' blue-patterned housecoat, had emerged from the farm.

"Don't worry", she shouted. "He won't hurt you". It turned out he was an ancient old thing, long retired and now completely harmless, but still useful to deter unwanted visitors. Like me. I still didn't quite believe her though, and so I stood rooted to the spot, afraid to even try to open the car door in case any sharp movement might spur the dog to action. It took her a minute or so to make her way arthritically out to the car, whereupon she grabbed the dog by the collar (I swear she had to reach UP to do so!) and pulled him away.

With the immediate canine threat out of the way, Sergio emerged from the car to explain why we had decided to drop in on her unannounced. As it happened the old lady was a mine of local information (they generally are) and soon told us where we could find sheep. And cattle. I am not certain, but I am pretty sure that both sheep and cattle belonged to some not-so-distant relative of hers, but she certainly knew where they were going to be. Back on the road I was, of course, the subject of some ridicule for my craven behaviour in the face of attack by a harmless old house-dog. I pointed out that we did not know that at the time, but no-one was interested and you could almost feel the story begin to grow as it would be embellished in the telling in weeks to come. That's why it's important for me to get the full, unadulterated facts down on paper here and now.

I also discovered that I had misinterpreted Sergio's hand movements. Apparently he had not been telling me to "take it slowly", but to "come back here". I had failed to notice that his fingers were being curled slightly inwards on the downward sweep of the hand. This is a gesture that doesn't exist where I come from, but is in common use in Italy. I should have recognized it because Tam had come across it a few years earlier in circumstances that were genuinely dangerous. But that's a story from the making of Wild Boar Stew, which was in Week Two of the Cookucina shoot, so there's a lot to get through before we get to that.

The PTCs with the cattle went like a dream. We found them grazing on a spot with the most wonderful backdrop of mountains disappearing, layer upon layer, into a blue afternoon haze. The cattle are a bit of a tourist attraction, so they're used to people getting up close with photographic equipment, and they just carried on munching gently away as Lia told Tam what makes this special local breed, the *Marchigiana,* such tasty meat.

The sheep however were another matter altogether, thanks to their Maremmas. Peter wanted a shot where the background was absolutely filled with sheep ("We've seen enough mountains for one show, Tam"), and for that we would have get quite close to them. And we needed to be able to see the Maremmas in amongst them. But every time we got close enough for Peter to start setting up the shot the Maremmas would pick the flock up and move them a little bit further away. So we'd have to grab all the kit again and start tip-toeing closer. By the time we had done this four or five times, we were quite some distance from the car and I, for one, was a little bit worried that the Maremmas might decide to stand their ground. And Tam was anxious to get back because we'd left Tinker locked in the car for obvious reasons. In the end Peter caved in, muttering "You win!" under his breath at the Maremmas. We got our shot, but I have say it is rather a peculiar one. Tam and Lia were getting a bit overheated by this time and when it came to recording it proved difficult for both of them to get their lines right at the same time. And when they did, of course, the flock had shifted and Peter couldn't see the Maremmas in the shot, so we had to go again. We got there in the end, but only by slicing bits of different takes together in the edit. I *think* it works. It's in Episode 5 - have a look for yourself, it starts at about 11 minutes in to the episode.

The Sibillini Mountains, by the way, now have a dish named in their honour. Lia called it *Pasta Sibillini* because it uses the *ricotta* cheese that was made right in front of our eyes in Episode 5 - in a country kitchen up in the foothills. Lia had taken us there so we could see how her friend Maria makes the *ricotta* we needed for the dish. In fact Tam and Lia got a double lesson - in making not just ricotta but the *pecorino* cheese that's part of the same process. And out in the farmyard they got to meet the sheep that produced the milk for both.

SIBILLINI PASTA

- *360 g. of dry pasta*
- *half an onion*
- *2 sausages*
- *200g. of ricotta cheese*
- *some saffron*
- *salt and pepper*
- *parmesan cheese*
- *extra virgin olive oil*

Chop the onion and soften them in a little oil. Chop the sausage roughly. Add it to the onion and sauté for a few minutes. Remove from the heat, then add the ricotta cheese and a little salt and pepper to taste. Dissolve the saffron in a little stock or the water you used to cook the pasta. Add it to the sausage, combine the mixture with the pasta (cooked al dente and drained). Sprinkle with parmesan before serving.

Delicious, and well worthy of the beautiful mountains that bear its name. Nasty moment during the shoot for this bit of the program, though. It was, as you can imagine I am sure, just a little bit hot in Maria's tiny kitchen while she was making the *ricotta*. Tam was clearly keen to get back outside in the mountain breeze as quickly as possible. And as soon as Maria produced the rich and creamy slab of *pecorino* from her pan, Tam was straight into her "Thank you very much, it's been delightful meeting you..." routine. Fortunately it was Lia who pointed out to her that we hadn't even **started** making the *ricotta* yet.

The Anchovy Horror

Arriving back in town, the kitchen suddenly felt like a safe haven. But Tam was in for a surprise. Lia had a job for her. One that she would put down as her most unpleasant experience in the kitchen throughout the whole hectic schedule. This afternoon they were going to make the *Acciughe al Verde*, anchovies with parsley, and the recording began with this exchange:

```
LIA
Ora, abbiamo comprato queste belle
acciughe.  Tu le pulisci

TAM
I have to clean them
```

Cleaning tiny fish was not Tam's idea of fun. In one swift and expert movement Lia showed her how to break the head off and remove the spine and the guts by running a finger up and down the body. Tam explained to camera...

```
TAM
I have to break the head off, oh my
goodness me. Scrape out its innards with one
finger in one direction and scrape up the
```

remainder in the other. Oh.

Tam's face was contorted with disgust. And this was a tiny anchovy she was disembowelling... it was hardly a Japanese whaling crew in action. Nevertheless, like a true professional, she had a go. Lia pointed out she might find it easier with her eyes open.

TAM
Then take out the spine. And pull it off.

LIA
Brava, molto bene

TAM
I can't look at the head coming off. Oh!

This word "Oh" taken from the transcript of the program does scant justice to the blood-curdling gurgle that emerged from somewhere deep inside Tamsen Courtenay. Sometimes television is a demanding mistress. Suddenly Lia stepped in. Clearly Tam was not up to the task.

LIA
No no, guarda, guarda

TAM
I broke it! And left some vital organs in

You can see this exchange for yourself if you go to 4.05 in Episode 2. Lia, though, had already seen enough. *Acciughe al Verde* should be a pretty dish, with the flattened fish laid neatly out in serried ranks like a herringbone army. She had apocalyptic visions of the glutinous mess it was likely to become if the job were left to Tam. Better find her something else to do. How about chopping parsley? Tam looked relieved. Soon we were back on track with the recipe, which was just as well because this was this evening's dinner. So the food was going OK, but what about Tam's culinary education? Not so good. Though we still had a good fortnight ahead of us to turn Tam into a competent cook. Lia did not look optimistic. Here's what we ate that night, and how it *should* be prepared:

ANCHOVIES in PARSLEY

- 800g. anchovies
- 2 glasses of white wine vinegar
- Parsley
- 1 clove of garlic
- salt, pepper
- extra virgin olive oil

Chop the parsley, cover it with oil, add garlic, salt and pepper and leave to rest. Remove the heads and entrails of the anchovies and fold them open like a book. Arrange them in a baking dish and add the wine vinegar until the fish are just covered. Add salt and pepper and set the pan on the hob for a few minutes. Remove from the heat, lift them gently out of the vinegar and lay them uniformly on a large flat serving plate. Drench them until covered with the prepared oil and parsley.

Ortos and Earthquakes

Next day was a Saturday and life in the Cookucina house was going to be even more hectic than usual. This was a cooking day. Mostly. Two recipes in the kitchen, morning and afternoon, and then dinner *al fresco* in the *orto*. Dinner in the allotment may not sound like much, but let me put it another way. Sergio's daughter Federica had dropped by from Tuscany for the weekend. Along with and her husband Rudi, their eight-year-old daughter, Rachele, and new baby Vittoria. It was a golden opportunity for us to build a typical family meal into the show. Sergio's allotment is a long thin strip of land that stretches out away from the Cookucina house following the contours of the old city wall. Our house is one level above theirs, and if we look out in the morning we can often see Sergio planting something out or fiddling with his roses or whatever people do in allotments. I generally call out a cheery "hello" in the hope that he'll get the hint and drop off a basket of tomatoes or something on the way home. When I say "drop off" I mean it. He'll leave them on the wall below our window and shout up to let us know they're there. That way it's me who has to do the fifty-three steps down, and then the same back up, to collect them. Sometimes, when I am feeling lazy, I will leave them there till I have to take the dog out. Can't do them any harm, after all. They'll just be ripening that little bit more in the sun. And living in a small community like this you don't have to worry that they will still be there - nothing ever goes for a walk like it does in London. When I was away Lia would occasionally bring round meals for Tam and just leave them on the front doorstep if she was out. All nicely wrapped, of course, but without the slightest worry that they might disappear. If you are in Sarnano one evening, hungry and caught short without any cash, it's always worth checking our front doorstep.

But I still haven't given you a proper picture of the *orto*. The small path along which Sergio walks back the hundred meters or so to his house is called the *via degli Orti*, the street of the allotments. There are ten or a dozen *orti* in two long strips below the *via*. Each of them has the same characteristic shape as Sergio's - long and thin, and following the gently curving contour of the old city wall. In fact the outer edge of Sergio's, bounded by a low wall, is actually right on the city wall itself. The view from our window high above is one of a patchwork quilt of thin allotments, the rich earthy colors of the land streaked with lines of tomatoes or beans, intersected with a regular pattern of low walls. Two or three sets of narrow steps run down between them to give access to allotments on the lower level. It is a lovely view and remarkably different from the vista of roof-tiles falling away from windows on the other side of town. But it wasn't always like this. These *orti* hold a sad secret, one which it took me many years to work out.

From the moment I first walked under the Brunforte arch and into the *centro storico* I had been fascinated by the history of this little town. I had learned about its founding in 1265, about how St Francis of Assisi had visited the area some forty years earlier during his travels across Italy, and how the town had been built on the castrum principle to protect itself against invaders. I also began to understand just a little of how a small medieval town like this might have worked. In the middle ages there were the same number of inhabitants as there are now, but all crammed into the tiny *centro storico* instead of spread out in the new development which has grown up around the old town in recent decades. I learned how taxes were based on the number of chimneys in operation on a dwelling. And how flour produced in the watermills of the surrounding countryside would be brought to the *Porta di Pesa*, the "Weighing Gate", to be stored in a communal granary (now re-purposed as the local cinema - where else can you find a seven hundred year old cinema?). But then, in thinking about the relationship between the town, with its tight little streets running between rows of tall houses joined in a single unbroken run, and the countryside, where everything would have been grown before being brought to market in town, I began to ask myself why would they have had allotments? Who would have wanted a vegetable garden in 1265? And then I read about the earthquakes.

Italy is a seismic hotspot, and down the years many earthquakes have ravaged this region. In 2006 we felt the ground shake, as much of the ancient town of L'Aquila, 55 miles away, was reduced to rubble. Ten years earlier Giotto's magnificent frescoes in the Basilica at Assisi, including a depiction of St Francis himself appearing before the Mamluk Sultan in Egypt, were damaged almost beyond repair by an earthquake whose epicenter was close to Serravalle del Chienti, about halfway between Sarnano and Assisi. Gentle tremors are something you have to get used to if you want to live in Italy. And you do. But you also know that there is always the possibility of the big one.

There are not much in the way of records to go on, but it seems there have been two REALLY big ones in Sarnano, one at the very end of the 18th century, the other in 1921. One day a few years back I woke up (possibly because the house was shaking slightly) with a revelatory thought. These regular shaped allotments weren't just gardens designed by someone with a liking for straight lines and right angles - they had once been houses. That morning I flung open the shutters and, looking down, I could see not allotments, but a streetplan, each *orto* the footprint of a house like mine, where people had lived, loved and died, some of them possibly as the earthquake brought down walls and roofs already more than five hundred years old. Now it suddenly became possible to conjure up a mental picture of how fortress-like this place must have been when the unbroken lines of solid brick houses wound round the hill on which Sarnano is built like so many lines of defense, each one capable of being held if the outer line below it had been breached. It was on one of these footprints that we were going to dine that night after watching the sun go down behind the mountains, in the balmy evening heat, by the light of candles and oil lamps.

Alfresco dining

Lia had chosen to cook two dishes that were perfect for an outdoor summer meal. Light and fresh but still substantial. And not a salad in sight. I am not sure whether it's a regular saying or just one of his, but when I was asking my friend Adriano if iPads were popular in Italy, he told me, "Yes, they're everywhere.... like salad." For a starter

Lia was going to teach Tam how to make *Pepperoni Grigliati con Labneh*, char-grilled red peppers with a rich and creamy-white Labneh served with roughly sliced *cotto a legna* toast. Fortunately this meant buying the bread from someone who had baked it in a wood-fired oven. For a moment I thought we might be baking it ourselves, in which case I was sure we would be needing the fire-blanket again. In fact the preparation and cooking of this dish went remarkably smoothly and Lia let us in on a little cook's trick. Having grilled the peppers until the skin had turned completely black she then put them straight into brown paper bags, folded them closed and put them on one side for ten minutes. After which you could pull the skin off them with no trouble at all leaving just the sweet and succulent flesh. It's the steam that does it apparently.

Labneh. I know what you're thinking. Isn't that an Arabic dish? Or from the Levant or the eastern Mediterranean at any rate? And yes, you're right, but any dish from that area comes from a historic melting pot of traditions that cross many modern boundaries. You'll find claims that Labneh is Greek as well as Arabic. Turkish too. But the point is all these places used to trade with one another, and people moved remarkably freely, and often, in times gone by. Lia herself has lived and worked in Lebanon, so maybe that's where she got the idea, but I prefer to think that Labneh is known here because this eastern side of Italy leans towards the eastern Mediterranean countries rather than the west. Ancona has been a major port for more than two thousand years and was Rome's gateway to the eastern empire. And we are just four hours south of Venice, whose economic power in the middle ages was largely derived from trading with the Levant.

Anyway, wherever Labneh comes from, it's a sort of strained yogurt (Greek for preference) and the trick is to leave it straining in the fridge for as long as you can - the more you leave it, the more liquid drains out and the denser and richer it becomes. It is the perfect accompaniment for sweet peppers.

GRILLED PEPPERS with LABNEH

- ½ kg. natural yogurt
- 2 peppers (red/yellow)
- 8 slices of baguette-style bread

Mix the yogurt with ½ tsp salt, pour yogurt into napkin in colander. Refrigerate for 4 hours (min). Put whole peppers under pre-heated grill turning occasionally until blackened. Place in paper bag for 10 mins. Peel, cut into strips and toss with olive oil, salt, pepper and herbs. Toast the bread slices, coat with oil.

The main dish of the evening was to be *Trota al Forno con Verdure,* which is fresh trout baked on a bed of vegetables. It was perfect for our outdoor dinner, because we could carry everything down in the one baking tray, but it's pretty revolutionary for Italians. They have a fairly dim view of English cooking. They seem to think we eat nothing but baked beans and pasty, tasteless sausages, with watery mashed potatoes and cabbage - and ALL ON THE SAME PLATE! This is what they *really* can't understand - why would you want to eat your vegetables at the same time as the meat? That's why it's such a nightmare in restaurants trying to get your grilled *zucchini* and peppers, or your *patate fritte,* delivered at the same time as your steak. It doesn't matter how many times you ask. They *say* they will, but the kitchens seem to be totally incapable of handling things that way. And the people who are letting you down here are hidden away in the kitchen, of course, so it's no good taking it out on the waitress. Nevertheless we once sat on the next table to an English woman who was angrily explaining to her uncomprehending waitress that "I don't *do* cold chips!"

We had bought the trout earlier in the day, on a trip over the mountains to the delightful little town of Visso. Just upstream from Visso where the river babbles prettily through town there is a trout farm whose fish are spawned yet further upstream close to the source, before being transported down to the farm where they swim in a constant natural flow of fresh mountain water. It is a far cry from your average lowland trout farm. As the flavor of the fish testifies.

Today, Lia was cooking them on a bed of tomatoes, zucchini and potatoes, which became gradually suffused with the delicate flavor of the fish as they baked in the oven. Tam acquitted herself perfectly in laying out the vegetables in the dish, pointing out that they were the colors of the Italian flag, something that Lia seemed unaccountably to have missed until now.

BAKED TROUT with VEGETABLES

- *Two trout of approx. 800g each*
- *3 medium-sized potatoes*
- *12 cherry tomatoes*
- *2 onions*
- *4 courgettes*
- *Rosemary*
- *Garlic*

Sprinkle the opened trout with salt, pepper, rosemary, crushed garlic. Place the trout on a layer of sliced potatoes in a pan on greaseproof paper. Halve the tomatoes, cut courgettes into sticks. Drizzle with olive oil. Bake at 180 degrees for 40 minutes.

Lia has that knack that all great cooks have. They somehow make everything seem incredibly easy. In fact much of the time food appears without her apparently having had to do anything at all. You can be sat in the kitchen chatting with her about life, politics, family, art, whatever, and be dimly aware she's doing a couple of background tasks. You might catch sight of something going in the oven. Then she'll make you a coffee, or maybe a small aperitif, and suddenly she's opening the oven door and out comes a fully-fledged meal. It was a bit like that on the night of the alfresco dinner. Even with all the paraphernalia of TV around her, along with rather demanding house guests, including an eight-year-old and a brand new baby, the food just seemed to materialize, and all at the right time. This is very annoying for someone like me. When I am trying to feed a large number of people everything seems to come to fruition in the wrong order. And unlike Lia, who was fresh and relaxed as we got ready to transport the food down to the orto, BIG cooking leaves me physically and mentally exhausted. Maybe I am cut out to be a professional chef - after all they're seldom required to turn up at the table to eat the stuff, something I find very difficult to pull off with good humor if I have cooked it myself. And then there's the mess. Lia somehow manages to leave none at all. My meals, on the other hand, emerge from the oven into a world of kitchen chaos. How on earth does she do it?

Down in the *orto*, Sergio had prepared the table. At the far end of the *orto* the old city wall protrudes outwards to create a sort of patio just large enough to seat eight people round a marble-topped dining table. Above the table there's a slender pergola grown over with honeysuckle. A couple of oil lamps hang from the pergola, with candles set every meter or so along the low wall. This protrusion, perfect though it was for an outdoor dining room, seemed a strange anomaly among the neat straight lines of the *orti*. Until, that is, Sergio explained that this was the remnant of a defensive tower jutting out so as to command views along the wall in either direction. The peaceful and pretty spot where we were about to dine had once been the vantage point from which raiders attempting to scale the city walls would be attacked. Possibly with boiling oil - though not the *extra vergine* kind. It was a poignant reminder of how life moves on over the centuries. And how the fabric of these ancient places once witnessed worlds so very different from our own.

There were seven of us for dinner, but when we arrived in the *orto*, Sergio had set eight places. I pointed out that Peter would not be eating. At least not with us. One of the perks of shooting a food program is that you get to film people eating instead of eating yourself. For some reason Peter did NOT see this as an advantage.

"It's not for Peter," Sergio gave me a withering look. "I realise that. No, we have an extra guest."

I hadn't bargained for this. The rest of us knew the drill - just pretend this is a normal meal, but do whatever Peter tells you, even if it means stopping dead in your tracks just as the food is about to enter your mouth so he can move the camera for a different angle. And do NOT, whatever you do, look at the camera. Now I would have to explain all this to someone new. Peter would not be pleased.

I shouldn't have worried. The guest turned out to be a young woman, Francesca, a cousin who worked in television herself. And she was gorgeous. So much so that Peter seemed to find it difficult to concentrate on the job in hand. But I didn't find that out until later.

The evening was a delight. The food was delicious, as we knew it would be. The company was stimulating and after a few glasses of local wine I felt a warm glow which perfectly matched the deepening red of a glorious sunset. You will have guessed, I am sure, that I had rather gone off duty by now. My job should have been to stand alongside Peter suggesting shots and helping him whenever he shifted the camera. But, being the generous man that he is, he insisted that there was no point in both of us missing out on a lovely evening and a nice meal.

"Go on," he said, "sit yourself down. Enjoy! I can deal with all this."

So I did. But not before making sure that he had a glass of wine to tide him over. So while the rest of us were pretty much done for the day, our jobs reduced to eating, drinking and having a nice time, Peter soldiered on for another hour and half behind the camera. Lia took pity on him right from the start, and made sure that his wine was topped up at regular intervals.

Next morning I was up early to check the rushes. It was clear from the start that Peter had done a good job, capturing the warmth of the occasion in some lovely shots. The wide shot showed the whole setup to perfection, the candle-lit group thoroughly enjoying the peppers and the trout-that-looked-like-the-Italian-flag against a backdrop of the town's towers silhouetted against the darkening sky.

Peter had managed some lovely close-ups too. Lia smiling as she sipped her wine. Sergio laughing. Tam tucking in to the food. Francesca tossing her thick dark hair. Francesca again, laughing this time. And another Francesca. Why hadn't I seen it at the time? Peter obviously had it bad. He couldn't take his camera off this girl, and she wasn't even part of the team. I had started the day feeling pretty good, but now I could feel myself slipping into a mild depression. Did we actually have enough shots of the rest of the dinner party? Were we actually going to be able to tell the story of a family meal *al fresco?* Or was I going to have to re-write the script to explain that we had decided to feed all today's food to a pretty girl we had never seen before. No wonder I was feeling a bit grim. Or was it just a little bit of a hangover? You can judge for yourself in Episode One, about twenty-two and a half minutes in. I *think* we got away with it.

Shooting the Titles

Television is a wonderful thing. It can be very forgiving. In the end you only need a small number of shots to make a sequence. And Peter had, like the pro he is, ensured that we had enough (just enough) shots of everyone else to make the sequence work. They were good shots too, which is just as well because the normal rule is that you need to shoot way more than you will actually need, to give the editor a choice of which ones to use, but also because some of them simply won't be any good. Whether by luck or judgment more or less everything Peter shot that evening was worthy of inclusion in the final piece. Mind you, it's only a couple of minutes in the finished program, whereas we could have made a whole half-hour of *Francesca Eats al Fresco*, and it might possibly have won some awards for the camera work.

I did indeed have a slight hangover that morning, but viewing the rushes of the *orto* dinner was enough to convince me that we really had something here, something that was actually going to work. I think it was being able to see the food in the context of the town and its surrounding countryside that did it. I had always wanted this to be something much more than an ordinary cookery show. It had to be something which made people fall in love with the whole atmosphere of the place, of which the food, of course, is such an enormous part. Seeing a table full of smiling faces, framed against the backdrop of town and rolling hills, and so clearly enjoying Lia's food, made the whole project come alive. I don't know what your regular cure for a mild hangover is (mine, bizarrely, is cooked ham and milk), but viewing these rushes did the trick for me in no time.

This new-found confidence in the project came at just the right time, because today we were due to shoot material for the Title Sequence. I like to think I am not, but I *must* be, a glass-half-empty sort of person. Because my approach to the opening of a TV show is that the job is to stop the buggers getting to the off switch (a task which became so much more difficult with the invention of the remote control). After all, the viewers have the TV on because they wanted to watch the *last* show, not mine. So if your opening shots can knock them back down in their seat, or even make the arm go limp as it gropes for the remote, then you are half way there. Lots of programs - documentaries and movies mainly - begin with a pre-title. This is a bit like cheating in my view. You just pick out the best shots from the rest of the program and jam them all together without making very much sense at all. We sometimes call it a "tease", which may be because what you get subsequently never quite lives up to the promise of the opening action. But we had decided to open *Cookucina* not with a tease or a pre-title, but with a full-blown all-singing, all-dancing Title Sequence, ignoring, for the time being, the awkward fact that these cost A LOT OF MONEY.

A Title Sequence for a show like this goes according to a fairly standard recipe. Take lots of pretty shots, plenty of sunshine, a bit of food prep, sprinkle with some glorious shots of the finished dishes, add the smiling faces of your two presenters and mix with some bright, quintessentially Italian music. Then hand it all over to a graphic designer - along with a very large check. The ingredients are relatively easy, but converting it all into a seamless and attractive Title Sequence requires some pretty expensive computer power. Right now, I wasn't quite sure where that was going to come from, but that was something to worry about later - today's job was shooting the pretties, and the day had dawned bright and clear, a perfect day to get shots of Tam and Lia in and around the old town. Perfect, that is, until the temperature began to rise.

It's times like this when you discover how actors earn their money. The first shots on the roster required Tam and Lia to be walking casually through some of the most picturesque alleys of the *centro storico*. Not too difficult you might think, but they needed to be carrying stuff - some local produce, and some fresh-baked bread. Gino had already set aside a selection of his finest fruit and veg, fresh from the market garden. And he had arranged them all nicely in a basket, a riot of summer color. Trouble was the basket was plastic. And ugly. Not quite the image we wanted to project. There was a short delay while we went in search of an old-fashioned wicker basket, which fortunately did not prove too difficult as Lia knew where to find one and promised to be back inside twenty minutes. She needed to be quick, too, because the morning sun would soon disappear from the *vicolo* we had identified for the opening shot. Meanwhile, Sergio went off to pick up some fresh bread. With the temperature rising relentlessly, the rest of sought out some shade. Sure enough, Lia was back with five minutes to spare. But the problems were not over because the basket was bigger than we had expected - about half as big again as Gino's plastic one. No problem. A quick dash to Gino's and Tam came back with another couple of kilos of glistening fruit and veg, arriving at just about the same time as Sergio - carrying a single small loaf. Well we tried, but it was never going to work. The two women looked ridiculous - one lugging a big basket overflowing with local produce, the other carying a small loaf. No - Sergio was packed off once again to the bakers, returning with an armful of bread. By now the sun was within just a few minutes of deserting us, so we had to go with whatever we had. And whatever we *did* have we would be stuck with for the rest of the shots in that sequence. I could see the shadow moving relentless along the *vicolo* towards our shot. The two women quickly took up their positions, Peter framed the shot and I shouted "Action". Tam and Lia set off towards the camera at what can only be described as the next best thing to a trot. They looked as if they were running for a bus. And frowning with it. I could sense viewers all over the world rising from their armchairs and reaching for the off switch.

"One more time!", I shouted. "And relax. Look like you're enjoying it. This could well be our last chance".

They did. And it was. But we got the shot, and I realised that we had a couple of born actors on our hands. They could "take direction", and managed to turn a fraught and panicky situation into a relaxed and cheerful opening to the Titles. But anyway, you can judge for yourselves. Go to the front of any episode and take a look at the two shots starting at nine seconds in.

It's often the way in television - initial plans begin to fall apart and you cobble something together, and then, in some magical way it just works. A TV friend of mine used to say that you could labor for days setting a sequence to a carefully-chosen piece of music so that the cuts and dissolves happened at EXACTLY the right moment to fit a beat in the music. Then if you strip the music off and replace it with something totally different it somehow seems to work. In our case, we were having to improvise with the props. The basket was obviously too big, and had to be balanced by the bread. Given another day or so I am sure we could have come up with something more elegant than a big paper bag for Lia to carry the bread in, but that's what we had, and that's what we used. And it's fine.

The next few shots in the old town were fairly straightforward (by comparison at any rate, and give or take some serious moaning by the talent about "having to work in this heat"), but then it was on to another difficult setup - this one just outside town. If you've taken the trouble to look at the Titles you'll know what I mean. It's the first few shots, with Lia and Tam hitching a ride on the back of an Ape, which drives away from camera to reveal the old town against the sun-drenched backdrop of the Sibillini mountains. All pretty straightforward you might think. But you would be wrong. The Ape is Gino's - he uses it to transport his produce from the market garden to his shop in the narrow streets of old Sarnano. Apes are notoriously tricky to drive, unless, as we know, you are either fourteen or very old. Or Gino. But Gino was not available to drive. He had gone off somewhere unexpectedly. Probably trying to find some fruit and veg to replace the stuff we had walked off with. So now one of the home team would have to drive the thing. Sergio. Peter and I were busy shooting and directing, and Tam and Lia were being the stars. Sergio, though, is not old. Like all Italian youths he drove an Ape when he was fourteen, but that was a long time ago, and driving an Ape is emphatically NOT like riding a bike, as we were about to discover. From the moment he came lurching down the road towards our camera position it was clear that Sergio would need to learn this skill all over again. And he had about ten minutes to do it in. At least that's what he told us to begin with.

"Give me ten minutes," he said, "and it will all come back to me."

Unfortunately, it turned out he needed the better part of half an hour before he had the thing even vaguely under control.

It is in the nature of schedules that they have to be re-written every now and again. I think that by the time we had finished shooting *Cookucina* we were on Version 11. That's part of the fun of the thing, although it never seems quite like that at the time. Re-writing the schedule is a sure sign that things are not going to plan, and maybe the end product is better on those productions that are able to stick rigidly to Plan A. But I somehow doubt it. Chucking the whole thing up in the air and re-arranging it brings a sort of energy to a shoot that you can't get any other way, and I think you feel it in the final programs. A living work of art, rather than painting by numbers. Our schedule for the day was falling apart by the minute.

We should have been finished with these shots an hour ago and off to lunch. But we had to hang on to get the job done because the sunlight bathing the town would disappear after lunch and our lovely backdrop of the steep walls of the *centro storico* would be in shadow. So all we could do was wait. Until Sergio had tamed the Ape. Which wasn't happening quickly. Every few minutes or so he would come kangarooing down the road gesticulating that he was almost there. Or possibly blaming everything on the Ape, it was never quite clear. So we waited. In the open. In temperatures that were still climbing towards the heat of the day. There was no shelter as far as the eye could see, and Sergio kept weaving past us making signs to suggest he would be ready next time round. The talent was slowly coming to the boil, in more ways that one. It was difficult enough for Peter and I to maintain our good humor, but Tam and Lia had to somehow try to look morning-fresh once we finally got to shoot.

Suddenly, just as Sergio came back into view, something else appeared right behind him - a police car. On a "professional" shoot this morning's exercise would have been planned and organised weeks in advance. Not over a glass of wine the previous evening, which was when Sergio had arranged the loan of the Ape. Those weeks would have been spent hiring the vehicle from a company specializing in film transport, arranging for it to be shipped from Rome, or wherever the right vehicle could be found, and, crucially, arranging insurance. All of this went through my head as the police car pulled up right behind Sergio, whose jerky braking did nothing to indicate he was fully in charge of his vehicle. Not only did we not have proper insurance for the shoot, I doubted that Gino's insurance would cover Sergio, and of course we didn't have a permit to film on roads that, though quiet, were definitely public. Perhaps the whole thing was about to go down the gurgler before we'd really got going.

But this is Italy. And small-town Italy at that. And these were the *Vigili Urbani,* the local police. If you're keen on becoming a policeman, Italy is the place for you. They have more kinds of police here than you can shake a stick at. And they all have great uniforms, of course. And nice cars too. I'll never forget the sight of a children's beach train following a top of the range Alfa Romeo police car with blue lights flashing as it escorted the kids along the front at Gabbicce Mare. They were the *Carabinieri,* a sort of quasi-military force. Then there's the *Polizia di Stato,* a national civilian force incorporating, among other things, the traffic police. The *Guardia di Finanza* are a special force dedicated to enforcing financial laws and regulations and tracking down tax evaders, though they seem to go missing fairly regularly when there's **serious** money (and politicians) involved. The *Polizia Provinciale* are a local police force, but they are only in some of Italy's 109 provinces. Maybe there's no provincial crime in the others. Their main tasks are to enforce regional and national hunting and fishing laws, wildlife management and environmental protection. But they are not to be confused with the *Corpo Forestale dello Stato,* who are responsible for law enforcement in Italy's national parks and forests. Their duties include enforcing poaching laws, safeguarding protected animal species and preventing forest fires. We know them affectionately as the *Mushroom Police,* because truffling rights are jealously guarded round here, and if you're up in the mountains looking for mushrooms, you can easily find your collar being felt by a man appearing over the horizon in a 4x4 Land Rover and a natty green uniform. But I am getting ahead of myself yet again, because our truffle recipe didn't crop up until much later in the shoot.

We were pleased to see that these guys were the *Vigili Urbani,* the local police. We know them well. One of them actually went to school with Sergio. So instead of carting us off to chokey, they were really keen to know what it was we were up to, and fascinated to hear we were making a cookery show set in their patch. In fact it was not long before they were swapping recipes, and I had to step in and stop the whole gang clearing off to a bar for a coffee. We had to get on, I pointed out, as the light was changing. Go ahead they said, and apologised that they weren't able to stay and watch. Presumably they had a coffee to go to.

That was probably a good thing though, because the *Vigili* were no longer there to witness our first few abortive efforts at getting the shots in the can. Once Sergio had brought the Ape to a (reasonably smooth) stop, Tam refused to sit on the tailgate. Gino's fruit and veg, coming as it did straight from the land, brought a lot of the land with it. And Tam was wearing a white skirt. Which needed to stay white. Ten more minutes went by while Sergio lurched off in search of a rug they could sit on. I say lurched because he seemed to be getting worse again, not better. Then once we had both women sat comfortably on the rug with the basket on their laps, it quickly became apparent that you couldn't actually see any of the lovely fresh produce in the basket unless it was tilted towards the camera at an alarming angle. And when I called "Action" for the first take, Sergio let out the clutch a bit sharply and both women fell off the back as the Ape took off down the road. Actually that makes it sound a lot worse than it was. In fact the back of the Ape is so small and low down that it was more like them standing up as the Ape drove away from underneath them. By no means a disaster, but not the shot we needed. We got the shot in the end though, as you will see from the opening of the show. The girls are smiling, the basket is overflowing with lovely fresh fruit and vegetables and the town behind them is bathed in sunshine. What you probably cannot see is the rope tying the basket in place, and you can just make out that Tam is desperately hanging on to avoid being dumped in the road. But one thing you will certainly not be able to see is the way those smiles disappeared as soon as it was over, Tam and Lia striding off towards town vowing never to do anything like that ever again. "Neither will I!", I shouted after them, my voice disappearing on the afternoon breeze.

It is what's on screen that counts. And by the end of the day we had all the shots we needed for the Titles. But what we still did *not* have was the large check. Fortunately we had a friend, an absolute genius on computer graphics. His name was Rob and I had worked with him a year or so earlier in one of my more bizarre jobs. It was in Qatar in the Arabian Gulf. It's a tiny sheikhdom ruled since the colonial British left some fifty years ago by a one all-powerful family, the Al-Thanis. It is place where there's money coming out of the ground. Quite literally, because it sits on one of the largest deposits of natural gas in the world - enough to mean that Qatar recently achieved the coveted title of the place with the highest income *per capita* in the world. Not that much of it filters down, because it is also home to a vast army of poorly-paid construction workers from Bangladesh and Nepal, laboring through appalling heat to build a forest of skyscrapers designed to trumpet Qatar's new-found status to the world. Most of the gas revenue seems to stick to the extended royal family, which means they have a lot of spare cash to play with and, by and large, they spend it on some interesting and worthwhile stuff. Al Jazeera Television, for instance, was created at the whim of the old Sheikh with a view to Qatar making its mark on the global stage. They have also hosted Human Rights Conferences (in buildings built by the migrant workers), and the UN Climate Change Conference (in a conference center lit by millions of lights and sporting moving pavements). And, famously, they won the right to hold the FIFA football World Cup in 2020 - in a place where summer temperatures can exceed 50 deg C. To cater for the hoped-for influx of fans from all over the globe they are currently building a whole new town and a Metro system with 65 stations. Let's hope there are enough football fans who want to spend three weeks roasting in an alcohol-light desert.

One of the more enlightened members of the royal family is the old Sheikh's daughter. She has something of an artistic bent, so she builds museums (fourteen at the last count), buys Art (she has paid the highest price ever for a single painting), and several years back decided she wanted a Film Festival. And so was born the Doha Tribeca Film Festival, an annual jamboree designed to lure Hollywood's finest to the Gulf. For a while it worked (perhaps because large sums were being pumped into "Bob" de Niro's Tribeca organisation), but after a few years much of the glamor melted away (along with Tribeca), leaving behind something much more valuable, a genuine attempt to foster new talent in the MENA region[3]. My job, for a couple of these Festivals, was to marshal a bunch of small video packages to post on the DTFF website in order to spread the message globally via the Internet. To be honest the website wasn't great, and neither were the packages we posted to it, but at least they looked really slick, and the man responsible for that was my friend Rob, the DTFF's top video editor.

Video Editors and Graphic Designers can be a miserable bunch, maybe because they see their job as making pretty ordinary stuff look really glossy. They see their role as a sort of institutionalized lying, which cannot be good for the soul. Nevertheless, for Rob it was one step up from his previous employment, which was editing porn movies. Unfortunately Rob is, as many of his female friends can testify, *profoundly* heterosexual, and the movies he was working on were the other kind. But, while glamorizing web videos in Qatar was a definite improvement, it wasn't exactly spiritually rewarding. Apart from being very talented, Rob is also a generous man, and when I told him what we were up to with *Cookucina* he immediately volunteered to sprinkle a bit of his stardust on our Title Sequence. If you have had a chance to look at it, he created the word *COOKUCINA* and how it assembles itself on screen, as well as the floating overlay and the general color tone. If the first thirty seconds of an episode of *Cookucina* give you the feeling that the next half hour is going to be a warm and enjoyable experience, that is largely down to Rob. Thank you, Rob Nield. And by

---

[3] Middle East and North Africa, for those of you as ignorant as I was when I first went there.

the way, that sort of work would cost tens of thousands of dollars in a SOHO post-production house. Rob did it for two hundred cigarettes and a large scotch.

Cooking the Ugly Fish

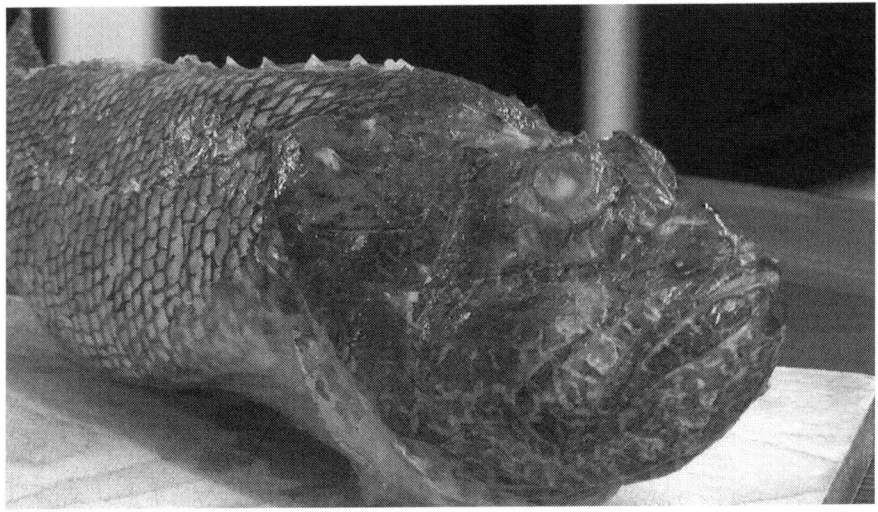

Monday was ugly fish day. Overnight Lia had defrosted the *Scorfano*, the 90 Euro fish. It had been kept under lock and key since we bought it from the Fish Pirate a couple of days earlier, and once out of the fridge an armed guard had kept it under surveillance during an overnight vigil. Only kidding of course, but we were still smarting from cost of these fish. I think because this was the single most expensive item in the making of *Cookucina* so far.

The *acciughe* experience had already taught us that Tam was not very good with fish. She had practically thrown up when asked to pull the spine out of a tiny little anchovy. Now she was staring down the gullet of the ugliest fish on the fishmonger's slab, its huge mouth gaping wide. The warty skin of the *Scorfano* is beautifully set off by its (almost human) eyelashes. It looks a bit like the marine equivalent of the old joke about a camel being a horse designed by a committee (a joke which somehow never got the laughs in Qatar). Lia was making what she assured us would be a light and refreshing starter, a *mousse di Scorfano*. First she boiled the fish for fifteen minutes in water flavored with onion, carrot and celery. Then it was time to remove the meat from the bone. The trick, she said, is NOT to use any kind of food processor, which would turn the fish meat into a cream and lose all the lovely texture of the flesh. Instead everything had to be done by hand. Tam's job was to pull the skin off, then tenderly tease the flesh from the bones, crumbling it gently into the waiting bowl. The look of disgust on her face said it all. I fully expected her to ask if she could be blindfolded for the task. Five minutes later she was able to announce that the job was done. Lia took one look and was clearly not pleased.

"You've missed a bit" she said. "There's more meat inside the mouth. The tongue is the most succulent bit. You'll have to get in there and crack the jawbone to get at it."

Tam blanched visibly. Barfing seemed inevitable. But Lia was winking at the camera. It was a joke and Tam was mighty relieved when she discovered she would NOT be required to pull the tongue out. Nevertheless, this cooking lark seemed to be losing some of its luster for her. This is the delicately flavored fish mousse Lia and Tam (reluctantly) put together that day:

FISH MOUSSE

- 400g. fillets of rockfish or grouper
- 2 stalks of celery
- 2 carrots
- ½ small onion
- salt, white pepper
- 4 tablespoons mayonnaise

Put the fish fillets and half the vegetables into a pan of lightly salted water. Boil for 10 minutes. Finely chop the other half of the vegetables. Remove the fish fillets from the water, drain them well. When they are cold crumble the fish with your hands, then mix well with the finely chopped vegetables, season with salt and pepper and blend with 4 or 5 tablespoons of mayonnaise.

Pizza and Restaurants

In a land of great food and fabulous home cooking, why would you go out to eat, to a restaurant? Because they are here, and there are lots of them. Well, there's the labor-saving aspect of course, and it helps that they are, by and large, really excellent value. There are also some things that will always be best when cooked in the right way and with special equipment. Like pizza. But the 'p' word covers a multitude of sins, and the pizzas you get here in Le Marche are a million miles away from the stodgy slice of dough you get in London or New York, covered with rubbery cheese (mozzarella-style) and dripping with something red that bears very little relation to a tomato. Pizzas here are thin and crisp. And hot, because you always have to wait for them to do the regulation 8-10 minutes in a wood-fired pizza oven. Light and easy to digest, they would clearly find no place in a "Hut". Just as the idea of a "stuffed crust" would cause a sort of pained incomprehension in any of our many local *pizzerie*. The puzzle of why you would choose to buy your pizza from a Hut reminds me of the old joke (as old as the Colonel himself, I guess) about Kentucky Fried Chicken, which asks, "why would you buy food that comes in a bucket?" Maybe the good people of Kentucky are as puzzled about what's happened to Southern Fried Chicken as we are about pizza. It is worth noting on the side, by the way, that not all pizzas are red. The menus here have two sections *pizze rosse* and *pizze bianche* - red or white. And if you've never tried one, you would be surprised how different a white pizza is from a red. Like white and red wines, maybe.

The physical surroundings are another very good reason to go to a restaurant here. They are often in remarkable old buildings - like eating in a museum - and sometimes have spectacular views. Several years ago we happened across a place called *Diulia* in a nearby hill-town, Sant'Angelo in Pontano. You drive up a steep and winding hill to get to the town in the first place, but then you have to park and carry on on foot, climbing up through narrow, twisting backstreets. Finally you go through a small and unprepossessing gate only to pop out on to a terrace with fabulous views away towards the sea. It was a balmy summer evening and we got one of the best tables right on the edge of the terrace with an unobstructed view across rolling hillsides neatly patterned with vineyards and olive groves. Stunningly beautiful in the rich early evening sunshine. But as evening drew on and the sun slipped gently behind the mountains, the darkening shadow which had fallen on the land began gradually to sparkle, almost imperceptibly at first, as growing clusters of tiny lights slowly appeared on top of almost every hill. We were new to Le Marche then and hadn't realised that the ancient towns of the region tend to be perched on top of hills. As our spectacular view began fading into night, so the towns came alive and the darkening hilltops began to twinkle like the stars above them. It was a magical moment.

Nobody much goes in for grand recipes round here, it is much more about the quality of the food. The *Agriturismo* is a popular format in Le Marche. This is agricultural country, and several decades ago the Italian government came to the rescue of an ailing rural economy with the *Agriturismo* concept which encourages farmers to diversify into tourism. A typical *Agriturismo* will be a large farmhouse converted to offer a few bedrooms alongside a restaurant open to the public and serving their own produce, along with products from other farms in the area. They must give preference to local produce and anything included in the national list of 'traditional food products'. They will also organise cultural, educational and sporting events designed to enhance the land and the local rural heritage. But it is the food that can sometimes make them really special. One restaurant local to us called *La Quercia della Memoria* which (very) roughly translated means The Old Oak, serves just two menus, one fish, one meat, in which everything is either grown or killed within a mile or so of where you are eating , which is quite something when you think there are up to eleven courses involved. And when you've worked your way through all that and the coffee arrives, it is accompanied by a forest of bottles of different colored *grappas,* each one flavored with herbs and berries grown around the farm.

Eleven courses sounds a lot, I know, but in fact it is just an example of something they go in for a lot locally - menus featuring a seemingly endless stream of small dishes, working your way through from *antipasti* to *dolci*. And with each course you are likely to get a detailed explanation of just exactly how and where the beans were grown, or the fish caught. Almost certainly this will be in Italian, so brush up your vocab before you sit down to one of these meals or do what I do and just smile and nod. A smile and a nod goes a long way. One man who pulls off this explanation thing with real aplomb (and who speaks a bit of English too) is Silvano Scalzini who runs one of our favorite restaurants just about twenty minutes from Sarnano. It's called *Il Picciolo di Rame* (The Little Copper Coin) and it is built into the fortified wall of a partly abandoned little village called Vestignano. Arriving after dark the village is a spectacular sight, because the steep cobbled streets you must climb after parking your car are beautifully lit at night, giving the whole thing the feel of entering a medieval castle. Step through the door of *Picciolo di Rame* and your sense of time slips further away, the stone walls and low beams framing a huge and ancient olive press.

Silvano's meals are never less than twelve courses and sometimes fourteen, and what makes them extra special is that the recipes are ancient and the food is cooked as it would have been in medieval times - give or take a gas oven. Some time during each course Silvano will appear alongside your table and explain the history of the dish in question. How, for instance, Italian *contadini* used to cook with fat not oil, because fat gave you the calories you needed for hard work in the fields. Oil was used for lighting. A visit to *Picciolo di Rame* has a touch of theatre about it and it has been a long time favorite of ours. So much so that we wanted to feature it in the show. But when I suggested that to Lia, she seemed strangely lukewarm to the idea.

"Silvano does a wonderful cream pudding," I explained, "perhaps we could get him to talk about how his medieval version differs from your *Crema di Nonna Giudi?*"

Not keen. I could tell.

"But it's perfect," I said, "Just right for our target audience. The English love that sort of thing. And the Americans.... the Americans practically wet themselves when they discover it. And Silvano plays to the crowd - he's a terrific character - larger than life..."

My words trailed off. She was unmoved. She wasn't saying no, but her normally smiling face had melted into something approaching sullen. If she were a child you'd have been tempted to describe it as a sulk. I changed tack.

"He makes this onion soup. Delicious. Absolutely yummy, but all he needs to make it is white onion, flour and some grated *parmigiano*. No fat. Nothing. Simple. So I was thinking... why don't we get him to teach Tam how to make it. Then she'll be able to make something all on her own. Maybe we could do it for the final episode, what do you think?"

A smile. I'd hit the nail on the head. She nodded in agreement. The smile, I noticed, had a little wicked edge to it. Like the *Mona Lisa*. She obviously knew something I didn't. But whatever it was, it was way in the future. For now I had got my way - a trip to *Picciolo di Rame*.

"I still want to do the cream pudding thing, while we're there," I said, pushing my luck.

"*Vediamo*" she replied. "We'll see."

Picciolo di Rame

The trip to *Picciolo di Rame* was exquisite. It was a beautiful day, and the road from Samano to Vestignano winds through rolling hills, a patchwork quilt of thick woodland and small rectilinear fields reclaimed from the woods over the centuries, their borders crisply defined as the farmers keep the fast-growing undergrowth at bay. There is not a single flat piece of land on this journey and the snaking road offers a constantly changing vista of vertiginous fields clinging on to the hillsides. There will always be two or three tractors working the land at seemingly impossible angles, and as the road winds so they seem to spring up first to the right and then away to the left. Is that the same tractor I saw a few minutes back? Or am I losing my sense of direction? By the time we arrived at Vestignano I felt almost dizzy as I climbed out of the car. And I had no idea in which direction Sarnano lay.

The steep cobbled steps up into the village offered us the chance to knock off a few pretty GVs of Tam and Lia climbing up to the restaurant. GV, as you know by now, stands for General View, and it is the TV term for wide shots you generally see before you cut to a close up of the house/office/cave/prison or wherever the next bit of your program is going to take place. The idea is give the viewer a sense of the wider environment around the house/office/cave/prison, and of course here it was a marvellous opportunity to see the surrounding countryside as the two women walked through the shot. Peter, though, is a bit of a perfectionist and he wanted to capture the view in all directions. This entailed Tam and Lia doing the same climb three or four times, with the camera in a different position each time. The final effect is great, and you really get a sense of the beautiful setting of *Picciolo di Rame*, but that is not the way the talent saw it at the time. It was early afternoon, in the heat of the day, as we had to interview Silvano before he started work on the evening's meal, so climbing up through the fierce sun was taxing enough once, let alone three or four times. I say three or four because, as I recall, Peter's call for a fourth angle provoked our first industrial dispute when Tam and Lia refused to do it. With some justification they claimed it was because they couldn't afford to be drenched in sweat for the interview itself, and that was much more important than Peter's GVs. Not for the last time I found myself playing peacemaker.

Silvano was waiting on the doorstep when we finally arrived at the restaurant. A big man, with a ground-length apron and a piratical headscarf knotted at the back, he cut an impressive figure. Stepping inside, the sudden change from bright sunlight to the darkness of heavy stone walls and tiny windows made it difficult to see anything at first. As the eyes adjusted it was possible to see the half dozen tables, with their strange three-legged chairs, dwarfed by the giant olive press. Silvano himself looked almost out of place, his size fitting nicely with the olive press but seemingly much too big for his tables and chairs. But he's a big personality too, and maybe this was all an optical illusion, and as our eyes got used to the darkness, so he seemed to settle back into place.

First on our agenda was Silvano showing Tam how to make his medieval onion soup (that's the soup that's medieval, not the onions). Filming it was to prove a bit of a challenge though, because when we followed him through a western saloon-type swing door we found ourselves in an absolutely minute kitchen, already occupied by Silvano's equally minute mother, who was beavering away at a chopping board. She was as small as he was big, one of those mother-son relationships that make you marvel at the human reproductive process. How on earth could such a tiny woman have produced such a bulky (there was no other word for it) man. I know he would have been a lot smaller as a baby, but nevertheless...

There were six of us trying to get into the kitchen by now. Me, Peter, Tam, Lia, Silvano and his mum. Plus Peter's camera and the lights. And to make matters worse Peter had to keeping moving around to get the shot, as Silvano's great chest kept obscuring the onions he was chopping or the saucepan on the stove. There was a lot of treading on toes and muttered (off-camera, I hope) curses. Tam was supposed to be learning how to cook this dish, but quite often she found herself more or less at the back of the pack, looking over the collective shoulders of Peter getting the shot, me getting the sound, and Lia discussing the finer points of the recipe with Silvano in Italian. We were getting the sequence (just about), but I doubted whether Tam would ever be able to repeat the recipe. She had, after all, only been able to see about half of what was going on - and that from a distance. The plan was that at the end of the series Tam would cook something by herself for the first time. We chose Silvano's onion soup because it was hard to imagine anything simpler, and as Episode Six reveals she did indeed produce an onion soup. And it was delicious. But I am pretty sure that Silvano would not have recognised it. Here's the recipe - for Silvano's Onion Soup, not Tam's!

A SIMPLE ONION SOUP

- *4 white onions*
- *100ml. vegetable stock*
- *50g. flour*
- *50g. butter*
- *Salt and pepper*
- *Extra virgin olive oil*

Roughly chop the onions. Put them in a heavy-bottomed pan and cover with water. Bring to the boil and cook until soft. Strain the onions and return them to the pan. Stir in the flour and continue to stir the mixture until it comes to the boil. Slowly add the vegetable stock, stirring it in thoroughly. Blend until smooth using either a hand-blender or food-mixer. Return to the heat, season with salt and pepper and cook with a little more water for 10 mins. Add the butter and blend it in with a wooden spoon. Serve with baked croutons, and drizzle with the olive oil.

The Italian being spoken in the kitchen was frankly a bit beyond my capabilities, but Lia and Silvano seemed to be getting on fine. So, with the onion soup lesson done and dusted we returned to the restaurant to get the other half of what we wanted from Silvano - the comparison of cream puddings. I had asked Silvano to have one of his ready, and I had sneaked the *Crema di Nonna Giudi* that Lia had cooked yesterday into the car. We sat down on our three-legged chairs for a mutual tasting. The other thing I wanted from this was a discussion of the philosophy of food - how each of these two people whose lives so revolved around food actually *thought* about it. This was a roaring success, as they seemed to agree on more or less every point. On the importance of natural ingredients, on the dangers of *gia pronti*, pre-prepared foods, and how too much fat was leading to increased obesity even in food-(and figure-)conscious Italy. So, with everything going smoothly, I introduced the two *dolci*, and the teaspoons with which to taste them. The two cooks, sitting opposite one another, were politeness itself. There was lots of *oohing, ahhing* and *mmming*, together with the occasional "*bellissima*", and "*che bel profumo*". They could not have been more gracious about each other's dish. I was mightily relieved. I certainly had not expected it to go this easily. Soon Peter had all the necessary cutaway shots (mostly close-up *oohs, ahhs* and *mmms*) and we were done. What I had thought might be a slightly tricky afternoon had passed off without incident. As we loaded the car I thanked Lia. It had been a really successful shoot, I said.

"And wasn't his *crema* delicious?" I added.

"*Schifo*", she replied tartly, sticking her tongue out. I could tell you what it means, or you could look it up in a dictionary - but you probably don't need to.

Partigiani

For several years I saw no reason to carry on beyond Vestignano, along the crumbling tarmac of the road that winds on up into the hills. *Picciolo di Rame* was one of my favorite destinations and the views along the way were spectacular. But when one day I did decide to venture further it was for a very specific reason and it took me somewhere I had never dreamed of going.

Growing up in England after the Second World War the prevailing attitude towards the Italians' participation in that conflict was to view them as at best hopeless and at worst cowards. They had the misfortune, of course, to be on the wrong side during much of that war, though it is little understood that until more or less the day that Mussolini took them in on the side of the Axis Powers, no-one knew which way he was going to jump. In fact as the possessor of one of the most powerful navies in the world, entry in the war on the side of the Allies could substantially have altered the course of the war. So in June 1940 Italian soldiers found themselves instructed to fight on the side of the Nazis when they could so easily have been fighting against them. Hardly surprising then, that the soul of the Italian fighting man never quite seemed to be in the job. Indeed throughout the war Italy remained a divided country, its regional variation affecting still further allegiance either to the forces of fascism, or to those who opposed it. Then in September 1943 came the Italian armistice. The Italian army laid down their arms and the gates of many of the prison camps housing Allied prisoners of war were opened. The suddenly released POWs now faced an extraordinary dilemma. Allied troops had already landed in the far south of the country and were expected to push north. Meanwhile German forces were pouring down from the north, establishing a series of strong defensive lines stretching across the country from coast to coast to prevent the Allies moving north towards

Rome and beyond. In many of those prison camps the men were ordered to stay put to await liberation by the expected arrival of Allied forces. But faced with the chance of freedom from captivity many soldiers broke out, or simply walked out of the camps to try to make their own way to safety in Switzerland in the north, or south to join up with the Allied invasion.

Here in central Italy that dilemma was at its most acute. Safety was a long way away whichever direction you chose to take. With no money, and not speaking the local language, the soldiers were reliant on help from the locals, and many Italian country families have a proud record of putting themselves in danger by taking in fugitive Allied soldiers. That danger was soon amplified as the Allied invasion became bogged down after the Anzio landings and by the harsh conditions of the winter of 1943-44. Families caught sheltering soldiers were dealt with with the utmost severity. But most of them continued to put their lives in danger, often moving their secret guests high up into the inhospitable mountain pastures. *Love and War in the Appenines*, Eric Newby's moving account of his experiences as one of those helped by the *contadini,* paints a vivid picture of these months; of the risks taken, and sacrifices made, by Italian farmers and their families.

The young men of the region faced another, equally dangerous dilemma - co-operation with the German occupying forces or resistance. Simply keeping your head down was not an option to many of them. Those who chose resistance joined one of many secret organisations that now sprang up operating under the broad banner of the *Partigiani,* the partisans. Here in Le Marche they were a mixed band of brave but callow local youths, escaped prisoners and seasoned Yugoslav partisans from the other side of the Adriatic Sea. The mountainous terrain facilitated guerrilla tactics, and the fighters relied heavily on the local people for food, blankets and medicine, sleeping in barns and abandoned farmhouses. Finding great difficulty in tracking down the small groups of *Partigiani* attacking their forces, the Nazis adopted a policy of reprisal. For every German killed by the *Partigiani* they would round up and execute ten Italians from a nearby village. It was designed to drive a wedge between the local populace and the partisans, but it had the opposite effect. When they did succeed in capturing *Partigiani* they were similarly ruthless. It was one such event that took me to the road beyond Vestignano some seventy years later.

After the armistice one group of partisans had based themselves in Montalto, a tiny village high in the mountains some ten miles or so from Sarnano. They called themselves the *Gruppo Nicolo'* and they were mostly from the nearby town of Tolentino. And mostly in their early twenties. In late March 1944, short of supplies, they descended on the nearby town of Caldarola to try to seize back the content of grain stores that had been confiscated from local villagers by German troops. They were caught in a brief firefight, but escaped back into the hills. Shortly after dawn on the 22nd of March a detachment of German troops from Muccia raided the group's hideout in Montalto. The partisans were taken by surprise. Thirty of them were rounded-up and taken to a stretch of track running through the woods below the town. There they were lined up, five at a time, and machine-gunned in the back. Their bodies were thrown down a bank at the edge of the road. An escaped British prisoner of war was being protected by the group, hidden in an old chimney. He managed to escape capture and made his way to a hillside overlooking Montalto from where he saw these tragic events unfold, as he recounted in a formal interview after the end of hostilities.

> *I succeeded in reaching the mountain top above MONTALTO and could see the Germans in the village down below. Following the raid, I saw them line up 25 or 27 rebels on the mountain road, which runs below Montalto Church. The rebels with rifles had to sling them across their backs; all had to place their hands on top of their heads; and 6 or 7 Germans, in charge of an Officer, machine gunned them from behind. After being shot, they were picked up and piled on a heap on the road side. I was less than ½ a mile away and could see everything plainly but could not identify any of the Germans taking part in the shooting of the rebels. I sat on the mountain top until the Jerries had left, then went down to the scene of the shooting. Stood looking at them was an old priest in tears. His name was Father Antonio. He told me to clear off as it was too dangerous. The dead rebels were all dressed in assorted civilian clothes, their bodies were piled up, one on top of the other, and covered with blood. I did have a look at them but not a close inspection as the priest told me not to interfere for my own safety.*

> *[Account of Forrester Hart, taken by Justice of the Peace Fred Page
> 12th September, 1946]*

Four other *Partigiani* had managed to elude the Germans, but as they tried to escape they too were captured at Vestignano, where they too were summarily executed.

This war crime was the reason I was now going beyond Vestignano and *Picciolo di Rame*. I was on foot, marching along with four or five hundred others from Caldarola through Vestignano to Montalto to the site of the massacre. The memory of this and other similar executions is a living issue here in Le Marche. Each year this march takes place, culminating in speeches from local dignitaries who, notably, direct their message to Italian youth. There is a very real sense in which the Italian post-war constitution was formed by the men who stood up against fascism. After the liberation of the region, Partisan commanders were appointed as mayors in many local towns. In marches like this, young Italians are reminded each year that they owe the freedoms they enjoy in modern Italy to those young men who died for the cause on a lonely roadside seventy years ago.

I had been living in Sarnano for some time before I began to really appreciate the significance of these events. The major set piece battles of World War Two seemed to have passed Le Marche by. After the unopposed Allied landings on the heel of Italy, at Taranto on 9th September 1943, the push up the Adriatic coast that followed, largely by British, Canadian and Polish forces, went smoothly enough until, just before Christmas 1943, near Otranto, they ran into the Gustav Line, a line of heavily fortified defensive positions stretching right across the peninsular from the Adriatic to the Tyrrhenian Sea. In land that favoured defensive positions, it was several months before the Allies were able to break through the line and force a German withdrawal, and it was this period of nine months or so from the armistice in September through to June of 1944 that saw the birth and flowering of the Partisan movement. It also marked the most painful time for the people of this region. In the immediate aftermath of the armistice German troops had swept south to occupy most of Italy. Now under German control, and lacking any guidance from the new Italian government, some *Marchigiani* decided to co-operate, willingly or unwillingly with the occupying forces. Others decided on resistance and took to the hills to form bands of *Partigiani*. The memories of that time, when the local populace found itself set neighbor against neighbor, still scar the towns and villages of the region. Italians have long memories for that sort of thing. Memories that can still be found in the fabric of towns like Sarnano.

Most mornings you can find me sitting outside *Bar Casciotti* enjoying a coffee in the sunshine. On the wall above the entrance is a plaque commemorating the deaths of twelve men who died in this town's resistance against the Nazis during this time. This plaque bears witness to the multi-national make-up of these bands. Most of the names are Italian, of course, but some are clearly Slavic. There are two names of English-speaking men, most likely British, American or Canadian. One of those names, which always puzzled us, was obviously English, but barely recognisable as such. The plaque recorded the death of a man called "Jefren Gordon". After my eyes had been opened by the march to Montalto I decided to find out more about "Jefren Gordon", and about how and why the others on that sad list died. The story I discovered brought that desperate period very close to home.

MEMORIAL PLAQUE OUTSIDE BAR CASCIOTTI

Exactly one week after the massacre at Montalto, just before dawn on 29th March 1944 German troops, accompanied by soldiers of *Battaglione IX Settembre*, a battalion of Italian Fascists, took up positions outside Sarnano. The *IX Settembre* were a crack troop who, after the armistice, had pledged their support to the RSI, the new fascist government established by the Germans under Mussolini in the north. As dawn broke they began to bombard the town with heavy mortars. Angiolino Ghiandoni, a young child at the time recalled that "all hell broke loose. It can only have lasted a quarter of an hour," he said, "but it seemed to go on forever". After the firing ceased the fascist troops rolled into Sarnano in force. The inhabitants were instructed to assemble in the main square, the *Piazza Vittorio Emanuele* - the same square where nowadays I sit enjoying my coffee beneath that enigmatic plaque. Houses were turned upside down in a search for evidence of Partisan sympathizers, and the men and women in the square were threatened with hanging unless they revealed the whereabouts of the partisans. One young man, Mario Catini, was killed in a small square a stone's throw from the main piazza. It is one of my favorite spots in Sarnano, with not a modern brick or window in sight, and a perfect view of the mountains. It is called *Piazza Perfetti*. I was sad to learn of this dark shadow from the past which taints its perfection.

As I look up at the plaque on *Bar Casciotti's* wall, I see the name of Mario Catini. I am pleased that I now know his story. Pleased that I can help to keep alive the memory of his suffering and the loss suffered by his loved ones. At the top of the list of names on the plaque is one other name - a name I knew carried special meaning for the people of Sarnano. As I researched the very particular, almost private, history of this town at that time, I discovered why that name, Decio Filipponi, is so revered. It is because of what happened that day, 29th March, as the people of Sarnano awaited their fate in the town square. The German action in Sarnano was part of a broader strategy. They had also dispatched troops into the mountains, to the tiny village of Piobbico high above Sarnano. Here they came across Decio Filipponi, the leader of the *Banda Piobbico* Partisan group. Filipponi and two Slavs, members of the group were killed. The exact circumstances are unclear, but at 2pm that afternoon the townspeople were suddenly told they were allowed to leave the square and return to their homes. There would be no further slaughter that day.

There is an ancient set of steps just below my house. Fifty-three steps that take you down through a dark arch, the *Porta di Bisio*, the last to be built of the main gates into the walled town. At the bottom you emerge into an attractive little piazza. It is called the *Largo Decio Filipponi*. Filipponi is a hero in Sarnano because of what happened that day in March 1944. It is a strongly held belief among the people of Sarnano they were released unharmed only because Decio Filipponi gave himself up to the Germans when faced with the threat of innocent civilians being hanged in his stead. Some time ago I met the niece of Decio Filliponi who confirmed the story to me. She also told me that her uncle was from Rome and had been a soldier in the Italian army. The armistice gave him the chance to throw his lot in with the *Partigiani*. So he made his way to his family's home in Le Marche and formed a band of volunteers based at Piobbico. His military training made him a natural leader. After giving himself up, she said, he was tortured before being hanged from a lamppost and left to die slowly. He was just 22 years old. I never discovered the names of the two Slavs who died with him, but they are certainly among the five Slavic names etched in stone along with Decio Filipponi.

I still needed to get to the bottom of the "Jefren Gordon" story, though - and, although I am not entirely certain, I believe I have. It is in the nature of resistance movements that every time you kill one of their fighters, two or three more will appear to take their place. Martyrdom is a very powerful motivator. In the weeks following the raid on Sarnano and the death of Filipponi, disparate small groups of *Partigiani* started to re-form and expand. Within a few weeks they had established control of the main road south through Amandola, a vital supply route for German forces now struggling to hold the Gustav Line south of Pescara. The German response was to dispatch the Italian fascists of the *IX Settembre* battalion to the area. Arriving in Sarnano they occupied the *Palazzo Brandi*, a large aristocratic residence in the *centro storico,* and a nearby school. Immediately they began a series of armed operations against the *Partigiani.*

By the middle of May the partisans, under the command of a Montenegrin, Janko Klicovach, learned that the *IX Settembro*, a disciplined and highly-trained force, had quickly established two habitual behaviours. Each morning one unit would form up for exercise drill on the town's football field just below the main square. Another would travel a half mile or so to a small-arms shooting range on the outskirts of town. On May 30th, partisans from the Piobbico group, along with another detachment named *Lucio,* the *Gruppo Nicolo',* and a group from nearby Gualdo, assembled in Cese, a small village up in the mountains.

Before dawn the following day they made their way in silence to Sarnano. One group set up a machine gun position overlooking the shooting range, while another positioned their gun above the sports field. This second detachment were to be disappointed, however. On that morning, May 31st, no German troops arrived for their usual exercise. It later transpired that their commander had spent the night with a woman and had not woken up to take his men out to the football field. Meanwhile, at the shooting range all went according to plan, and in the firefight that followed eight fascist soldiers were killed. In the meantime, the football field detachment had shifted their machine gun to a position covering the windows of the *Palazzo Brandi* and opened fire on soldiers reacting to the distant noise of heavy firing at the shooting range.

Altogether, eight soldiers from *IX Settembre* died that day. In the fighting at the firing range two of the partisans were killed. One was Dusan Labovic - another of the Slav names on the plaque in the square. The other is reported to have been an Englishman, an escaped prisoner called George Godfrey. To English ears most Italian names have a beautiful, mellifluous tone to them. I bought my house from a man called Zeo Zega, which seems to me to put any English name in the shade all by itself. Sadly, it doesn't work the other way round. Italians just don't seem to understand why we have incomprehensible, ugly names, like Clive, or Douglas, or Stephen. And as for surnames like Phelps... well, forget it. Whether they can't actually DO them, or just don't make the effort I am not sure, but we get called all sorts of strange things here. My builder always called me "Stin" (pronounced Steen), even on official documents, and I have never been able to change his mind, even by writing it out. So the idea that a local stonemason back in the 1950s should have rendered George Godfrey as Jefren Gordon seems to me to be entirely plausible. But maybe someone out there will prove me wrong. I hope not.

All that has been a bit of a diversion, I know, but it started with *Picciolo di Rame* and the commemorative march going on up past the restaurant. But I make no apologies, because this is serious stuff, and interesting too. We forget these stories at our peril. For nigh on three-quarters of a century there has been peace in Europe, a continent ravaged by war over and over again in previous centuries. That is because the generation in charge in the aftermath of war were determined these regular bloodbaths should be ended, and in doing so they created the European Union. It has its faults, and it has all sorts of benefits too. But the prime reason for giving it more or less unquestioning support is that it signifies the desire to end the internecine slaughter that was being acted out even here on the quiet streets of Sarnano seventy years ago. The Nobel Prize Committee knew what they were doing when they awarded the Peace Prize to the EU. Good for them.

But this is Italy, and we must get back to food. Not difficult, because here in Le Marche even a memorial march to honour the region's martyred partisans finishes up with a delicious bowl of free pasta served from a giant vat in the crypt of the ancient church in Montalto. It was a *Penne all'Amatriciana* that day, and it was mouth-wateringly delicious. Oh, and there was a band. And the singing of partisan songs. *Bella Ciao* sung alongside the memorial to the twenty-six executed men, at the very spot where they died for their cause, made the hairs stand up on the back of my neck. Try it for yourself...

https://www.youtube.com/watch?v=4CI3lhyNKfo

Driving Shots

By now we were just about a week into our shoot, and it was the height of August. And heating up. By the middle of the day the temperatures were well into the upper 30s, and the talent was getting fractious. One key piece of advice for young people joining the new and "exciting" world of TV for the first time is to pass on that sage warning that most of the time you spend on a film shoot you will be *waiting*. Waiting for some piece of kit to arrive, waiting for the sun to come round to just the right angle, waiting for Make-Up to powder down the star's ever so slightly shiny face, whatever. Waiting. There always seems to be something you have to wait for. And on a shoot like Cookucina, celebrating the great outdoors of Le Marche, much of that waiting time was spent standing in the blistering sun. And when they weren't waiting, Peter's perfectionism meant that the talent were being asked to "go back and do that walk again". He was not popular.

Day 7 was the hottest so far. The hottest day of our shoot and the hottest day of the year. I am tempted to say it was the hottest day EVER, but I would be lying. It just *felt* like that. To start with things weren't so bad. First thing on the agenda was to film some driving shots up in the mountains. These would be used for little music sequences to get out of Sarnano and into the hills - specifically to illustrate the journey across the mountains to the trout fishery near Visso. Driving shots are a fantastic way to show off BIG SCENERY. You try to build what's known in the business as a "sequence". You see sequences all the time, but if they're good you won't notice them. Unless you are a professional. Basically a sequence involves shooting the same thing from a number of different angles then cutting it together so it looks like one continuous piece of action. That's fine if it is just a politician walking into a building (and how many times have we see THAT!). But if you are up in the mountains things get a bit more complex. To start with, you need a minimum of three shots to make a sequence. More if you're doing driving shots. For a top-dollar driving sequence you need:

1. A big wide shot of the whole view with the car driving across the scene in the far distance.

2. An "up and past" shot, where the camera is on the roadside and the car comes along the road towards it and on past.

3. An in-car shot of the driver at the wheel. Plus (if there's a passenger) a "reverse" shot of the passenger sitting alongside.

4. A driver's POV shot. POV stands for Point Of View, so this is basically pointing the camera through the windscreen at the road ahead.

5. Car-to-car, where you put the camera in a car traveling in front of the "target" car and film backwards so the camera is effectively the view back from an "imaginary" car in front (because in the wide shot and the POV there will **be** no car in front).

166

Have you managed to follow me so far? I hope so, because I've got one more to add. The icing on the cake is:

6. A bonnet-mounted camera shot looking back, as though the cameraman is sprawled across the bonnet hanging on for dear life - which is exactly what happened in our case, but more of that later.

All this is not *too* difficult you might think, except when you realize that for Shot No. 2 (the "up and past") the camera has to be right next to the car's wheels as it passes, whereas for Shot No. 1 (the wide shot) you have to be quite some distance away. And when you are shooting a mountain backdrop you need to get off the road and tramp about half a mile up a hillside before you can even start. Take a look at the very first shot after the Title Sequence in Episode One and you will see what I mean.

But that's when the difficulties start, because once you are in position, camera focused and recording, you have to "cue" the driver of the car to set off. Sometimes you can manage it by giving a BIG WAVE of the arm, but maybe you want the car to come *into shot*, which would mean they need to start by being out of sight, and therefore couldn't see you waving to start them off. Solution? Yes, you've guessed it - walkie-talkies. And of course, we had organized a pair of walkie-talkies before we set off up into the mountains. The secret of TV success, you see, is in the planning.

But it's a contrary business, television. On the morning in question Peter and I struggled up the hillside under a fierce sun and managed to find a lovely vantage point. Away to the right below us the road came round a bend then snaked across the side of the mountain. We had had a little planning conference before Peter and I set off up the hill with the camera and sticks, and a big heavy bag with all our lenses, filters and tapes. Lia and Tam had gone off in Sergio's Fiat Panda, which by now had become the Cookucina Car, to wait out of sight where they couldn't see us - essential, of course, so that the camera would not see the car until it came round the bend. So by the time Peter and I had reached our spot and set up, the car was hidden round the corner, Tam and Lia waiting patiently for us to call and cue them to drive. Breathing a little heavily after the climb we set up the camera and Peter focussed tight on the bend where they would appear.

He switched the camera into record. A quick nod indicated that he was ready to go. I pressed the TALK button on my walkie-talkie.

"Standby!"

"What was that?" said Peter, a note of alarm in his voice.

"What?"

"There it is again... Your voice."

"My voice?"

"It's coming out of the bag."

"What bag?"

"Our bag."

"Our bag?" I was beginning to sound like a particularly talkative parrot.

"It's the other bloody walkie-talkie. It's in the bag."

We had never actually agreed whose responsibility it was to ensure that the walkie-talkies were fully charged and in the right place, but the look on Peter's face said he was pretty clear it was my job. It didn't seem like the right time to argue, so I just shrugged and apologised. Five minutes later Tam appeared on foot at the bend. Hands on hips in a rather menacing manner. She and Lia had just made the same discovery. She looked a good deal angrier than Peter. I was glad to be half a mile away. I gave her the BIG WAVE, but she didn't recognize it immediately as the Alternative Cue I intended, and waved back in an exasperated sort of way. So I did the BIG WAVE again. This time I think she stamped her foot, but on the third go she finally understood what I was doing and returned to the car. Peter switched the camera into record and two minutes later the Panda duly appeared round the corner and we got the shot. It worked perfectly and it does a fantastic job of showing off the sheer size of the scenery up in the mountains, but it was not an auspicious start to our driving sequence.

Next came the car to car shots (No. 5 on the hymn sheet). Eight minutes into Episode One is where you'll find these for the first time. A really super-professional crew (with the kind of money we DIDN'T have) would have hired special camera mounts for a shoot like this. A bonnet mount (that's for Shot No. 6), so that you can fix the camera firmly on the bonnet and it will record the view back through the windscreen at the driver and passenger as they travel along. And for the shot looking backwards from a car traveling in front, maybe even hiring a special camera car, adapted so that you can mount a tripod in the back - generally a station-wagon or a pick-up. Once upon a time a lowly Citroen 2CV was the cameraman's favorite, because it had the world's softest suspension and you could just roll the roof back to turn it into a convertible. We, of course, had none of these things. But we did have Peter. And Peter is nothing if not resourceful. I said we'd just have to make do without those shots somehow, but Peter was having none of it.

"I'll sit in the trunk," he volunteered.

And he did. We used the sticks to prop the trunk open and Peter sat like a Buddha holding the camera on his shoulder. The shots are a little wobbly when we went over the occasional bump, and you can only *just* detect the moment when the sticks shifted and the lid of the trunk fell on his head, but overall it was a classic piece of improvisation.

And he was not done yet. Flushed with success, he decided he was now going to have a go at the bonnet mount shot.

"But we haven't *got* a bonnet mount" I protested.

"Don't worry," he said, "I will *mount* the bonnet." And that's what he did. He climbed up and took up the Buddha position once again - this time on the bonnet itself. This position was even more precarious than his last, so we tied him on with a piece of rope, and Lia and Tam set off (rather gently) down the road.

"Faster, faster", shouted the crazed Buddha, fully aware that traveling at 5 miles an hour wouldn't cut together with all the other shots. Above and beyond the call of duty, I told him when it was done, but Peter just shrugged it off. It was a good job we were up in the mountains, though, with no *carabinieri* around. I wondered what other wild schemes Peter would come up with before the shooting was over. One thing to remember about television is that you never see what's going on *behind* the camera. Good thing sometimes. The shot works beautifully, Lia and Tam smiling and laughing to one another as they drive along. It brings a lovely feelgood factor to the sequence. But only Peter and I know that the laughter is in fact hysterical. The one and only time in her life that Lia has had to drive along a narrow mountain road with a man strapped on the hood.

The Heat

At least in the mountains there was a bit of a cool breeze. But there's not much shade, and Peter and I were developing the beginnings of a nice tan after clambering up hillsides and, in his case at least, being strapped to the bonnet of a car for half an hour or so. Inside the car, meanwhile, Tam and Lia were coming to the boil - and I am not referring to the hysteria, rather the fact that eighteen year old Fiat Pandas, while they may have four-wheel drive and be able to go anywhere, are distinctly lacking in modern creature comforts. Specifically, air-conditioning. Inside the car the talent was hot. But not in the Hollywood sense of the term. And they were about to get hotter. Because our next appointment was back down in the foothills, at one of the finest of the many local *cantinas*. A *cantina*, in Italy at least, is a winery. A sort of outlet for a family-run vineyard or a small local cooperative. Generally you can buy anything from award-winning bio-ecological reds, to the local *Montepulciano* or *Falerio* which are delivered on tap into 5 liter flagons. Serious drinkers, or restaurateurs, or large families - or maybe restaurateurs with large families - sometimes turn up with a 25 liter flagon for a refill. An English friend of mine got a nasty shock when he first arrived at one of these places and saw a local apparently filling his car's gas tank with wine from a hose. In fact he was bent over one of these giant flagons that he was very sensibly filling up without moving it from the trunk. Lifting an empty 25 liter glass bottle out of the trunk is no problem. Getting it back in when it is full with 25 liters of wine is another matter. You only get caught that way once.

We needed a bottle of a really nice local red for the *dolce* Lia was going to make when we got back into the kitchen, *Pere al Vino Rosso*, pears in red wine. Of course when you are cooking with the stuff you don't need a really expensive wine, but it was a good opportunity to showcase some of the high-class wines being produced locally, and beginning to make themselves felt on a wider stage. To start with the visit went well. As soon as we arrived at the *Cantina di Saputi* Alvaro Saputi whisked us straight into a temperature-controlled environment where the wine is aged in oak barrels before being bottled for the market. After several hours roasting in a Fiat Panda, Tam in particular looked very much happier here. So much so that we couldn't shut her up. The idea had been to knock off a quick interview indoors then go and do the bulk of the piece in the *Saputi* vineyard. But Tam was clearly intent on staying in the cooler for as long as possible and kept asking more and more questions, going deeper and deeper into the arcane processes involved in wine-making. Much more than we needed for the short clip we would be putting into the program. But maybe I am being uncharitable. Tam is a good talker and very inquisitive. Maybe she really DID want to know all the intricate details, and it was nothing to do with the cool conditions. Or maybe she just knew what it was going to be like when we got out among the vines under what had by now become a merciless sun. If that is what she was afraid of, she was not disappointed.

It was a Mad Dogs and Englishmen moment, but we had to do it. Despite the blistering heat we had to get out there amongst the vines. You cannot do a visit to a vineyard and stay indoors. Peter wanted the classic vineyard shot, looking down a long line of vines extending down the hillside with a hilltop town off in the distance. Tam and Lia, along with Signor and Signora Saputi were to walk towards the camera, chatting in a leisurely way about the secrets of making such delicious wine. Which meant they were all walking uphill, and, as you will know by now, they had to do it several times, so Peter could get the different sizes of shot, and the close-ups, that would be needed for the edit. And then, when they reached the end of their walk, there would be a short recorded interview.

In fact it is a **very** short interview. Generally cutting an interview is a matter of picking the really good bits and leaving the rest on the cutting room floor. But in this case, if you look at the interview, which is about sixteen and a half minutes into Episode One, that's all there is. It is one minute and fifteen seconds long, and absolutely nothing went to waste. If you look closely at Tam's face at 16 minutes and 40 seconds you can see her thinking "WHEN is this going to end!". And as soon as the one minute and fifteen second interview was over Tam and Lia were back into the cool of the winery in the blink of an eye. Signora Saputi was very understanding and fished out a large glass of their top grade white *Castru Vecchiu*, chilled to perfection. Lia still talks about it as one of the nicest glasses of wine she has ever drunk.

After a morning spent outdoors under a fierce sun the wine went down a treat and half an hour later we left the winery with several bottles and a couple of slightly tipsy stars (see the evidence at 18:14 into Episode 1). But at least we had a nice red, as recommended by our host, and so it was back to the Cookucina kitchen where Lia was fortunately able to teach Tam how to make a delicious *Pere al Vino Rosso* without too many mishaps. "That's because it couldn't be simpler", she said. Well, see for yourself...

PEARS in RED WINE

- *4 pears*
- *3/4 liter red wine*
- *Cinnamon*
- *6 cloves*
- *1 orange*
- *5 tablespoons of sugar*

Peel pears without removing stems, stand them in a narrow pot, cut the orange in half and squeeze. Place orange in middle of pears. Add wine, cinnamon, cloves and sugar. Lift pears out when soft. Reduce wine to a syrup. Slice pears and drizzle with syrup.

Monterotti

It was an *afa*, an *ondata di caldo,* a heatwave. We couldn't have timed it worse really. Day after day of record-breaking temperatures, a fierce sun burning down from clear blue skies. Ideal for the beauty shots (television pictures have no temperature at all), but murder when you are standing out in it trying to catch that perfect composition. And there was no respite indoors, of course. The Cookucina house itself is cool enough (kitchen apart!) - thick brick walls take care of that, and the back wall of Lia's *ingresso* is built into the living rock which is cold to the touch whatever the weather outside. But we were on a schedule - Peter and his camera had a date on a luxury yacht which he wasn't going to miss. And that schedule said that every time we came back to the house it was straight into the kitchen and on with the oven! No air conditioning, of course.

Every year I go through the same routine - for ten months I pat myself on the back at regular intervals about living in a house that has changed very little in seven hundred years. But for the other two months, when the thermometer starts to bubble and the main topic of conversation in town is which of the roadside temperature gauges is most accurate, I begin to vacillate. It starts with breaking out the electric fans that have been tucked away since last summer, moving on to actually *reading* the fliers from electrical stores that get stuffed into the letter box on a daily basis, trying to make sense of the air conditioner ads and their BTUs and COPs (that's a Coefficient of Performance). Then there will be the conversation about how it's not really much of an expense, and it's a small price to pay for comfort in your own home. But thankfully I am always slapped down by Tam. She will not even begin to entertain the idea of contaminating the outside of our house with an AC exhaust unit. She makes the point she spends much of her life campaigning against satellite dishes, so she couldn't even if she wanted to, and of course, she's right. Anyway, in the normal course of events these discussions go on for long enough that the heat breaks and the beautiful September weather arrives - long sunny days with the temperature just about ideal. Soon the fans will be tucked away at the back of the cupboard ready for next July - along with the discussion about buying an air conditioning unit.

Out among the vines in the heat of the day I had not been the most popular person. It was my job to devise and maintain the schedule. I'd built it all a couple of weeks earlier, when the weather was more normal, and it seemed to me it would just about hang together. If we stuck rigidly to the spreadsheet in the front of my bright green Director's folder we could just manage to assemble all the material we needed for the series. It had taken me two sleepless nights to pull it all together and I was convinced (possibly, I now see, unreasonably) that there was no room for manoeuvre. The talent, however, didn't buy into this idea at all, and were constantly trying to rearrange things (sometimes behind my back) so that shoots requiring them to stand out in the sun were postponed. Until when it was never quite clear, and of course it was baking hot every day so if they had had their way we would have finished up with a series set entirely indoors, and the wonderful vineyards, mountains and lakes of Le Marche would have been entirely invisible. Come to think of it, if they had sniffed victory they would probably have started to complain about being *indoors,* in the kitchen, and we would have been in danger of achieving nothing at all. So, unpopular though it was, I had to insist on sticking to the schedule come what may.

That evening, though, I changed abruptly from villain to hero - and all because of the schedule.

"Tomorrow," I was able to announce, "we will be spending the day in a cold store."

It wasn't quite true, but it had the desired effect, and anyway we were indeed going to be visiting a cold store for about five minutes as it happens - but it had much the same effect on the talent as that glass of chilled *Castru Vecchiu'.*

Simple Food, Beautifully Cooked was the mantra Lia had brought to Cookucina. The whole ethos of the series was to show hard-pressed cooks how they could make something special without spending hours in the kitchen. We had broken the content down into three new recipes in each show - a starter, a main course and a *dolce*. One of the starters she hadn't originally intended to include was *Crostini with Ciabuscolo and Stracchino*. You might remember Lia served it up to us for lunch earlier in the shoot and Peter and I were so impressed we insisted she include it in the series. It's basically just slices of bread toasted with salami and cheese. *Stracchino* is a soft spreadable cheese they use a lot round here, but the *ciabuscolo* is really the key ingredient. It's that soft salami that you can only find in the foothills of the Sibillini, and Sergio had arranged for us to visit a place where they make some of the finest *ciabuscolo* in the region.

There's a fast food joint in Sarnano. Of a very Italian sort. It's a van which parks up in the corner of the main square on a daily basis. It sells homemade cheeses, salamis, *prosciutto*, *ciabuscolo*, and all sorts of cured meats. You can get anything and everything can be made up into a *panini* for a kind of workman's lunch. My favorite is that *porchetta* which they slice off a whole piglet stuffed with fresh herbs and roasted over a spit. The van is a family concern run by the Monterottis from a small factory just outside town, and this was where we were going today, to find out how they made their *ciabuscolo*. Signor Monterotti, Fabrizio to his friends, had suggested we start in the cold store where the salamis and hams are hung up to age - for months, even years, at a time. It is a bit like entering an underground cavern with long thin salamis hanging from the ceiling like stalactites. *Lonza, Lonzino, Salami di Fegato* (liver), this is a veritable cornucopia of cured meat. Giant hams stamped with their date of origin were swung aside to reveal yet more curtains of hanging meat. Tam (who likes a slice of salami) looked like a kid in a toy store. This was a lifetime's supply of *affetato misto*. And what is more the toy store was *cold,* and I mean really cold. This was pretty much heaven for Tam - which is why she so regretted asking to see how the *porchetta* was made. "*Venite,*" said Fabrizio, "*vi faccio vedere*". And following his lead, we stepped out of the cold store, up some stairs, through a heavy plastic curtain, and into a furnace.

Monterotti's *porchetta* is a work of art. Fabrizio was very keen to emphasise that they use only their own pigs, reared pretty much in the backyard before being trucked down, when their time was up, to the local *mattatoio*, Sarnano's very own slaughterhouse. All as natural and eco-biological as could be. The herbs are local too. So much so that they are collected fresh every morning. But not, it turns out by

Fabrizio. This is a job for Nonno Monterotti, Fabrizio's dad, who nips out shortly after dawn into the fields and nearby woods to pick the freshest selection of herbs that could be. He's a sprightly old chap and I'm sure he be doing it anyway, but Granddad has to get out there at the crack of dawn because the *porchetta* has to be roasted and shipped down to the van in town in time for lunch. People round here don't seem to retire - there's always something keeping them productive. Generally their son. We had missed the herb harvest of course, but we were here now for the final act - the roasting.

It's hard to explain the effect on Tam. Down in the cold store she was all sweetness and light, entrancing Fabrizio with her genuine fascination about the age-old secrets of Sarnanese salami. But as we stepped through that plastic curtain to be confronted by an open spit oven and what looked like a wall of orange flame, she came quickly back to the boil.

"Stand there." I said, "Next to the oven... so we get the flames in the background". She was not amused. Particularly when Peter decided he needed to put the wide angle lens on so that Fabrizio, Lia, Tam and the roasting pig were all in shot.

"No, don't move," I shouted, "the set-up's perfect. Changing lens won't take a minute".

Well it didn't. It took about five. During which the right side of Tam's face began to cook nicely, taking on the same sort of color as the roasting pig. My jokes about crackling didn't make matters any better, but once the lens was on we were able to go straight into the interview with everyone in just the right spot and the fire roaring away. This interview is short, too, but I have to say that was nothing to do with Tam, just that Fabrizio told us all we needed to know about *porchetta* in record-breaking time. Maybe he was getting a bit warm too.

Leaving Fabrizio's furnace was about the only time the talent felt good to get back out into the blazing sun. It didn't last, of course. Pretty soon they were agitating to get back into the cool somewhere. We had, however, left with a *ciabuscolo* tucked under our arm (complete with secret ingredient) so Peter and I were happy we were at last going to get our Crostini with *Ciabuscolo* and *Stracchino*.

CROSTINI with CIABUSCOLO and STRACCHINO

- *200g. of stracchino or any soft white cheese*
- *200g. of ciabuscolo or sausage-meat (if you must!)*
- *4 slices of crusty white bread.*

Use a heavy fork to mash the soft cheese and the sausage-meat together. Spread the mixture thickly on the bread slices and put them under the grill for 7/8 minutes, or until golden brown.

The secret ingredient? Oh yes, I forgot. But you didn't *really* think I would tell you that, did you? Signor Monterotti swore he would kill me if I told anyone. And you know what they're like about vendettas round here.

Massimo, Adele and the Sagra

It took me a few years to realize it, but there is one fundamental difference between life in Italy and in Britain. Here in Italy life is, as much as possible, lived outdoors, while in the colder, damper, grayer environment back in the UK life is mostly spent indoors. Here in Italy people return to their houses to eat and to go to bed - generally twice a day, once to sleep and once to rest. But the rest of the time they will be outside pretty much whenever possible. In the mornings they're out for coffee in one of the bars (early, if they're off to work), then it's home for lunch and a *riposo*, an afternoon rest. After that it's back to work, then home for *cena*, the evening meal. By which time the sun is on its way down, the heat of the day has passed and the countryside is bathed in early evening sunshine and washed by a cool breeze. This is the best bit of the day, and the average Italian will much prefer to be outside rather than indoors where the house will still be stuffy at the end of a hot day.

I am generalizing of course. And I realize I am talking about the summer (in winter we spend much of the evening wrapped up in front of the *stufa.*) But the point is a real one. Whenever they can, Italians will take to the open air. In the *campagna* you will see whole families sitting outside their farmhouses on white plastic chairs. Or clustered round an ancient wooden table under an old oak tree. In town they'll be sitting on the doorstep, or, more likely, wandering about, bumping into friends and chatting about, well.... mostly football, food or their latest visit to the doctor, as we know. This is an institution called *la passeggiata*, and it's evident in its many different forms all across the country. A couple of years back I traveled down to Molise (a region even less well-known than Le Marche) to stay with a friend of mine who had gone back for a couple of weeks to the village where she was born. Molise is only about four hours south of us, but

179

it's like a different country (that's the glory of Italy). More parched, wide open spaces, shallow-rising hills stretching off into the distance. A bit like the central plains of Spain (the ones where it hardly ever rains!).

Cristiana's home village is built on the side of one of these hills, and it's pretty much a strip of houses along a single road that winds its way gently along the hillside. So there's not really very much choice on where to go for your *passeggiata*. But nobody is much bothered by that. Certainly not Cristiana, who was happy to slot back into old habits (she lives in London nowadays). At about 5.30 in the evening, she grabbed my arm and said,

"We're going for a walk"

Which is what we did. We turned left out of her parents' house and walked a mile or so through the village and out into the countryside. Along the way we passed elderly couples sitting outside their houses on the obligatory white plastic chairs, and lots of other people, again mostly in pairs, who passed us going in the opposite direction. Cristiana had something to say to just about all of them, but not enough to stop *la passeggiata*. After a mile we came to a halt, turned round and walked back through the village, and straight out the other side. And as we did so, we passed the same elderly couples and the same walkers we had passed before, only this time coming back in the other direction. Then, of course, a mile out of town we turned round and walked back ourselves. One road - out, back through the village, out the other side, turn round and back home. Perfect length of walk to work up an appetite and just enough engagement with friends and neighbors without getting into anything too deeply. And that's what they do. Whenever the weather allows. That's *la passeggiata*.

At Monterotti's this business of getting out into the fresh air in the evenings came in handy. As Tam was roasting slowly in front of the furnace I was able to assure her that we had a nice cool evening ahead of us. We were going to a *Sagra*. *Sagras* are a big institution in these parts. They're a sort of annual village fair, held in most of the tiny villages up in the hills round here. They mostly center around food (of course!). Within a few miles of Sarnano we have *Sagras* in honour of *polentone* (big *polenta*), fresh-water prawns, *strozzapreti* (pasta that's shaped like a priest's collar. Its literal meaning is "priest throttler") and even frogs. That evening there was a Sagra on the road up out of town in honour of *vincisgrassi*.

This is a real local treat. Legend has it (and you can read this in one or two cookbooks) that it was named after an Austrian General Alfred Candidus Ferdinand zu Windisch-Graetz who fought in the Napoleonic Wars. It is true that the Napoleonic Wars extended throughout Northern Italy and even down into the central provinces. Indeed one of the most celebrated of its battles took place just down the road from us at Tolentino in 1815. But it seems to me highly unlikely that this is the real derivation of the name. The Windisch-Graetz family were originally from Styria in modern Slovenia and they were a substantial aristocratic family in first the Holy Roman Empire and then the Hapsburg Empire of Austria-Hungary. But why a flying visit by this one general should be worthy of the invention of a special dish escapes me. It's not even that *vincisgrassi* sounds or looks much like Windisch-Graetz - unless you take your glasses off and squint a bit. And anyway, Silvano, who runs *Picciolo di Rame* and specialises in cooking like they did in medieval times, makes a fantastic *vincisgrassi*, and I am pretty sure he would rubbish the idea that it wasn't invented till 1815. I certainly wouldn't want to persuade him otherwise since he'd be obliged to consign the dish for ever after to his medieval trash can, and I for one would miss it hugely.

I have my own theory. *Vincisgrassi* is a dish that's a bit like lasagna. Wafer thin leaves of pasta sandwiching layers of a *ragu*, a special meat sauce, and bechamel sauce. The *ragu* is made with very lean meat, and the whole thing is incredibly rich without you feeling you've eaten a heavy dish. So I think the name goes back way beyond Napoleonic times and comes from corruptions of the two verbs *vincere*, to win, and *sgrassare*, to degrease. Seems to make more sense than the Slovenian general story, but I am sure there are plenty of you out there who would like to argue about it - and you will! One final little wrinkle.... it seems that the English minor royal, Princess Michael of Kent (strange name for a princess!), is descended from the Windisch-Graetz princes. I only mention that because it might help you to decide which side of the fence to come down on, dependent upon whether you are a royalist or a republican.

So on the night of the *porchetta* furnace interview I had us down to pay a visit to the *vincisgrassi Sagra*. I had been to it in previous years so I knew what we were in for. Apart from delicious *vincisgrassi* (and I am prepared to bet that none of the people who made it that night had ever heard of Alfred Candidus Ferdinand zu Windisch-Graetz) served with a glass of local *Rosso Conero* or *Verdicchio di Matelica*, all for a knockdown price, there would also be dancing, music and a fresh evening breeze coming off the mountains. Tam would be happy! What I hadn't realized, though, was that we would make a major breakthrough that evening in what the whole series was going to feel like. More accurately, what it was going to *sound* like.

There was dancing. There's always dancing. Mostly it's good old-fashioned hang-on-to-your-partner sort of dancing. But I was taken a bit by surprise when we arrived to find the locals were line-dancing. And looking as though they were having fun. Which struck me as unusual because normally line-dancing sends a chill down my spine. My father took it up at the ripe old age of 75 and it sounded as though it was quite a laugh. Then I discovered that my cousin was practically a professional, so it seemed that she was going to be a good way into it, once I had decided I wanted to see what all the fuss was about. The chance came when I got an invite to my cousin's wedding anniversary. I was late (I generally am, I must be turning into an Italian) and I walked into the room to find that the line-dancing had started, about forty of them moving in perfect unison across the floor. The trouble was it didn't look like fun at all. In fact they were so intent on getting it right, so deep in concentration, that it looked more like the march of the living dead. I have never seen a bunch of people looking so miserable doing what they enjoy. In the space of about two seconds the urge to get into line-dancing had left me forever. Which is why it came as such a surprise to see a bunch of Italian country-folk laughing and smiling and chatting with each other as they moved across the open-air dance-floor in, well, not **exactly** perfect unison.

But that wasn't the biggest surprise of the evening. It was the music they were dancing to. Provided by a duo from a village about 30 miles away, as I discovered later. There was a guy in his forties playing the *fisarmonica*, the squeezebox which is the basic instrument of traditional *Marchigiana* music. He was brilliant, and could play anything from Bach to the Beatles. I expect I am exaggerating a bit, but not much. He was great. But if anything he was eclipsed by his partner, a stockily-built, twenty-something girl singer with a truly wonderful voice. I don't watch X-Factor programs, but if I did I would not have been surprised to see her sweeping the board. But, of course, she lives in rural Italy and sings in Italian, so there's not much chance of that.

A singer we did **not** need, but it suddenly dawned on me that Massimo and his *fisarmonica* were just the thing we needed for the soundtrack to the series. There's the better part of three hours television in the six parts of the Cookcucina series, and most of it has music on it. Strange how music has become a central part of our lives, instead of a high value optional extra. It's everywhere - shops, elevators, phone lines ("you are number... seventeen ...in the queue", cue Music), and it's all over just about every television program. Trouble is, if you use commercial music this can get very expensive, so most production companies tend to opt for one of the free libraries (I generally use Audio Network). They're great, don't get me wrong, but the music is sometimes a bit bland (elevator music?) and after a while you begin to hear the same track over and over again. Maybe it's because that track is really good, but I tend to think it's because television producers are basically lazy, and don't attach too much importance to music - just slap it down and make sure there's plenty of it. It's human nature really, though, because when you type in the "genre" of music you want, and maybe a couple of other parameters, like "instrumental" and "celtic" you will be presented with a list of about three hundred possible tracks. Actually *listening* to all those tracks is the labor of Hercules, and it will always come at a time when you've got better things to do - like lunch. So music gets picked on the Google principle, which is to say if it is not on the first page it's never even going to get opened.

Massimo and his *fisarmonica* came therefore as a godsend to us. Local music played on a typical local instrument and everything either *trad.* (traditional) or written by Massimo himself, so that he was able to grant us all rights, in all media (currently existing or yet to be invented), everywhere, and forever (we are nothing if not comprehensive, we TV producers). And he signed it all over for a very reasonable price, too - presumably in expectation of fame and fortune. Luckily, we wanted only instrumental music, so there was no need to cut a deal with Miss X-Factor, though maybe we would have stood a better chance of making money if we had.

In fact Massimo's music works brilliantly for the series, conjuring up just the right degree of tradition and history without making the series feel like something from the archives. Massimo and Miss X-Factor are two very talented individuals and deserve all the success they get, though I suspect they are quite happy living their normal life here in Le Marche and turning out for the occasional *Sagra*. Miss X-Factor looked a bit like Adele, who is one of the few huge stars/talents who has been able to keep the insanity of the music business and international fame in its place, maintaining her ability to live the normal life from which she was plucked. One of the few truly great talents to emerge in recent years, she often disappears from public life for months, maybe years, at a time, carrying on with normality who knows where. Come to think of it Miss X-Factor *sounded* a bit like Adele too - do you think it's possible...? No, surely not...

But before we wave goodbye to music and the *Sagra*, and the burning controversy over the derivation of the name *vincisgrassi*, I ought to leave you with the recipe. Now this is not one of Lia's, perhaps because everyone wants to keep theirs secret, and it is not one that Silvano, the owner and chef at *Picciolo di Rame* would recognise, but it **is** a serviceable version, and one that you should be able to cook anywhere in the world.

VINCISGRASSI

Ragu

- 1 tbsp extra virgin olive oil
- 50g chopped onion
- 50g chopped carrots
- 50g chopped celery
- 1 garlic clove
- bay leaves
- 1 glass of dry red wine
- 400g lean minced beef
- 100g minced duck (pork will do)
- 50g chicken livers
- 50g chicken giblets
- 500g peeled tomato
- 1 tsp tomato paste
- 250g egg lasagna sheets
- Butter
- 250g fresh sheep's cheese, crumbled
- 100g grated Parmesan

Béchamel sauce

- 60g butter
- 60g plain flour
- good pinch of ground nutmeg
- 1 liter milk, warm

Heat the olive oil in a frying pan over medium heat. Add the onion, carrot, celery, garlic. Add the bay leaf and gently fry until the vegetables are golden brown. Add the beef, duck (or pork), chicken liver and giblets, and cook until it starts to stick to the pan. Add the wine, allowing it to evaporate completely. Add the tomato, tomato paste and wine glass of water and simmer for 1 hour.

Meanwhile, to make the béchamel sauce, prepare a roux by melting the butter in a small saucepan. Add the flour and nutmeg. Cook for few minutes. Add the roux to the warm milk, whisking very quickly. Bring to the boil and cook for 10 minutes, stirring with a wooden spoon. If too thick, add cold milk and whisk gently.

Blanch the lasagna sheets in boiling water for 5 minutes, strain, then place on a clean cloth to dry.

Grease a 30 x 45 cm baking try with butter. Spread 1 ladle of béchamel on the base and arrange the lasagna sheets to cover the bottom of the tray. Add a layer each of ragu then béchamel (there should be twice as much ragu as béchamel), and sprinkle with the fresh sheep's cheese. Repeat with the remaining ingredients – you should end up with about 6 layers. Sprinkle with grated parmesan cheese and dot with extra butter. Bake in preheated oven at 200°C (180°C fan) for 30 minutes.

At *Picciolo di Rame* Silvano uses a totally different *ragu,* one made solely from chicken and duck. As I recall you use no oil or fat for the *ragu* either, but instead throw the chicken and duck, bones, giblets and all, into a big pot, cover them with water then boil until the liquid has almost disappeared. Remove from the pot then pull all the meat from the bones, chop it finely and cook gently in a frying pan with whatever liquor remains in the boiling pot until you have the consistency of a nice *ragu.* It's a bit more tricky and you need *really* good quality poultry (such as you can find easily here in Le Marche), but it's truly worth the effort. Especially when Silvano does it!

Fiastra and the Wind

The *Sagra* was a lovely way to wind down at the end of a busy day. But, as ever, it was work too, because we were filming it for a brief clip in Episode Five. The last couple of minutes of Episode Five is where to go if you want to see Massimo, "Adele", the *Sagra,* and right at the end you'll catch a glimpse of the somewhat chaotic line-dancing. If you're quick you can also see a moment which threw a little extra bit of light on small-town Italian life for me. It's the moment when we bump into an old friend who comes up to us while we're sitting tucking into the Vincisgrassi. He's called Luigi. He's our *geometra* and you've already met him right back at the beginning of this journey. He's the guy who left us sitting in the bar one beautiful spring morning after deciding it was much more important to disappear up into the mountains to walk amongst the wild flowers than it was to turn up for the meeting we had arranged the day before. He is still a very good friend because we've come to understand that business arrangements have to take their proper place in the life we're now living. Anyway, Luigi was spending that evening at the *Sagra,* and when he saw us he came over to say hello. Tam invited him to join us and there's a nice little sequence in the program of cheek-kissing hellos (TIP: always *both* cheeks here, and always the left one first) and then we're all sat down together sharing a drink and a chat. Except. Except what it *doesn't* show you is that as soon as was decently possible Sergio got up and wandered off.

"What's the matter?" I whispered to Lia.

"*Mal di pancia*", she whispered back. That, you will remember, is a stomach ache. Like the one he got when the olive oil man let us down at the *frantoio*. But I couldn't see quite how he could have got one of those at such short notice. Turns out it is a family euphemism - Sergio gets *mal di pancia* whenever there's someone around that he doesn't want to be with.

"What's the problem?" I asked, "Luigi's a really nice man. One of our closest friends here."

Apparently Luigi wasn't the problem. It was Luigi's dad. It seems that several years Antonio (sadly no longer with us) and Sergio's father (also now passed on) had fallen out over something or other, and Sergio has never forgotten it. Which is to say he's not forgotten the sleight to the family honor though he may well have forgotten exactly what it was (Lia said he doesn't like to talk about it, but I suspect he can't remember).

It was all over without any fuss of course, and the evening carried on as jovially as ever, but it was a salutary reminder of a) how family loyalties run deep in this society, and b) how they can carry a grudge around for a very, very long time. The flip side, however, is that loyalty spreads way beyond family and you can call in a favour years after you've helped someone out. They will never forget.

Next day we had a pleasant trip in store - into the *Parco Nazionale dei Monti Sibillini,* the National Park. Sarnano lies just on the edge of one of Italy's least-known but most exquisite National Parks, seven hundred square kilometers of wonderful mountain scenery matched by the variety of its flora and wildlife. Here you can find eagles and wolves, a curious little lake up among the mountain tops that boasts its own unique crustacean, a freshwater shrimp that goes by the snappy name of *Chirocephalus marchesonii,* and dozens of different varieties of orchid. For just a glimpse of what the Sibillini National Park has to offer try:

https://youtu.be/K05Zw3a5RTE.

One of our favorite places in the park is a different lake, much bigger and easier to reach (it's a twenty minute climb out of Sarnano by car). It's the *Lago di Fiastra* and it's where we go to swim and relax - no serried ranks of sun-loungers here. In fact it is a man-made lake, created by a huge dam at one end of a deep gorge that snakes along the valley of the Fiastrone river. It is one of many such lakes in Italy designed to harness the potential of the Appenines to deliver hydro-electric power. The little village of San Lorenzo was drowned when it was created in the 1950s, which must have disrupted more than a few lives, but let's hope they were sufficiently rewarded for giving up their ancestral homes to the need for electricity.

What it has done for us (apart from knowing the lights are going to stay on most of the time) is to provide us with quite the most relaxing place you could wish to find. Tam is in the habit of going up there to swim whenever she gets the chance, and she is often entranced by dozens of (confused) butterflies who congregate around the flowers on her bikini as she lies soaking up the sun. But it is the trees that blow me away. I have worked on and off for several years in Doha, on the shore of the Arabian Gulf, where any trees (and there are indeed a few) have been brought in on the back of a pick-up truck to be planted outside a five-star hotel, or along the elegant Corniche that curves round the bay in a giant semi-circle. But when I get back home to Italy, and up to the lake, I am simply astonished by the number of trees in my field of vision. Mountains rise up on all sides of the lake, with bigger mountains rising behind them - and every centimetre of them seems to be wooded. There must be literally millions of trees in this huge, unbelievably rich, vista. No wonder they are big on wood-fired stoves round here.

The lake is one of the most beautiful spots in the area and we wanted to show it off to its full potential in the series. So I had scripted the opening of one of the shows to take place up there. There is a rustic little *punto panoramico* at one end of the lake, with a couple of picnic tables and a fantastic view along the lake as the reflection of the late afternoon sun shimmers on the surface of the water. The Italians go in for picnics quite a lot, though they don't involve sitting uncomfortably on a rug. That is *not* the Italian way. Sunday lunch is a big institution, often with the extended family and friends gathered together. Sometimes it will be outside the farmhouse, sometimes in a restaurant, where lunch can easily go on until five o'clock. But in the height of the summer, in the heat of summer, they often choose to get out of town and up into the mountains for a picnic where the air is cooler and fresher. Which is why you find picnic tables in the most unlikely places - in the middle of woods, or hidden in bushes just a short climb up from a riverbank. Most of the time they are pretty ancient, but someone, in some previous, more communally-minded era, must have spent a lot of money providing for picnics and Sunday lunches in years to come. Echoes, they are, of a bygone era.

You can see these tables, the ones at the end of the lake, at the beginning of Episode 6. My script called for Tam and Lia to be walking across the grass towards the picnic tables carrying baskets with the food for their picnic. The wide shot would reveal the lake in all its glistening glory. Then there would be a couple of links with the two women sat at the table putting the final touches to the picnic food before them. Lia had brought a nice table-cloth, because that's an important part of the tradition. They wouldn't dream of eating off the wood. There always has to be a *tovaglia*. Generally of the paper, disposable variety. Incidentally, this once caused what was close to a diplomatic incident when Tam and I gave Lia as a birthday present the beautiful marble-topped table which sits elegantly in their outdoor dining room on top of the old city-walls. Lia was thrilled and invited us to dinner the following evening to give the table its first serious outing. We were looking forward to seeing it in position, where, we thought, it would sit much more harmoniously with the pink brick of the city wall than did the previous green plastic version. Imagine our surprise, then, when we turned up to find the marble covered with a paper table cloth with hideous floral designs all over it. Words were exchanged, but it was all pretty amicable and we arrived (I think) at a wonderful compromise where a tablecloth is used for all dinners except the ones to which we are invited. Goodness knows what the other guests make of it.

So getting a table cloth onto the picnic table was, at least in Lia's eyes, an absolute essential. But we had not reckoned on a minor difficulty that we should, perhaps, have seen coming, given that we were sitting at the end of a long, steep-sided valley. The wind. Just getting the table cloth spread out was like something out of Laurel and Hardy (I think Tam must be Laurel, because she's taller). Every time they got one end spread out nicely, the other end suddenly billowed up in the air. And we hadn't even got any food onto it yet.

"Aha!" shouted Tam, "That's it. We'll position the food carefully so that it holds the tablecloth down. Cutlery too. No problem."

I pointed out that the idyllic lakeside picnic effect might be a little spoiled by having everything on the corners of the (large) table instead of in front of the diners, where it might more naturally be found. But Tam was not to be deterred and we spent a good fifteen minutes arguing over whether there could be a logical explanation for the bottle of wine being three feet away, and right on the edge of the table. While the cheeseboard was three feet in the other direction. We tried scattering some cutlery around the corners of the table, but we didn't even get the chance to discuss the logic of that one because the wind picked the tablecloth up anyway and sent them flying. No matter what the distribution, we couldn't find any way of holding the cloth in place without it all looking like some kind of art installation instead of a picnic.

But there was a solution. There's always a solution. It was me. I think it was Peter who suggested it.

"Perhaps, Steve, you could lie under the table holding the cloth down. I can keep the shots nice and tight, so you can't be seen."

This, as you can imagine, was a bit of an affront to my dignity. I pointed out that I was not only the Director (note the capital D), but also the sound recordist.

"I need to be able to see the shots," I argued, "and I'll need to get the microphone in close with all this wind."

"Perfect" said Peter, "I'll take care of the shots, and you'll be able to get much closer with the mike if you're lying under the table. I'll shout if the squirrel starts coming into shot."

There was a remorseless logic in all this, and it had the side benefit that the talent seemed to find it funny - which would mean nice smiley shots (in the face of windy adversity). So the final vestiges of my senior status as the Director (capital D) went out the window as I lay on my back under the table holding a microphone boom (or broomstick) in one hand and four corners of a tablecloth in the other. It's a glamorous business, television.

A final, linguistic, note on this debacle. During the couple of weeks we had been shooting so far, Lia's English had come on in leaps and bounds (well, that might be stretching it a bit - it was more like "one small bound for mankind"), but when she was talking about the conditions that day up at the lake she kept saying it was very "windly". Which struck we three English as such a charming word that we agreed not to correct her. And now, of course, it's too late. She's stuck with it, until some helpful English acquaintance points out she should be saying "windy", and then there will be hell to pay.

The Truffle Hunt

This is truffle country. Some friends from London came to see us recently. They're a couple of keen *gourmets* who spend a large proportion of their collective income dining out at some of London's top restaurants. We wondered what they were going to make of the simple, natural food here in Le Marche. They arrived on our doorstep with wide eyes and open mouths. They'd stopped for a bite to eat at a little roadside restaurant on the way from the airport. That makes it sound a bit like a diner on an American freeway, but in fact (I know the place well) it's in a lovely wooded valley with views up to an enchanting hilltop castle whose crenelated tower seems to burst up out of the woods. They'd ordered pasta with *funghi porcini* and couldn't believe their luck when the *cameriera* asked if they'd like truffle shaved onto it. Their latest culinary adventure was off to a good start.

The Cookucina dog, Tinker, is a bit of a star in Sarnano. She's a Patterdale terrier from the north of England, and they have never seen anything like her here. Patterdales are hunters and diggers. They are reputed to be the only dog that can burrow into a badger sett and come out alive (though we have studiously avoided checking this for ourselves, and dachshunds must be in with a shout since in German *dachs* means badger and *hund* means dog). Patterdales spend their entire time sniffing things out in the undergrowth, then trying furiously to dig them up. Strong sense of smell, front paws like little spades and easy to train. In fact the ideal truffle hunter, at least that's what we're often told when local *contadini* stop us in the street to ask if she's for sale. She's not, but every time this happens it sends Tam into a sort of frenzy about getting Tinker trained so she can make us rich when she finds that elusive huge and perfect white truffle. In case you are not familiar with the world of truffles the idea that you can get rich just by finding one is no joke. In 2010 a man called Stanley Ho who runs casinos in Macao paid $330,000 at auction for two pieces of rare white truffle together weighing just 2.87lbs. He must enjoy truffles (or demonstrating how obscenely wealthy he is) because three years earlier he had paid exactly the same amount for a single white truffle weighing in at 3.3lbs. Looks like this one must have run out by 2010.

You are very lucky, of course, if you find a white truffle like that. The truffle hunters in Le Marche, while always remaining hopeful, are mainly on the lookout for black truffles, and, in the summer a seasonal variety called *scorzone*. But where to find them is a closely guarded secret. A good truffle-hunter will have an expert dog, preferably trained since birth, and an encyclopedic knowledge of the local terrain where truffles are most likely to be found. These are almost invariably a kind of ancestral hunting ground, with precise locations passed down from father to son. Lia had chosen to cook *Tagliolini with Truffles*, and this gave us the opportunity to get out into the countryside with a truffle hunter and his dog. Sergio had found us just such a man.

"Tonino" he told me.

"Tonino? What, the Tonino who works for the council? Checking the street lights, putting up flags for *Ferragosto*, that sort of thing?"

"Yes. Tonino with the restaurant... the one that does only Sunday lunches."

"Except if you book in advance."

"For a large party, that's right. That's Tonino."

"So it's the guy with the honey shop. Who make his own *vin cotto*?"

"That's him", said Sergio.

"And he goes out hunting truffles in his spare time, does he?"

"Yes, but it's business. It's not an 'obby"

Sergio, of course, was talking to me in Italian, but they use the word "hobby" just like we do. Except they drop the 'h' and say 'obby. This is not just because they don't have an aspirated 'h' so much as they just can't seem to get an 'h' in the right place when they're using English words. It drives Tam up the wall when she's trying to teach them English. A prized possession on her mobile phone is a saved text from a student who wasn't able to make his lesson. It says "I cannot leave my bed. I am hill". They have a lot of difficulty with the 'u' (as in 'rugby') as well. Italians talk about playing a game of *regby*. In an Indian restaurant they'd be eating a *kerry*. And if they were going on to a nightclub they'd be going to a *cleb*. Although, confusingly, they would call it a *night* (perhaps to avoid having to say 'nightclub'). I guess some Italians must even be members of a *regby cleb*. But I digress. Again!

OK, so this truffling is serious business then. But where was Tonino going to take us to find truffles? Well, that was the problem apparently. Sergio said Tonino was happy to show us how it was done, but he couldn't take us to any of the places he went to find truffles.

"So, we won't find any truffles then, will we?" I pointed out helpfully.

"Exactly."

I told Sergio I thought this wasn't really going to do the trick for us. In the world of TV there is no such thing as an unsuccessful hunt. There always has to be something new, some discovery never before made. Like all those endless documentaries about Pompeii (or even Bombay) which start with the assertion:

"Tonight, Window On The World (or whatever the series is called) can reveal for the first time ...."

...as if the program's researchers have managed to uncover something that the people who have been researching this stuff for half a lifetime have unaccountably missed. So we could not possibly go truffle-hunting and come back empty-handed. Especially as we need some for the *Tagliolini with Truffles*. Sergio volunteered to go back and negotiate once more with Tonino. If he could figure out where to find him.

The deal Sergio came back with wasn't ideal, but it would do. Tonino was going to go out into the country and "plant" a truffle for his dog to sniff out. I wasn't wildly happy about this, pointing out that I had spent many years making programs that exposed the planting of evidence by rogue policemen. I didn't like the feeling that whatever credibility I had achieved while doing investigative journalism was now going to be lost on a cookery show. But Sergio convinced me that it was OK because Fiuto, the dog, wasn't going along with the burial party and so, when he found the truffle it would be genuine. OK. All I had to worry about now was whether the dog *would* actually find it.

In the event Fiuto had no trouble finding the truffle, though it was touch and go for a while since Tam insisted on taking the Cookucina dog along on the trip, and for the first twenty minutes or so Fiuto was much more interested in Tinker than truffles. The interview we did with Tonino went rather well, particularly as the whole issue of how valuable truffles can be had passed Tam by, and she was genuinely amazed when she discovered how much money they can fetch. For a moment I think she got the idea that the one Fiuto had dug up was worth thousands of Euros, but then it clicked that he wouldn't have risked burying one like that in case he (and Fiuto) never found it again. In fact the one that Tonino held in his hand was a *scorzone*, and it went into the absolutely delicious dish that Lia cooked for us that evening.

TAGLIOLINI with TRUFFLES

- *320g. of tagliolini or spaghetti*
- *50g. Butter*
- *4 tablespoons grated Parmesan cheese*
- *Salt*
- *A black truffle (fresh if possible)*
- *One small clove of garlic.*

Put the noodles into boiling salted water. Meanwhile, melt the butter in a large frying-pan with the garlic. While the butter melts, clean the truffle with a small brush and cut it into thin slices (using a vegetable peeler if necessary). Then toss it for a few seconds in the pan with the butter from which you have removed the garlic. When the pasta is cooked **al dente** *lift the pasta from its water and add it to the truffles along with a little of the pasta cooking water (an important tip for ALL pasta dishes). Take it off the heat, add the Parmesan cheese and mix gently until the pasta is coated with a creamy sauce.*

Urbs Salvia and Strange Names

Rome is an extraordinary place. Walking around that vibrant, modern capital you constantly find yourself bumping into bits of the ancient city. They seem to be just lying around. Left where they fell sixteen or seventeen centuries ago. And the astonishing thing is that everything is so BIG. The scale of the Colosseum dwarfs anything else built for hundreds of years after. But it is not just the major monuments. A couple of years ago I was wandering the back streets, when I had to jump out of the way to avoid being hit by a (typical) Roman driver. The traffic and the drivers are not quite as insane as in Naples, but this certainly isn't Cheltenham, or Washington DC where drivers will pull up if they see you about to cross the street fifty or sixty yards ahead. Anyway, I had just turned a corner into what felt like it *ought* to have been a pedestrian zone when he came at me. I leapt up on the pavement to get out of the way and bumped into a giant foot. That was it. No other way to describe it. A huge, anatomically precise, marble foot. Maybe twenty or thirty times life size. And there it was, just round the corner tucked up against a wall, all on its own, with no other feet anywhere to be seen. I never did discover what or who it was, but whatever was attached to this foot must have been pretty impressive in its heyday.

Rome, of course, has this in spades. But this same thing applies in a lesser way to the rest of this country. A few kilometers from Sarnano for instance I once stumbled across half a small amphitheater in someone's garden. And just up the road from that is a bigger, more complete, Roman theater that is still used for theatrical performances. I went to see a delightful version of Carmen there a few months back which disappointed only in that (as an honored guest) I had seats in the front row instead of being sat up at the back with a view of the whole ancient auditorium.

And then there is *Urbs Salvia*. This is about a twenty minute drive from us along the SS 77. The 77 is the main road north out of Sarnano and it goes straight through the middle of the remains of the Roman town of *Urbs Salvia*. It is an astonishing place. It was a major settlement of maybe ten thousand people until it was sacked by the Visigoths in the fifth century. There are well-preserved remains of temples, shops, houses, roads and a theater. But perhaps the pride and joy is the amphitheater. Built in the first century AD it's where gladiators used to do battle in front of up to 5000 spectators. It is just a remnant of the real thing, of course, but it retains the whole shape and enough of the auditorium that it is used every summer for a theatrical and opera season. If you wander around it on your own you can pick up the sense of what it must have been like in the days of the gladiators. You can walk down their special entrance directly into the arena, and see the medical room where they were taken when they got injured. You will need someone to point them out to you, but on one side of the arena there's a water inlet and on the other a drain, which allowed whatever Roman entrepreneur ran these things to flood the whole place and stage "sea battles".

We wanted to show off our own mini-Colosseum in the series, so (as you may remember) I had scripted a couple of PTCs for Tam to record. They were simple enough - walk out of one of the dark entrance tunnels, into the light, look to camera and start delivering your words. There weren't too many (words, that is) and it shouldn't have been a problem. But television is always waiting to catch you out, and sometimes the simplest things can turn into a nightmare. I was directing a sequence for a program for Channel 4 Television once which involved reconstructing a car crash on a narrow road running through dense woodland. We had found the perfect location, the access road to a private estate. And we had hired an experienced stunt driver whose job was to crash the car into a tree at some speed. Then we were going to put our "star" into the driving seat and do a series of artistic shots of him slumped unconscious over the steering wheel as the car radio continued to play Crazy by Patsy Cline (if you don't know it, check it out - it's wonderful).

The trouble is, you only get to crash the car once, and when our stunt man drove it head-on into the tree (very successfully, and at what seemed like breakneck speed), the back of the car reared up, slewed crazily sideways and landed smack across the narrow road, blocking any possibility of other vehicles getting past. Now this was a night shoot, and in fact it was already later than we had intended because it had been a difficult day. So by the time we got to crashing the car it was already nearly midnight. We had arrived at the location a couple of hours earlier, and fed the crew straightaway as we were already two hours behind schedule and the caterers wanted to get away as soon as possible. The food had been served up at the big house and then the crew had all come down for the crash scene while the caterers washed up and packed away. So no sooner had the car come to rest blocking the only exit from the estate than the caterers' vans appeared coming down from the big house, the staff all keen to get away and home to their beds. But the car could not be moved because we still needed to get our Patsy Cline shots.

And that's when the wind and the rain started. Within ten or fifteen minutes we were being bombarded by a storm of hurricane proportions which meant that everything was taking ten times as long as it should. I won't burden you with the details, but it was two o'clock in the morning before the caterers were able to get away and they spent most of that time telling me how unhappy they were, and that it was all my fault (which it was). We finished the evening four hours behind schedule and soaked to the skin. And what I forgot to mention was that I was coming down with the flu as all this was going on and couldn't get out of bed the following morning. Standing in the woods, in a howling gale, with rain dripping down inside my parka at 2 o'clock in the morning with incipient flu, trying to placate an irate catering manager, was one of the most miserable moments of my career. I distinctly remember being absolutely convinced that I would be better off dead.

So things could always be worse. That's what I tried to remind myself as we struggled with Tam's PTCs outside the amphitheater. Walking and talking is not difficult. We all do it many times a day without any trouble at all. But try doing it for a TV shoot and suddenly it becomes incredibly hard - at least for ordinary mortals. It's a talent that a few people have naturally, and that's what makes them successful television presenters (just as much as their ability to put a senior politician on the spot). Tam, of course, is not one of those TV professionals, and the first couple of times we tried it she stalled half way through the words. Now this wouldn't have mattered much except that we were late (you will have gathered by now that I am one of those directors who is always running behind time) and the light was beginning to go. It was my fault, I'm sure, but I seemed to somehow convey my anxiety about getting it done to Tam, which meant that the more she tried the harder it got. And then when we *did* get a good take, it would be drowned out by the noise of a passing truck (I never realized there were so many noisy trucks going up and down the SS 77). We got there in the end, of course - you always do. But the last PTC we recorded was something of a compromise. Not Tam's best performance, but devoid of traffic noise. And moody in the extreme as the sun was disappearing behind the hills and Tam was having to squint at the camera, the dying embers of the day softly lighting her face (or as my editor later described it, "in the dark"). So not exactly ten out of ten for that one. But one thing I have learned over the years is that television is the art of 90%. You can **never** get everything perfect, and if you get to 90%, or even close, then you should consider that a success. I reckon this last PTC that day was about 75%, but I will leave you to judge whether that is success or failure (Episode 4 at 12.15).

The next thing on the agenda was a trip up to Urbisaglia, the new town established on the hill overlooking the Roman remains after the Visigoths had come to visit. And fortunately it was a visit to a *birreria artigianale,* an artisan brewery, so Tam's frayed nerves could be settled with a glass of their deliciously strong lager called *Route 77.* This is the beer that Mick Jagger and The Rolling Stones don't yet know about but would probably enjoy. The name is a play on the fame of Route 66, immortalized by the Stones as well as many films and TV series over the years. Together with the fact that the *birreria* is just off the SS 77, of course.

The SS 77 doesn't have a great deal to recommend it for anyone planning a road trip, but the interesting thing about a beer called *Route 77* is that the English language *sells* here in Italy. In fact the Italians give English (or English-sounding) names to lots of things. I believe it adds a certain class, or cachet to a product, or a pet, or whatever. The problem is, it can have funny results - sometimes verging on the unfortunate.

The other day I had to take the Cookucina dog to the vet for a check-up, and there in the waiting room was a woman with the cutest little puppy. Of course puppies are wonderful icebreakers the world over, so we fell into conversation.

"What's he called?", I inquired after a while.

"*Nobby*" she replied.

"Nobby!" I laughed, "great name for a dog!"

"*No, no.*" she corrected, "*Si chiama Snobby*".

Well that was it on the conversation front. I think she probably (and perhaps understandably) misinterpreted the strange face I pulled at this point, because she turned to talk to her friend in rather a barbed way. I thought for a moment of trying to explain what *snobby* meant in English, and why it didn't really work as a name for a dog (at least to English ears), but I thought better of it. Too difficult, and anyway I couldn't really expect her to change the dog's name just because it sounded weird to an Englishman. Mercifully I got called into the surgery within a minute or two. *Snobby* isn't the only odd-named dog in these parts either. I once came across a terrier called *Drunk*. Which would make for a rather unusual scene if he escaped and the owner was running round town calling his name. But that hasn't happened yet, to my knowledge.

Supermarkets and drugstores the world over are treasure troves for connoisseurs of strangely named products. And the ones here in Italy do not disappoint. A recent trip to the shops produced a household cleaning product called *Rio Bum Bum*. Which shared a shelf with *Smac*. Then, in the food aisles there was *Saddam* sugar, and something called *Succoliva* which sets the imagination racing in most unfortunate ways.

And there was the advert for a GoPro-alike sports video camera. You know the sort of thing, stick it onto your helmet and film your out-of-control rush down the mountain so you can replay it in your sitting room to show your mates how much fun you were having on the ski-slopes. They are designed to appeal to young people having a good time and throwing caution to the winds. But why would you call your camera a *Foolish*? It might be rather an accurate description of what it is going to be used for, but I don't imagine that was the intention. You sort of know what they were getting at, but surely it would be worth opening an English/Italian dictionary wouldn't it? Do we do this sort of thing in the anglophone world? I don't think so. We give things Italian-sounding names, for sure, because the ad-men think it gives their product class, but somehow we seem to avoid names which just sound ridiculous. Or do we? Italian readers please help me here.

This trip to the *birreria*, by the way, wasn't just about necking a refreshing beverage at the end of a hard day. It was all about getting the right beer for *Chicken in Beer,* the meal Lia served up on Peter's first day here. It filled the bill perfectly for Cookucina, because we wanted recipes that would "travel" - something that you can have a go at wherever in the world you are. But of course it also had to be special to Le Marche - and that's where locally brewed beer comes in. If you want to have a go yourself look for a beer that's a bit hoppy and flavorful rather than a bog-standard lager. And (it goes without saying) buy the best quality chicken you can afford. After that, it's simple...

CHICKEN in BEER

- *800g. small pieces of chicken*
- *a stick of celery*
- *1 carrot*
- *1 onion*
- *salt, pepper*
- *flour*
- *olive oil*
- *600ml lager*

Finely chop the celery, carrot and onion, then sauté them in olive oil until they are soft but not brown. Coat the chicken in flour, add it to the pan with the sautéed vegetables and cook gently until the meat is lightly browned. Season with salt and pepper, then gradually add the beer and cook for 20 mins.

The Boar Hunt

Gestures are a big thing in Italy. My first baby steps in learning Italian were taken at the Italian Cultural Institute in London. I signed up for a three week intensive course. I had already been to Italy a couple of times, and I had bought a book. A teach-yourself book. I was good at languages. I had studied them at school. French and German, though not, I'm afraid, Italian. But that was a long time ago, so long ago in fact that some of our German textbooks were in Gothic script - although maybe that's just a function of the priority English governments have given to funding education over the years. Anyway, I have always thought of myself as having a bit a talent at picking up languages, so I had bought myself that teach-yourself book. And I seemed to be making good progress.

But when I walked into the Cultural Institute I was immediately on the back foot. These people were speaking Italian. Right in the heart of London! It shouldn't have come as a surprise, I know. But it did. And straightaway I was faced with a decision - what level did I want to sign up for? Beginners, Intermediate, Conversational, Expert?

"Intermediate", I foolishly replied.

"*Che fai alla fine settimana?*" the nice man asked me.

I told him (in quite reasonable Italian, I thought) that I had gone to see my father in his house on the south coast. Flushed with success, I told him what we had done over the weekend. That we had watched football on the television and had enjoyed seeing Arsenal beat Manchester United 2-0. This was going really well. Until the nice man told me he had asked what I was going to do *next* weekend. Embarrassing. And then the nice man started to write BEGINNERS in his notebook, with what looked a bit like a smirk on his face. Maybe not so nice after all.

He was right of course. I learned far more in the beginners class than I would have done in intermediate. In fact I probably wouldn't have stuck it out in intermediate, which could well have turned out to be a miserable, out-of-my-depth experience. In fact it was just what I needed and consolidated what I had already learned - as well as correcting a few things I had got wrong. The course lasted three weeks and was a really solid grounding, largely because it was conducted entirely in Italian, with not a word of English spoken.

I do think, though, that there was one thing missing, but it didn't occur to me until I had come and spent some time here in Italy and amongst Italians. There should in fact have been *fourth* week in which they taught us how to use our hands as part of speaking proper colloquial Italian. I am not sure that an Italian would know how to communicate at all if you tied his hands behind his back. Everything is accompanied by gestures which serve to accentuate or mitigate what is being said. Tam is always on at me to buy a man-bag, rather than stuff everything into my pockets in the usual English way. She seems to prefer a man with a little leather bag slung over his shoulder, than one with pockets bulging in a manly fashion. I wonder why. In fact, though, it dawned on me recently that the true function of the Italian man-bag is to allow full use of the hands while talking, so now it all makes sense. Still not sure it's for me, though.

There's another problem with gestures. Sometimes they mean something different in one culture from another. Tam found that out the hard way. Tam is a very persuasive woman. With big brown eyes and a beaming smile she's always been able to talk her way into (and out of) things. One of the local delicacies is *cinghiale*, or wild boar. There are hundreds of them in the woods round here, and they are big. And dangerous. Normally they keep themselves to themselves, but if you go anywhere near them during the breeding season they will attack. And every year two or three people locally write off their cars by hitting a boar that has run out into the road. The general view here is that the only good boar is a dead one, not just because of the risk to cars, or because they are very tasty, but because they do tremendous damage to farmland if they get onto it and start to tear it up in search of food. So they are hunted. Each fall, in the hunting season, you can find small parties of men gathering outside a bar ready for the hunt. You can easily spot them. They will be dressed in camouflage clothes, carrying high-powered rifles, and driving small 4x4s with two or three yapping dogs in the back. And not a woman in sight. Until Tam decided she wanted to go on a hunt.

At the time, we had befriended a local restaurant owner who also happened to be a builder (they are nothing if not versatile, the *Marchigiani*). His name is Aurelio and he is short and stocky with long hair and a gnarled face. You feel he could have walked straight into a part in Lord of the Rings. He's a crack shot and he does a lot of hunting. Which is why it is always a good idea to go for the *Salmi di Cinghiale* in his restaurant, *L'Ermitage*. Tam cornered him one evening, after finishing rather a delicious plate of *Salmi*, and said she'd like to go hunting with him. He explained that women don't go hunting, but she wasn't to be put off. She fixed him with the brown eyes and smiled that big, persuasive smile. And he caved in and agreed that she could come along the next morning. At least, that's what Tam will tell you. Personally I don't think he thought he had agreed to it at all. I think he thought that after he had told her a) she would be all on her own, b) it would be dangerous, and c) it started at 6 o'clock in the morning, he had seen her off at the pass. What a surprise he must have got when she turned up outside the bar at 6 o'clock the next morning armed with her video camera.

To do him credit Aurelio recognised he was a beaten man as soon as he saw her outside the bar. And like the decent chap he is, he explained patiently to all the other hunters that Tam wouldn't be actually *hunting*, but that she was a TV producer who would be videoing the event for posterity. Which seemed to break the ice, because most people seem to be taken in by the idea of being on the television. What Tam didn't tell Aurelio (or anyone else) was that it was the first time she had ever handled a video camera, and that (at that stage) there wasn't a television program in sight. But the camera did the trick and it was enough for the rest of the hunters to agree that she could accompany them into the woods for the next few hours.

First though, there was a safety briefing. Tam was allocated to Franco, one of the most experienced (and nicest, as it turned out) hunters, and told to stick with him at all times. As long as she was by his side there was no chance of her being accidentally shot at. This was no idle threat. Tramping through the woods in search of *cinghiale* who are doing their level best to stay out of sight can leave you very disorientated. The dogs' job is to find and flush out the boar, but following their tracks means constant changes of direction, going up and down hills and in and out of dense woodland. Tam's video shows men in camouflage clothes popping in and out of the woods in the most unexpected places. And, of course, these swift and fleeting movements are exactly what you will be expecting if you are lucky enough to sight a boar. Every year there are two or three sad cases where one hunter has loosed off at another after mistaking him for a boar. One unfortunate guy managed to shoot his own brother a couple of years back. I can't help thinking it would be better if they all dressed in day-glo orange or something, but then the boar would see them coming I suppose.

Tam's outing with the hunters was a big success. Three boar went to meet their maker (one of them a giant that it took several men to load onto the back of a pick up truck), and she even got film of the carcasses being skinned and prepared for the freezer. And all of the hunting party survived unscathed. But, as you can imagine now that you have got to know Tam a bit, the day was not without incident. It happened like this. Half way through the morning they had decided to shift operations to a different part of the woods. So everyone piled into their respective vehicles and off they went in a ramshackle convoy of pick-up trucks, ancient Fiat Panda 4x4s, and yapping dogs in the back of what looked like mobile kennels. After about five minutes they reached a small steep clearing on one side of the road, and everyone pulled off into whatever space they could find. One or two of the hunters immediately set off into the woods to see if the dogs could pick up a scent. Franco told Tam to wait by his Panda while he walked across to one of the other cars to check what was going on. She would be safe, he explained, if she stayed alongside the car. It was an opportunity to draw breath, so Tam lit a cigarette. Suddenly the dogs began to bark away in the distance and a shot rang out. There was a bit of a commotion going on up ahead where Franco had gone to join the others. Holding his rifle in one hand he started gesturing to her with the other. It was a sort of grasping gesture, palm down. Like someone trying to pick up a handful of stones on a pebbly beach. What could it mean? Well danger for sure, because there were more shots now. He did it again - more urgently, with a sort of a downward motion. She figured it must mean get down behind the car. So she crouched alongside the door. He did it again. She got down on her knees. Again, but he was getting more agitated every time. She lay down on the road. He started to jog across towards her. He must be really worried about her safety. So she shuffled her prostrate body as far under the car as she could go, by which time Franco arrived.

"*Che cazzo fai?*" he asked in a puzzled sort of way. (I won't translate it, it wouldn't be nice.)

It turned out that Franco's gesture didn't mean "get down" at all. It's what Italians do when they want you to "come here". But it's a gesture unknown in England and completely the reverse of the palm-up version we would use. All it meant was "walk across to join me over here", so Franco must have been a little perplexed by Tam's attempt to crawl under his car instead. I don't think that little episode did much for Tam's standing as an international television director.

In fact, even though Tam had never used a video camera before, she turned out to be a natural, and when she showed me the footage she had got I was mightily impressed. Sadly, though, no-one had been around to film the crawling under the car sequence. But what she *had* shot was to come in very handy now we were approaching the end of our filming schedule. Lia had been keen from the start to include *Salmi di Cinghiale* in the series. This is not the only place they make it, but the Sibillini mountains version is a bit special. I felt it was going to be difficult to visualise in the series because we were shooting in the height of summer and the hunting season doesn't start till October. But Lia was insistent.

"What's so special about the Sibillini version," I wanted to know. "I've had wild boar stew all over the place."

There is a magic ingredient, she told me.

"What's that then?"

"It's magic."

"And secret?" I asked.

Not exactly, was the answer, but it still took me another ten minutes to wring it out of her. And I have to say I was underwhelmed. The answer - the secret, magic, ingredient - turns out to be pickled onions. More or less. It was a bit like discovering that a top Michelin-starred chef likes to spice up his *Chateaubriand* with just a *soupçon* of pork scratchings. But then she cooked it for us, and I was won over straight away. We had to get it in somehow.

But I still couldn't figure out what we were going to do to make it come to life, without being able to go out on a hunt. Until Tam reminded me of the footage she had shot a couple of years earlier. Bingo! That's the answer. And so Tam's first and only home movie did, finally, make it onto TV. At least in Croatia - but that's another story, of which more later.

I am not sure how easy it's going to be to get wild boar where you live (or pickled onions for that matter) but in case you can, here's how to make *Salmi di Cinghiale alla Marchigiana.*

WILD BOAR STEW

- 800g. wild boar meat
- sage
- rosemary
- 5 juniper berries
- 2 carrots
- 2 onions
- 2 sticks of celery
- 2 cloves of garlic
- 150g. of pickled onions
- 2 tbsps balsamic vinegar
- olive oil
- salt pepper
- ½ liter of red wine
- beef broth

Roughly chop half the carrot, celery and onion. Prepare a marinade with the wine, the chopped vegetables, and all the herbs and spices. Cut the wild boar into small pieces, put it in the marinade, make sure it is well covered, and leave it for at least 12 hours. Remove the vegetables from the marinade. Finely chop the remaining vegetables, put them in a pan with the oil and soften them for a few minutes. Add the boar and brown gently. Season with salt and pepper and cook slowly for about 40 minutes until the meat is lightly browned. Now add the broth, and the drained and rinsed pickled onions. Add the balsamic vinegar and cook until the meat is soft – approximately 2½-3 hours.

Aurelio, by the way, hasn't ever spoken to us in quite the same friendly way since the boar hunt. And Tam certainly hasn't been invited back. It is just possible she may go down in history as the only woman ever to go out boar hunting in Le Marche. Quite a claim to fame!

Medieval Night

Shooting the series in August had both good and bad points. It was (as we know) blisteringly hot, and the town was crowded with tourists. But those tourists had come because August in Sarnano is a month-long party. There is some form of live entertainment every night, and to say it is eclectic is to understate the matter quite substantially. There are jazz bands, cover bands doing everything from the Beatles to Nirvana (and it's often the same band) and tribute bands to Italian stars you've never even heard of, except if you're Italian. Generally the English are a bit snooty about these last, but it's amazing, when you listen to the canon of work of some obscure Italian singer from the sixties, how many of them have been re-worked into old favorites in the anglophone songworld. My respect for Italian song-writing grows every year.

But it's not just music that is on offer. There is a town about forty minutes from here called Treia, and every August in Treia you can experience an extraordinary ball game called *Bracciale*. It's a cross between real tennis, squash, cricket and pelotta (or jeu de paume, or jai-alai, depending on where you live). It was the national game in Italy for hundreds of years until it was supplanted by soccer. Imagine a giant tennis court with three men on either side of a line on the ground which takes the place of a net. Now put that court up against the 20 meter high city wall, so that the wall runs along one side of the court. The scoring system is much like tennis, but the ball must bounce off the wall before hitting the ground in the opposition side of the court. Now, here comes a surprise. The ball is about the size of a handball and it's made of wood with a leather covering. Like a huge, over-sized baseball. And instead of rackets, the teams have their playing hand inside what looks like a giant wooden pineapple with studs all over it. So that when the ball comes flying off the wall at some crazy angle, they take a big round arm swing, pineapple meets giant baseball with a crack of wood on wood, and the ball flies back at about a hundred miles an hour. It's exciting. And picturesque too - the teams are dressed all in white linen with colorful sashes, and it's played in the shadow of a medieval fortified town. Far more exciting than soccer.

In fact, it hasn't always and only been played against the town walls. In Macerata, our provincial capital, there is an extraordinary building called the *Sferisterio*. Nowadays it is an open-air opera venue. Its annual *Stagione Lirica* is one of the true gems of Italian opera. It is considered to be the third most important Opera House in Italy after La Scala and Verona. It was built in the early 19th century and it is a unique design. The auditorium consists of a limited number of stalls seats inside a massive banana-shaped curve of boxes three stories high and separated by 56 neo-classical columns, opposite a flat brick wall 18 meters high and nearly 90 meters long, running the whole length of the building. But that massive wall, with its wonderful acoustic, was not designed for opera. When the *Sferisterio* was built back in 1827, after the money had been raised by public subscription, it was intended to be the country's finest *Bracciale* court. An amazing place to watch an amazing game, and nowadays just as unusual and unique as an opera venue.

The Italians are good at re-creations and evocations of their history. There's lots of it, and they extremely proud of it. And tourists love it. Every August here in Sarnano the *centro storico* is transformed for ten days into the medieval town of six or seven hundred years ago. The ancient cantinas under the houses are opened up as the shops they might have been in the past, with locals in medieval dress making candles or soap, combing and spinning wool, or selling herbal concoctions. There's even a blacksmith's forge. The little *ortos* are turned into pens for sheep, cattle or donkeys and there are roaming musicians performing on traditional instruments. Oh, and the streets are lit by tallow candles. It is a magical experience.

We had built a Medieval Night into the schedule, and we were not disappointed. In addition to the usual archery, and sword-fights between men in armor we came across some unexpected gems. It's difficult to film at night in amongst crowds. Hard to keep control of the situation when there are three or four of you trying to set up a shot. Peter, as ever, had an answer, quickly volunteering to go off on his own with the camera.

"Leave it to me, I know the shots we need, and it will be so much easier if I am operating on my own. I'll be just like any other tourist with a handycam."

"Except that yours is three times the size of anyone else's."

"I'll just tell them I'm from America," he said.

Despite the fact that Peter looks, and sounds, like the perfect English country gentleman, he wasn't to be talked out of it.

"So what's the first shot you're going for?" I asked (I was once told that this was the first thing you should agree with the cameraman on any shoot).

"I thought I would start with the belly-dancers." Suddenly it all came clear.

In the *Piazza Alta* Tam discovered the most delightful family who kept a strange collection of animals. There was a little compound with bales of hay and a roped-off area with a donkey called Napoleon. You will remember that Napoleon figures highly in local history, but I am not sure he would appreciate having a donkey named after him. The most unusual members of their menagerie were a couple of completely tame owls. Lia had spotted them first, and she called Tam over to take a look. Tam is a big animal fan - any animals, big ones, small ones, furry ones, feathery ones. She's a bit of a cat rescuer (we now have five, including one who had to have one of his eyes removed after she found him, as a kitten, at death's door). And then there was the swift.

Swifts arrive here in the spring, and it is wonderful to hang out of the window and watch them swooping and diving in the lee of the town walls. They seem to have a sense of fun, and sometimes they will fly right up to the window, wheeling away at the last minute in what looks for all the world like a game. Swifts, of course, are magical in that they live life on the wing, so it was a big surprise when we found a baby one cowering in a doorway with a damaged wing. Tam brought it home, and for two weeks our shower became a swift sanctuary. This was more than I had bargained for, especially when we discovered that we shouldn't have been feeding meat to Buzz (don't ask why he got called Buzz). The proper food for a baby swift (should you ever need to know) is live crickets, and Tam, being the good researcher she is, discovered a place they could be bought. Would I mind going to get them, she asked. No problem. I was happy to go and pick them up - provided I didn't have to do the feeding - until I found out that I would have to drive to Civitanova Marche to get them, and that was over an hour away. The journey there was not too bad, but coming back with a box full of live crickets on the seat next to me was beyond the call of duty, I thought.

After Tam had spent a week sitting in the shower feeding crickets to Buzz to fatten him up, his wing seemed to have come good, so we took him out into the country to release him. Except that he wouldn't go, because by this time he had decided Tam was his mum and he clung onto her tee shirt for dear life. Time to consult the Internet. We discovered somewhat unexpectedly that there was a real, dedicated, swift sanctuary in Italy. Tam called them and explained the problem. They said she had done well, but this was really a job for the experts, and if Tam could bring Buzz in, they would take over his rehabilitation. The trouble was, they were in Trieste, right up on the border with Slovenia. Well we were too far down the line to turn back, so one morning Tam set out on what turned out to be a fourteen-hour round trip to take a bird to Slovenia. All in a good cause. She was exhausted by the time she got back, but delighted by the unique experience of spending a few hours in a swift sanctuary, where she was introduced to the extraordinary private lives of the recovering swifts - seeing them doing swift gymnastics, squat regimes on their tiny legs, and watching an older bird literally take young Buzz under her wing. It is odd what can follow from finding a tiny bird cowering in a doorway, but after three weeks we finally got the shower back. And we fashioned a nice joke out of it, too. We would ask friends,

"What has 15 eyes, 26 legs, 2 wings and a beak?"

The answer is, "Our house".

You can imagine then how entranced Tam was to meet two tame owls. And when I say tame you could actually stroke their heads. If you wanted to, that is, because up close you realized that these things could do you some serious damage if they cared to. The male of the pair was about three feet tall. His beak was clearly designed for tearing small animals apart. And the claws were absolutely terrifying - curved scimitars, powerful and obviously extremely sharp. Personally I kept a respectful distance, but Tam gamely moved in to stroke his head and the beautiful silky down that adorned each claw - he was a truly impressive beast. I didn't like the look of him though. Ever since I first saw *The Exorcist* I have been wary of anything that can revolve its head through pretty much 360 degrees. And his eyes! Huge dark eyes that seemed able to transfix you. Come on, Steve, snap out of it - this is Medieval Night in Sarnano, not a Hitchcock movie!

In fact I felt a bit of a wimp when Tam got to know the background to these two owls. They belonged to a family with two young daughters, maybe 4 and 6 years old. These girls had grown up alongside the owls and had absolutely no fear of them, despite being only a little taller than the birds. And apparently the owls were a mating pair, and were likely to remain together for the rest of their lives. They were released at night and came back to spend the daytime in the house along with the two young girls. And here they were, perfectly comfortable in a large crowd the bravest of whom, like Tam, were stroking them as they perched on their respective logs. It was a delightful scene, bathed in candlelight and made all the more attractive because the entire family were dressed in medieval clothes

You won't find any shots of the owls in *Cookucina* though, because we couldn't find Peter. We went off to look for him, wondering where he might have gone after filming the belly-dancers. But he was nowhere to be found, and, it being the end of a long day, we decided to cut our losses and wrap for the day (technical term!). An hour or so later, Peter still hadn't appeared, so I went out looking for him again. I found him, of course, still filming the belly dancers - Peter is a sucker for a pretty girl.

Dinner with the English

We were exhausted. We had been at it now for almost three weeks. But at least the end was in sight. I mean the end of shooting, of course. There was still a great deal to do to turn hours and hours of rushes into a serviceable series. Not to mention the months and months of work that would go into trying to sell the thing. But when we woke up the morning after Medieval Night we didn't know anything about that. All we knew was that there was just one more day of filming left. At least that is what the Schedule, my Bible, told us, and - amazingly - we were on target. We had just two more recipes to shoot in the kitchen, but yet another night shoot to do. I wasn't sure that Peter would make it, as he had been up late drinking with the belly dancers. But Peter is made of stout stuff and comes up smiling even on a hangover and about three hours sleep.

We were moving towards the climax of the series. Today we were planning to shoot most of the material for Episode 6 - the final episode. And it was going to be a bit different. The first recipe was going to be the one that rounded up the whole *shtick* of the series, the idea that Lia was teaching Tam how to cook. To be honest, it didn't seem to me she had learned very much. She certainly showed no signs of having developed a desire to become a domestic goddess who liked nothing more than crafting works of art in the kitchen. Fair enough, there had been a lot of television "work" for her to do, and what with things being shot two and three times, and the general flow of the cooking process constantly being interrupted, these were not ideal circumstances in which to learn. But it didn't seem to me that she had any real *desire* to learn, and she had lost none of her appetite for restaurant meals. Maybe it is something to do with her American blood. I don't think I've told you yet that Tam is American. She *sounds* completely English, but the first eleven years of her life were spent mostly in America. Her father was American, her mother English, which Tam seems to think allows her to claim to be whichever of the two nationalities suits her at any particular time. I guess soon she'll have Italian to choose from as well. I remember reading somewhere that Americans eat 64% of their evening meals in restaurants. I am not sure if that's true, and it depends very much, I suspect, on your definition of "restaurant", but Tam certainly does her best to keep the numbers up.

Nevertheless, for the purposes of *Cookucina* we had had to ensure that Tam actually learned how to cook *something*, and a week or so earlier we had settled on what it would be. It was when we visited *Picciolo di Rame* and Silvano showed us how simple it was to make his delicious onion soup. Tam had known all along that she was going to have to cook something and so she had latched onto this on the grounds that it would be difficult to screw up. But if Tam was going to suddenly turn cook we would need to put her new-found skills to the test. I am not sure who came up with idea but we decided it was best to try her soup out on the English. A few of the ex-pats who, like us, have discovered their own little paradise here. It might have been Lia who had the idea first, because I think she was worried (with some justification) that Italians, who all see themselves as food critics, would be a little bit too honest when asked to pass judgment on Tam's onion soup. In fact, thinking about it now, it's clear that this is what Lia had in mind when the onion soup first came up as we were discussing a possible visit to *Picciolo di Rame*. She must have decided right back then that Tam's onion soup would be fit only for the English.

The plan was to round the series off as we had started it, with an alfresco meal in Sergio's *orto*. The English love that sort of thing, so it should be easy to get them to come along. But the big question was, who to invite? There are plenty to choose from round here, so we tried to narrow the field down a bit. The best idea seemed to be to figure out the parameters for the ideal TV dinner guest and compare it to our English friends and acquaintances. So we did what we often do when faced with a problem - we made a LIST!

1. First of all they would have to have a genuine appreciation of Italian food (they were going to get Lia's *Salmi di Cinghiale* as well as Tam's onion soup). That ruled out Iain, who spends most of his time trying to work out the cheapest way of importing baked beans and Marmite.

2. They had to speak fairly good Italian, as the rest of the guests would be Lia's family and friends. That ruled out Iain, too, as he seems to take a perverse pleasure in having lived here for ten years but still not being able to speak the language. He even lived with an Italian woman for a while, but that didn't seem to help - although her English improved no end. Iain's friend Mark has an Italian girlfriend too, and he has learned to speak excellent Italian, though with a rather incongruous Salisbury accent. In fact it turned out that neither of them could come anyway because they were going to the football that day (I am going to call it "football" because "soccer" just doesn't seem right to an Englishman). They had both been mad keen football supporters in England, and since coming here they have adopted the team at Ascoli Piceno, an hour or so south of Sarnano, as their principal love. Iain made a banner that they faithfully take down with them every other Saturday, but they still stand out a bit - a couple of middle-aged Englishmen bobbing up and down in the midst of the Ascoli *Ultras*. I went myself a couple of times, but it all got a bit too complex for me. The Italian football authorities tackled the hooliganism threat by making it virtually impossible to buy a ticket for an away game. Buying a ticket for a home game is easier. It's only *practically* impossible. You have to buy it well in advance, from specially designated bars (that's a good way to control the threat of excess alcohol consumption at football matches!), and you'll have to show about five proofs of who you are and where you live, or at least it seems that way. The net result is that the crowds are not what they might be, and with Italy being a difficult country to get around, sometimes the away contingent is tiny. The security forces never drop their guard, though. I once saw the entire away section of the ground completely empty apart from one traveling fan waving a huge banner and chanting his team's songs all on his own. He was encircled by six policeman. Needless to say they managed to control the situation, and the potential for trouble was nipped in the bud. An Italian will tell you, by the way, that there were six policeman because they always come in threes - one who can read, one who can write, and one to keep on an eye on the two intellectuals. But hang on a minute, I was making a list...

3. They would have to be meat-eaters. That ruled out David and Jayne. They're vegetarians, so why they chose to come and live in Le Marche, which is pretty much the heart of meat-eating Italy, I am not sure. They would be OK with the onion soup, and with the dessert

no doubt, but we couldn't have them turning their noses up at the wild boar. Someone suggested Tony and Jackie, but she declined the offer on the grounds that the dinner clashed with East Enders. And anyway, she's the woman who sent back a plate of chips back when they arrived *after* the meat (as they normally do in Italian restaurants), saying "I don't do cold chips". Actually that raises an interesting issue about Italian food. It's quite often just warm when it arrives at the table, and not piping hot as the English seem to require. First degree burns to the roof of the mouth is a particularly English eating hazard in my experience. The only way to get them here is a premature assault on a pizza that's straight out of the oven. It applies to drinks, too. Edna, a visiting American, always sent her cappuccino back on the grounds that it wasn't hot enough. While my Italian friend Cristiana, who lives in London, invariably sends London coffees back because they are too hot.

In the end the field was whittled down to just one couple, Damien and Sharon. They are crazy about Italian food, good cooks in their own right and they speak excellent Italian. And they are close enough friends that we could be sure they would not be *too* harsh on Tam's onion soup. You will remember that Silvano had shown us how to make something we called A SIMPLE ONION SOUP. It seemed the ideal dish for Tam to cook, and to be fair she made a pretty good stab at it. Fortunately Lia was on hand to pick up the pieces and get her back on track on a couple of occasions when the recipe was not quite "simple" enough for Tam. She got there in the end though, and Damien and Sharon were kind enough to give it eight out of ten when Tam went out on a dangerous limb during filming and asked them to *rate* her soup. Personally, I thought they were being a bit generous, but then nobody asked me, which was probably just as well.

The whole evening went off well, in fact. It was one of those balmy evenings at the end of another blistering August day when it was just perfect to be eating in the fresh air watching the pink glow of dusk wash gently across the rolling hills. The company was congenial, Sergio had dug out a really delicious *Rosso Piceno,* and the food was a rising crescendo of special treats. We kicked off with Tam's creamy onion soup, followed by the rich, dark, melt-in-the-mouth *Salmi* of wild boar (and pickled onions) that Lia had been lovingly creating for much of the day. But the climax of the whole meal was pudding. Lia knows I have something of a sweet tooth and she had been telling me for the last fortnight that she had something special up her sleeve for the last dinner. I was not disappointed. What she produced was *Torta di Mele* with *Vino Cotto Zabaione*, and it was simply magnificent. On the face of it, it's just a sort of upside down apple cake with a rich and creamy *Zabaione*, but sometimes the simple things are best. *Vino Cotto*, of course, is a bit of a magic Marche ingredient, but even without it you can have a go yourself. Here's how it's done:

APPLE CAKE with VINO COTTO ZABAIONE

For the cake:
- 5 *golden apples*
- 200g. *Flour*
- 200g. *Sugar*
- 100g. *Butter*
- 2 *Eggs*
- 200ml. *Milk*
- *a tsp of Baking Powder*
- *Cinnamon*

For the zabaione:
- 150ml. *Vino Cotto (use Vin Santo Or Marsala if you cannot find Vino Cotto)*
- 3 *Egg-yolks*
- 3 *tablespoons of Sugar*

To make the cake:
Peel the apples and slice them thickly. Beat the eggs and sugar together, then add the melted butter, milk, baking powder, cinnamon and flour. Mix everything together with the apples and pour the mixture into a baking tray covered with baking paper. Bake for 50mins at 170°. Push a cocktail stick into the cake to check it is fully cooked – it will come out dry when the cake is properly cooked.

To make the Zabaione:
Whisk the egg yolks with sugar, add the Vino Cotto and heat gently in a **bain marie** *or double saucepan until the mixture becomes thick and creamy.*

Delicious. And with a couple of glasses of that *Rosso Piceno* and Tam's soup scoring eight out of ten, everyone was felling pretty mellow by the end of the meal. But though this was the last supper, we still had one more job to do - we had a party to go to. A *Sagra*. In a lively little town about twenty minutes down the road called Loro Piceno. And this one was dedicated to guess what? Yes, *Vino Cotto*. 10pm and it was back on the road - but this assignment sounded like it was going to be fun.

Fireworks and Vino Cotto

As you know, most of these *Sagras* are held in tiny little villages out in the countryside, but when they happen in the local towns they include an extra special treat. Sarnano is unusual because many of the houses in the *centro storico* are occupied all year round by people (like us) who have chosen the place as their principal residence. Most of the houses in the other medieval hill-towns, though, are weekend and holiday homes for families who now live and work in the big cities. Maybe the parents were part of a major demographic shift in post-war Italy when the Italian economy transformed itself from agrarian to industrial and a large percentage of the population moved away from the countryside and into the cities. Often they simply walked away from the old family farmhouses which represented the unrelenting toil of making a living from a smallholding. Such houses can still be found dotted across the countryside, in various states of preservation - or, more accurately, disrepair. They are exactly the sort of place that tempt buyers from Britain or Holland who come across them on a country walk one sunny summer evening and fall madly in love with the idea of retiring to an old country house in Le Marche. They are also the sort of place where you can get cut off by the first big snowfall, and cost an arm and several legs to heat when the winter winds blow down from the north. And then there's the rain. The rain here often arrives in biblical quantities, transforming the rolling hillsides from an estate agent's wet dream into a nightmare of mudslides and landslips. One English family who bought one of these old farmhouses a few years back arrived one day for an autumn break to find that their access road had been completely washed away down the hillside. For the next few weeks they needed crampons just to get out for a pint of milk.

This same process of abandoning the family home happened in the towns too. Either because young families set off to seek work in the cities, or just because they moved into new-builds down the road that were a lot easier to look after. The end product is that when you walk around a town like Loro Piceno, or even Sarnano, you will see only the outside of houses many of which are shuttered and closed. But when the *Sagra* comes to town the doors are magically, invitingly, open. A while ago I made passing reference to a town called Amandola. It's just to the south of us (the other direction from Loro Piceno, but hang on - I *am* going to get there) and it's got a charming and attractive medieval heart with narrow streets that wind their way up towards a fabulous view from the big church at the summit. It's delightful, but it is one of those places that feel a bit like a museum. Until, that is, the festival comes to town. In this case it was a festival called *Diamante a Tavola,* Diamonds on the Table, by which they mean truffles. It happens in the first week of November and the lure of the truffle attracts people from all over the region, so the place is suddenly heaving with visitors. And the old town is, for that one week, thrown wide open, as all those centuries-old doors are opened up and the cellars and hallways behind them are turned into impromptu eateries, truffle stalls, bars and even lottery posts. And as you wander into them you have this magical feeling of dipping into other lives. The dank brick vaults of the *cantinas*, one-time medieval shops, half underground, half spilling onto the narrow alleys. Or the occasional glimpse of an elegant rococo hallway with ancient frescoes and ornately decorated ceilings, hidden for fifty-one weeks of the year behind a forbidding heavy wooden door secured with vast iron bolts. And the magic of it is, that everyone wants to show off their *cantina* or their stairwell. You can peek and poke to your heart's content.

This, too, is what it is like during the *Vino Cotto* sagra in Loro Piceno. With one significant difference. Loro is the home of *Vino Cotto* and just about everybody there seems to have been making the stuff for about three hundred years. So all the *cantinas* opened up for the *Sagra* turn out to be miniature *Vino Cotto* factories. Stepping in from the brightly-lit streets you can find yourself time-travelling back to an earlier era, in the musty gloom of a cantina lit by a single bare bulb, or even a suspended hurricane lamp. All around you are ancient barrels lying in wooden cradles on the bare earth beneath. Each barrel has a faded paper label with a date. Looking around we see 1915, 1929, even 1863. What do they mean, we ask? Apparently it is all to do with the method of producing the very best *Vino Cotto*, and it means these barrels have been constantly on the go since that date - up to more than a hundred and fifty years. Each year when the *vendemmia,* the grape harvest, is in, they will make another batch of *Vino Cotto* and add it to the barrel, which is never allowed to fall below the level of the tap. So when you buy a bottle of the 1863 vintage you know that some tiny proportion of it actually went into the barrel over a hundred and fifty years ago.

As you can imagine, knowing the Italians as well as you do by now, getting any of them to explain exactly how they make their *Vino Cotto* was like getting blood out of a stone. Everyone likes to think they have some special and magical technique that has been passed down from father to son since... well, since 1863 I suppose. We did find one man willing to tell us about it though, and that was the multi-functioning Tonino, who had learned to trust us (a bit) when we went truffling with him and his dog Fiuto. He took us out to a rundown shed deep in the countryside, opened up a creaking barn door and ushered us inside - into a world of copper cauldrons, oak barrels and a strange device that looked like an upright mangle. All of which looked as though they would already have been a bit second-hand back in 1863. Peering suspiciously down the lane as the last of us stepped inside, he carefully closed the doors to keep his trade secrets safe from prying eyes.

The barrels, he said, were oak. *Quercia nera,* a dark oak, ideal for making *Vino Cotto.* His favorite barrel, he told us, was a hundred and twenty years old. Personally, I found it a quasi-religious experience to find myself in the presence of a wine that pre-dates my great-grandparents. The method goes a bit like this...

The grapes are harvested, brought to the cantina and pressed using the *torchio* (the upright mangle) to squeeze out all the must. Meantime, you've lit the fire underneath your giant copper cauldron and set it to start heating up. Copper is important apparently both because it distributes the heat uniformly, and also because it neutralizes the sulphur with which the grapes have been treated to protect them from diseases. Then you boil it all up - and here the information started to get a bit hazy. Tonino had taken some persuading to take us into his confidence, but I was beginning to think that he was holding quite a lot back. It all seemed just a bit too easy.

"How do you know when it's ready?" Tam asked.

And then Tonino started to tell us about the ancient method, which seemed so implausible that I am not sure to this day whether he was winding us up. He called it The Egg System. The time-honoured way, he said, of checking if the sugar content had reached the right level. You take a fresh chicken's egg and float it on top of the must on the surface of the wine in the cauldron, and if the egg floats then you know you have reached the right sugar content. Now, I am great believer in the acquired wisdom of the ages, but it did strike me that there was a problem here in that, if you attempted to float the egg too early it would sink, and then you'd have something a bit more like egg nog than *Vino Cotto*. Tonino laughed. And that was it. No more information was forthcoming, and now he diverted everyone's attention by cracking open a bottle of the stuff, which I have to say was absolutely delicious. So that's it. That's how you make *Vino Cotto*. Or at least that's *some* of the instructions. Best to remember the old warning, I suppose: "Don't try this at home, children."

We had arrived at Loro Piceno with a bit of a warm glow, having 99% of the series "in the can". All that remained were a few "wallpaper" shots of Tam and Lia strolling around the narrow, crowded streets of the town checking out the cantinas. At least that is all that *I* thought we needed. Peter, ever the professional, pointed out that I must a bit demob-happy and insisted on making a proper sequence out of it.

"This place is just too good to throw away on wallpaper," he insisted, "we've absolutely got to get inside these cantinas."

Now I realise I have lapsed into a bit of TV-speak here. And I am sorry about that. "Wallpaper" is how we describe general shots of something that are used when the voiceover is talking about that same thing. A sequence is a few shots that cut together so they look like continuous action. And a sequence will often include "actuality" (people talking) which come through to break up the voiceover on the soundtrack. All clear now? I doubt it, but hey, we've got to retain *some* of the mystique of the TV profession in these days when anyone with a iPhone is a cameraman.

The sequence Peter wanted was in fact a series of shots of Tam and Lia inside the cantinas sampling the *Vino Cotto*. We got it OK, but we never got beyond the first one we went into because the old boy who ran the place was so taken with Lia and Tam that he insisted they try *un goccio* from each of his barrels. As I said, they had arrived with something of a warm glow from the *Vino Cotto Zabaione* and the *Rosso Piceno*. And we had topped it up on arrival in Loro with a *Mazzotto M'Ubriaco* which turned out to be a sweet sponge cake into which they pour a small glass of *Vino Cotto*. So by the time Lia and Tam had "tasted" three or four of the barrels they had become a little difficult to direct. Not exactly Marilyn Monroe difficult (there was no Winnebago in which to lock themselves), but enough to prompt us to call it a day. The sequence wasn't quite as expansive as Peter had wanted, but it does the trick, and you can get a sense of where things began to get difficult by taking a look towards the end of Episode Six, just before the closing titles at 24.10.

In fact, though we thought we had packed the camera away for ever, those closing titles reveal there was one last thing we decided to shoot. Just as the evening was drawing to a close and we were about to head off home we realised everyone was moving towards the main town square. This was the final night of the *Sagra*, and it turned out that they wrap the thing up each year with a firework display, and we were told that it was going to be pretty spectacular. Now I've been round the block a few times when it comes to fireworks. London for the Millenium, the Fourth of July in Washington - that sort of thing. But I have never, never seen anything quite as spectacular as this. It started with a bang. It always does in Italy. The start of the show is signalled by an enormous aerial explosion which makes you jump right out of your skin and sends all dogs within a five mile range into mental meltdown. There's no warning. A gentle sort of *pouff* as the thing is launched into the air which you *might* notice if you are lucky, and then this almighty bang that echoes round the mountains in a terrifying cacophony. They do the same thing to signify the end of the display, too. Only this time it is *three* explosions - just to finish off any dogs who have survived the display intact.

The display was not only spectacular, it was long. It seemed to go on for about half an hour - a constant stream of ever-changing multi-colored bursts lighting up the night sky and the fortifications of the old town. I don't know how you judge these things, unless you are a pyrotechnician (if that's the right word), but we reckoned it must have cost about a quarter of a million Euros. OK, maybe that was the *Vino Cotto* speaking, but anyway it must have been a small fortune. And all this from a town of just about two and half thousand inhabitants. By my reckoning that would be about a hundred Euros each, so I doubt I am right. Nevertheless, either the good citizens of Loro Piceno just love their fireworks, or they have found some mysterious European Fireworks Fund. Because, like the vast majority of open-air public entertainments here, it was free. Fireworks never come across particularly well on television (the point, after all, is that the stuff is exploding over, above, and all around you, rather than on a 32" flat-screen telly) but you can get a flavor of quite how magnificent it was from the closing credits of our final episode. And at last the shooting was finished. There's nothing like going out with a bang!

But that's when the trouble started.

DOLCE

Finding an editor

IT WAS OVER. The following morning Peter woke me up early with a cup of tea and a reminder that he had to be at the airport in a couple of hours. I had a bit of a headache (I can't imagine why) and this was the last news I needed. But as we had built the entire schedule around Peter's trip to the South of France for his week on the most luxurious of luxury yachts, I knew it had to be done. Peter was his usual, smiling self. But he had to be concealing a headache, I knew that, and in a little over ten minutes he had slung all the equipment into a bag and was ready to go. On the way to the airport Peter brought up an awkward subject.

"What" he asked "are we doing about editing this stuff?"

We had both known this question was coming but we had been so busy for the last two and a half weeks collecting the material that the issue of how exactly we were going to convert hours and hours of raw rushes, including numerous cock-ups and re-takes, into a polished TV series had not been discussed. An editor is a vital part of making any kind of documentary program. The director and cameraman try to make sure they've got the action fully "covered" from lots of different angles and preferably several times over. The director then takes all this stuff into the edit for the editor to kind of tidy up a bit, and maybe give it a bit of extra gloss by cutting the shots nicely to music. At least that's the way directors see it.

Editors themselves generally think of the job in a rather different way. As far as they are concerned some hapless, and generally inexperienced, director is going to walk into their edit suite with a collection of virtually useless material that can only be "saved" by his own skill in crafting a watchable TV program out of all this rubbish.

The truth, as ever, is somewhere in the middle, but what is absolutely certain is that if you don't have a decent editor you will not end up with the slick and professional program you want. And editing is one bit of the process that is best not left to an amateur. The better your editor, the more he is going to be able to make of your rushes - be they good, bad or indifferent. She can turn good stuff into award-winning and make the totally unwatchable good enough for daytime TV.

Editing is therefore a vital part of the television process. Personally, I have always enjoyed that bit more than the filming. When you are out on the road filming a series there is constant sense of dissatisfaction. There is always something *else* you could have done at the end of the day. Mostly I found I used to think of something extra just after the cameraman had packed all the kit away. It earned me a bad reputation in the BBC, where I came to be known among the camera crews as "Just One More Shot", always asking them to get the camera out again.

But when you go into the edit suite you take in a complete set of material. That's it. If you haven't shot it, you haven't got it. And you have just x weeks - whatever you've been allocated (or can afford!) - to turn this limited, incomplete, inadequate material into an award-winning show. At least that's the way your editor will generally describe your material once he's had a look at it.

In fact editing is one of the most constructive and creative parts of making a TV show. Television is a kind of community project. Unlike, say, a book, no one person "owns" a piece of television. The joy of it all is bringing many skills together. Some years ago I was working at the BBC directing a live Current Affairs studio show. It was the big daily morning show, called *Breakfast Time* - the one that Selina Scott used to present. The full crew was about 25-30 people - cameramen, sound, lighting, gallery crew etc. As the Studio Director you are the spider in the middle of the web - telling everyone what to do and when. They all look to you to "call the shots". Now I was well aware that the sound crew, the floor managers and the cameramen were highly trained and experienced and could all do their job much better than I ever could. That's obvious. The satisfaction of being a Studio Director is bringing together a whole range of talents like those into a single coherent whole. But quite how much I, as the Director, relied on other people's talents came home to me one day after I had already been doing the job for a couple of months. I went to the studio a little earlier than usual, while the crew were setting up for the show, and as I wandered about I found a door labeled RACKS. Pushing it open I found two men sitting inside staring at some knobs and dials that I had never seen before, doing a job I didn't even know existed. And they were making *me* look good by doing it. Racks, by the way, is something to do with balancing the color levels. Or something like that.

On filmed programs like Cookucina the relationship between editors and directors is a strange one. Neither of you can make a show without the other, but both of you have a sneaking feeling you could do the other guy's job better than he can. Directors, nevertheless, rely on editors to get them out of a whole load of trouble. That infamous phrase "We'll fix it in the edit" falls lightly from a director's tongue when things haven't exactly gone to plan. Fixing it in the edit is all very well, but it means relying on the skill of your editor. And right now, as we barreled down the *autostrada* on the way to the airport, it seemed to me we had no editor and nowhere to edit. Peter, as you will have come to expect by now, had an answer.

When I was a lad edit suites cost millions of dollars. Not literally, but almost. Nowadays, you get free edit software with every computer operating system. They are not professional systems, of course, but you get the point. And even professional software edit packages can be bought for a few hundred dollars. Chuck in a professional monitor (that's a kind of super TV) for a few hundred more and you are in business. And that, Peter announced, was what he had done. A few days earlier he had sloped off to bed early. Most unlike him, and we had thought it a bit unusual at the time.

"I got on the internet," he said, "poked around a bit on Ebay (Peter is something of an expert on Ebay) and picked up a couple of monitors and a little sound mixing desk. I'm going to set up my own edit suite."

"Where?" I asked.

"In the attic over the garage. It's a little self-contained flat and office combined. I thought I could let it out to production companies who've had enough of paying an arm and a leg to edit in some dingy basement in Soho. Make a change, don't you think?"

Well it certainly would make a change, because the attic over the garage is the east wing of a rather palatial old farmhouse in Hampshire. There are peacocks and guinea fowl strolling around the gardens, and views out across fields where polo ponies graze, towards the Hampshire hills. This is Jane Austen country you are looking at, not the fire escape on the back of a crumbling office block in Wardour Street. When I first walked in I knew the editing process was going to be more than usually enjoyable. I was right, except for one thing. It was still going to cost an awful lot of money.

OK, Peter's investment had saved us the cost of the equipment, but most of the cost of editing is the guy (or girl) who does it for you. These are talented, highly trained (and therefore expensive) people. But we, of course, were trying to do everything on the cheap. We needed someone who would do the job on deferral, which as we know, is TV-speak for being paid not only late, but less. And possibly not at all. Now obviously we are honorable people, so we had to find an editor who would work for maybe half-price now, with the balance coming out of the profits. But where would we find an editor desperate enough to go for that somewhat speculative deal? After all, we didn't even have an end-product whose chances of selling they could judge for themselves. That was going to be *their* job. No-one sprung immediately into my mind. But Peter had ideas. Two to be precise, and they were very different propositions.

Rick (not his real name) was a tubby, homey sort of guy who liked to work with Peter because, living-in as it were, he could work the peculiar hours that seemed to suit him. He would get up at about 1030, make himself a hearty fried breakfast which took the best part of an hour and a half to knock up and consume, and start work shortly after midday. If you were lucky. Somewhat disconcertingly, he always had a laptop open alongside the edit machine on which he was constantly trawling East European dating sites. He would work deep into the evening, to be sure, but he also expected an equally hearty lunch and dinner as the day wore on. Rick didn't go out much.

James, on the other hand (his real name, by the way) was a hunter. A real one. He liked working at Peter's place because Peter has about seventy acres of woodland where James can go hunting things. I am not sure, but I think he kills them with his bare hands. Or a bow and arrow or something. Then he cooks them. And sleeps out at night in hammocks slung between a couple of trees. He runs survival courses in Peter's woods when he's not editing. He'll be a great guy to hang on to when the nuclear winter arrives. James likes to start editing as the cock crows the dawn, and disappears down into the woods at sundown. I am not sure when he washes, and brushes his teeth - but maybe he doesn't need to. Rick, on the other hand, wears carpet slippers.

Rick v. James

So far we had been doing everything ourselves. The only costs had been flights, petrol and meals. But if we had to hire one of these two editors (even on deferral) the cost was going to get serious. At first I thought I could persuade Peter to do do it. He trained as an editor, working at the BBC's famous Ealing Studios where some of their greatest documentaries were made. Not to mention the movies - all those fabulous post-war Ealing Comedies starring Alec Guinness. Not all of them, but about 95% I am sure.

But Peter had pretty soon graduated from editing to directing, which is a bit like being elevated to the House of Lords - you like to quietly forget you were once a lowly MP in the Commons. He laughed when I suggested he might be the right man for the job, pointing out that the last program he edited was before the invention of videotape. If we had shot the whole thing on film he might be in with a shout, but then it would have either cost a fortune or looked like the 1970s. Lord Peter of Hampshire can do email and Ebay, but wouldn't know where to start on a digital editing system. No, this was going to cost money.

You might be wondering why this seemed to have come as a shock, as we must have known all along that it would need editing. The truth is, I don't think any of us ever really thought we would get this far. And for the last three weeks we been working flat out - worried only about what we doing in the next two or three hours. And there was a fly in the ointment, the "Distributor" who had egged us on to be more and more ambitious with our idea. You'll remember that when we set out on this path the general thought was to make a series of short packages we could sell to broadcasters as *interstitial* material. Nasty word but, to remind you, these are those short items that fill in the gaps behind programs made for American TV. There's a concept in television called the TV Hour. It is sixty minutes minus the amount of time taken up in each hour by adverts and promotions of upcoming programs. In the USA, as you will know if you've ever had the pleasure of watching their TV networks, there are an awful lot of adverts. So many, in fact, that an American TV hour is going to be something like 46 minutes, whereas on the BBC, with no ads, it will be about 58 minutes. Hence the need for small, *interstitial,* packages to fill in the 8, 10 or 12 minute gap when broadcasters outside the US show American programs.

David, the "Distributor", had rubbished that plan, "No, no, no - this is a great idea. It's a cookery program, and I can sell cookery programs like falling off a log. Enough with the silly little *interstitials*, stick them together and give me six half-hours." And that's when he told us to "cut out all that 'learning some kitchen Italian stuff', that's **educational** programming (he said it with a nasty sneer in his voice) and *no-one* wants that."

As an aside, I sometimes wonder what John Logie Baird would think if I could bring him back from the grave and show him the TV schedules.

"What have you done," I can hear him asking, "with my invention? Why have you trampled on the most powerful educational medium ever invented?"

"Sorry, Mr Baird. It just got out of control."

"Well, I don't think I shall invent this after all," he thunders, "I'll come up with something else - how about an electronic information web, letting people all over the world share the finer things in life? I doubt you people will make a mess of that!"

But the genie, of course, is well out of the bottle, and now we had decided to join in - in our own small way. We had signed up to the goldrush of cookery programming. Or so we thought. My phone rang. Peter. This will be good news - he's got one of the editors to commit to the project.

"Both of them," he told me. "Rick can do the first episode, and James will pick it up from there."

"But they are such very different characters," I protested. "We need a consistency of style through the series."

"Come on," said Peter, with just a hint of exasperation in his voice, "this is a cookery show, not *Lord of the Rings*."

And so we set out on the long journey to make a six-part cookery series, where Episode 1 and Episodes 2 to 5 looked vaguely like they were the same thing.

"And one other thing," said Peter, "Rick needs to start right away, and, as you have no doubt remembered, I leave for my week on the yacht tomorrow. So you'll be doing Ep. 1."

"Thanks a bunch", I grumbled. "When does he arrive?"

"He's here now. We having a game of Bridge with the neighbors - Rick's a bit of an expert apparently."

A Bridge player who didn't get up till late morning and spent most of the day in carpet slippers trying to find a Russian wife. I wasn't looking forward to working with Rick.

The Chopper

In fact we got on fine, Rick and I. Notwithstanding his strange working hours, he put a good shift in. And he worked fast. But the most important thing is that Rick is *creative*. And he brought a lot of that to the series. In Episode One he set a style that was pacey yet informative. I had always been a bit worried about how we were going to shoehorn three recipes into a half hour program. Especially as the preparation and cooking time for each one often added up to nearly an hour. And that's not to mention the trips over the mountain to meet the people and buy the produce.

"Leave it to me," said Rick, with an air of calm authority. "Why don't you go off and make us a bit of lunch, and I'll tell you when I've got a cut you can come and look at."

I know Rick likes his food, but it was 10.30 in the morning, and I recognised the true meaning of this speech - "Please get out from under my feet and leave me to have a go at it by myself. Your suggestions are not helping!"

So I did. I went down to the kitchen and whipped up a delicious pasta lunch. But not before I had spent an hour and a half reading the newspaper. This is the life! And at 3 o'clock - after our pasta lunch - Rick called me back to the edit suite to show me his first cut. He had achieved miracles as far as I was concerned. Really good editors know how to truncate the action so that only the really significant bits are there, while at the same time the viewer feels that they are still getting the whole thing. It's not just "and here's one I made earlier." It's much more sophisticated than that. A good editor can make you believe that the eggs have somehow magically beaten themselves. That's it... they are magicians really. Have a look for yourself. The first recipe Rick put together is the *Trota al Forno con Verdure* at 10.15 into Episode One, and it is very close to the first cut

238

that Rick showed me right back at the beginning. Massimo's music helped a lot, but the whole effect lifted me out of a bit of a depression - wondering how on earth all this was going to go together. But then that's all part of the natural life cycle of an edit - the editor bailing the director out of a black negativity about his own work. *They* may be magicians, but *we* are artists, you see...

The pinnacle of Rick's achievement was the chopper.

"We need a device," he said.

"What sort of device?" A *device* is a visual gimmick, short and sharp, that lets you move from one topic to another. A sort of new chapter heading, but quick and stylish. And no words. If it's got a little bit of music that transforms it into a sting. A *device* is like a sting, only even shorter. You get the picture?

"Something crisp. Something that says *kitchen*... Like a chopper."

"A *chopper?*"

"You know, a meat cleaver."

Brilliant. But those things cost money. A **cut** from one picture to another is instantaneous. A **mix** dissolves one picture into the next, but something like a chopper is much more complicated. In slow motion you need to see that it is *cutting* into the picture as it falls across the screen. Stop it half way through, and the top half is the outgoing picture, while the bottom is the blade of the meat cleaver. Step on a bit further and once the chopper fills the frame you can **cut** straight to the incoming picture. At normal speed the whole effect is of the cleaver "chopping" out of one scene into the next.

"But we'll need *green screen*," I mumbled, "and there's no way we can afford that. That's how they put men onto Mars in the movies."

"Forget about that," said Rick, "I have an idea. See if you can find a cleaver somewhere."

Peter keeps turkeys. And lambs. And he eats both of them. In fact it's pretty much the freshest meat you'll ever eat, because he butchers them himself. So I was optimistic, and after rifling through his kitchen drawers I was soon able to return to the edit suite with a cleaver. I was greeted by a strange sight. The camera was set up on a tripod about 18 inches above the ground. It was pointed at a small coffee table with some green baize draped over it. Behind it, butted hard up against the coffee table, was Peter's green baize card table lying on its side.

"What's all this?" I asked.

"Our green-screen studio," said Rick, matter-of-factly. "Have you got a chopper?"

The next couple of hours we spent happily filming the source material for our *device*. We needed a floodlight from Peter's garage, but apart from that nothing but the tables and the chopper. And the green baize. Rick imported the shots into the edit system, pressed a few buttons (to make the system see anything green as transparent) and by mid-afternoon we had a "device" that could have cost about $50,000 in Hollywood. Maybe there was something to this do-it-yourself TV after all.

Translating the Fish Pirate

The chopper is a vital part of **Cookucina**. We use it over and over to get us instantly from one "set-up" to another. Or to suddenly flash forward 30 or 40 minutes while something is cooking. It pops up all through the series, but if you want to see what it looks like right now, just look at beginning of the recipe I referred to just now (10.15 into Episode One). It's one of my favorite places where the chopper is used to terrific effect.

I have to confess I hadn't seen it coming. The need for a chopper, that is. A *device*. And there was something else I hadn't seen coming - though I felt pretty stupid when I finally realised. I mean how can you embark on a TV program in two languages without giving any thought to the issue of translation? Well *I* did. And, in my defense, I have to say that none of the rest of the team had thought of it either. My Italian is serviceable but rudimentary. Tam's is better, but not very grammatical. Lia's English, as you may have noticed by now (and as is pretty fundamental to the series), is just about non-existent. As for Peter and Sergio neither of them had the faintest idea about the other language. Peter started most days with a cheery smile and a "good morning" in something a bit like Spanish, but we didn't like to discourage him so we let it go. Sergio seems to think that learning *anything* in English would be the start of a slippery slope to eternal damnation.

It's all about subtitles, you see. Right from the start we knew this was a series aimed at an anglophone market. When we're in the kitchen Tam is on hand to translate on the fly anything Lia says. The idea is that we, the viewers, learn the recipes and a little bit of kitchen Italian through Tam. So everything Lia says gets repeated by Tam in English. Simple. But when we're out on the road pretty much everything is in Italian. With subtitles. And subtitles are notoriously tricky.

What I learned fairly quickly once we started the edit was that we couldn't do it on our own. First of all, there's quite a bit of colloquial Italian, which needs to be rendered into similarly "natural" English. Towards the end of Episode One, while they're making *Pere al Vino Rosso,* Lia asks Tam to add some cinnamon to the dish. "How much?" asks Tam. "*Un bel po'*" she replies, which makes no sense at all as a literal translation, but gets used quite a lot, meaning something like "quite a bit... but not *too* much." Most of the translation, of course, would be relatively straightforward, but when you are making a TV series you can't just muddle through as you would in ordinary life - things have to be *correct.* It was clear we were going to need somebody who was just about fluent in both languages. Fortunately, I had someone in mind.

By now, basking in the afterglow of the chopper device, Rick had ridden off into the sunset returning to his proper job at the BBC putting the laughs into unfunny comedies (sometimes literally). He left us with a 90% completed first episode and a great template for the rest of the series. Rick, we are forever grateful.

James was uncontactable for a few days, according to his wife. He was out in the woods, she said, killing things and living off the land. I had a sneaking suspicion that he was probably a few hundred yards away in the thick undergrowth down at the bottom of Peter's lane. But I certainly wasn't going to go looking, tramping about in the woods searching for a man with a rifle and a sharp eye for the quarry that would provide his next meal. Tam's video of the boar hunt was still fresh in my mind. And frankly a hiatus of a couple of days was just what I needed if I was going to sort this subtitle/translation thing.

When we first jumped off the cliff of making a new life in Italy I was working in central London, just round the corner from the Italian Cultural Institute. That's how I came to walk in one day to sign up for one of their intensive courses. The *Istituto Italiano di Cultura* turned out to have two wonderful things going for it. The first was the cafe in the basement. A real treasure, proper Italian food (made by proper Italians) at knock-down prices. Quite simply some of the best Italian food in London, and certainly the most authentic - right down to the manageress's three-year-old daughter rattling around the place making a nuisance of herself all day. The only thing missing from the genuine Italian restaurant experience was a TV showing a constant stream of inane gameshows featuring impossibly attractive showgirls in impossibly short skirts. And a bloke called Carlo Conti, who seems to present **everything** on Italian TV. One of his quiz shows starts with four girls in identical dresses jiggling about to loud music for about a minute and a half. And this is a *quiz* show. Perhaps the *Cultura* bit in the name of the Institute means that Italian TV has to be banned from the cafe.

The second thing was Cristiana. You've met Cristiana before, when we were doing the *passeggiata* through her home village in Molise. She arrived in our lives as a bonus. Literally. Halfway through my intensive (Beginners!) course we were suddenly offered ten extra lessons (after school) with half a dozen young women who were also studying at the *Istituto*, to become teachers of Italian. They needed students to practise on and we Beginners had been chosen. In truth they were a bit of a mixed bunch, but Cristiana was one of the better ones and seemed like a really nice person. Our own teachers had already made it clear that we needed to try to find someone with whom we could set up a *scambio*, a language exchange. An Italian learning English with whom we could meet regularly for conversation in both languages. I plumped for Cristiana. To be honest, her English was quite a bit better than my Italian, but she didn't seem to mind and we started to meet every week. Each of us would bring along a newspaper article for the other to read and ask questions about. It worked really well - until I moved to Italy.

Cristiana, then, was the ideal person to call on to help us with the subtitles, particularly because she's very generous and I knew she wouldn't want paying. And as I expected, she was happy to help. But in the absence of remuneration we thought it would be good to try to give her a really nice time.

"Come and have a relaxed weekend in the Hampshire countryside." I said. "Lots of fresh food, and walks in the woods - it'll be lovely. And bring a friend."

So she did. But (poor woman), she hadn't realized quite how much of this there was - three hours of subtitled programs takes a lot of checking. And some of it, like the Fish Pirate, was even in dialect, which made it extra difficult for someone from a different part of Italy (her family home in Molise is about a 4 hour drive south of Sarnano). And it rained. So much for the walks in the woods. In the event she was hard at it in front of a computer for the whole weekend. But Peter cooked us some fabulous meals, and her friend Alessandra played the piano while we worked, so it was a pleasant weekend, even for the over-worked Cristiana. Peter, of course, fell in love with Cristiana. Or was it Alessandra? Or maybe both. And I can't say I blame him.

The Voice

Subtitling was just one of a whole string of minor difficulties we hadn't seen coming when we set out on this thing. *Cookucina* is a bit of a metaphor for life in that respect. I mean if you could see, right from the start, all the problems that a particular course of action might hold in store, you'd be paralyzed, wouldn't you? We make our way through life tackling the individual difficulties as they crop up, one at a time. If you start trying to *anticipate* the problems, life suddenly becomes a minefield and it seems the only safe course of action is to stay right where you are. Sadly, it's something to do with aging, too. The older we get, the more we seem compelled to look for the problems before they arrive.

The next tricky situation we ran into was to do with Commentary. James pointed it out about five minutes after he arrived. Commentary (or Comm. as we usually call it) is the out of vision voice-over that kind of knits everything together. You know the sort of thing... those vacuous TV programs in which a bunch of "celebrities" get together to try to pull something off (like living as a "homeless" person with a TV crew in constant attendance) which always seem to include the line:

"The team have just ... days to... [FILL IN THE GAPS]"

I have often thought that line (and others like it) must be on a macro in the TV Producers' edition of Word.

Comm is really get-you-out-of-trouble stuff. And it's very powerful. When you're out on the road filming you generally try to shoot something that will tell its own story. Sequences. All the bits (you think) are going to fit neatly together like pieces of a jigsaw. But when you get into editing somehow it's never quite like that. Either there are bits of the jigsaw missing, or when you have finished putting it together the jigsaw is about the size of a football pitch. Either way, the solution is Comm! Tightly written Comm can fill in those gaps or condense whole chunks of action into a skilfully crafted couple of words. And, of course, we soon found we were in need of Comm.

But Comm is a living, breathing thing. You write a couple of pithy sentences, get your Presenter to record them and cut them into your program. And then you discover you could have done it better, more sharply. Or it needs to be even shorter. Or there's a fact missing. The general progress of an edit is to continually whittle the material down until it fits the slot available, hopefully without losing anything significant. It *should* be getting better and clearer as you go along. And constantly refining the Comm is an integral part of that. The trouble was, we were in Hampshire and our Voice (Tam) was a thousand miles away in Sarnano.

Ten years ago this would have been a complete disaster, but in the modern world we knew that we could start sending Tam bits of Comm which she could record into her computer and email across to us. Simple, except that the one thing you really cannot do without when recording Comm is a "squirrel". That is, a decent microphone. And where was she going to get one of those in the middle of the Italian countryside?

Peter was back by now from his luxury yachting experience. Tanned, bleary-eyed and with a permanent smile, I suspected he had enjoyed himself even more than was usual, or possibly even legal. But there was no time to find out what he'd been up to (which I am sure would have induced a nasty bout of envy in me, whatever it was). No, we had a problem to solve.

"I've a confession to make," said Peter.

"This is not the time" I said, with a bit of a sour tone in my voice. "Some of us have been hard at work in the edit suite while you've been.... well, whatever it is you've been doing."

"No, no," said Peter, "Remember when we had to race off to the airport at the end of the shoot? And we both had a bit of a hangover from the *Vino Cotto* at Loro Piceno the night before?"

"Yes."

"Well when I got onto the yacht and unpacked the bag, I discovered the mike was missing."

"You've lost it?" I must have sounded a little bit uncharitable at this point.

"Not exactly. I think it's still in the house in Sarnano. Probably down behind my bed. I wasn't quite with it that morning and when I picked up my bag to leave, I missed one of the handles and everything fell back out on the bed. You were waiting by the door in a hurry to leave, and I thought I had got it all, but when I got to the other end there was no mike, so my guess is, that's where Tam will find it - down behind the bed."

"Why didn't you bring it up before?"

"We didn't need it before, but hey, sometimes the world works, doesn't it?"

And that, in fact, is where it was. Though Tam rather churlishly seemed to think it was all bit unprofessional to have to rummage down behind the bed for a key piece of equipment. Nevertheless, by early that afternoon we had Tam recording bits of Comm and emailing them across. It was a technique we would refine over the coming weeks, and without it the edit would have been a whole lot more difficult.

For James, this was the final piece of his editing toolkit. Over the next three weeks James worked pretty much flat out stitching together Episodes 2 to 5. This was a man with a hunger for work, or maybe just a hunger to get this boring editing stuff out of the way and get back to nature. In any event he had us all hard at it. I was constantly re-writing scripts, emailing new bits of Comm over to Tam who would record them and have them back within an hour or so. Sometimes four or five times a day. Peter, back from his holiday, was lending his own ideas to the edit, but more importantly, cooking lots of nice meals and supplying the edit suite with endless cups of tea and coffee.

Inside a month we were done. Our motley crew of part-timers, multi-taskers, Bridge players, yachtists and hunters had, against all the odds, crafted a really quite entertaining and informative TV series. The question now was, how would anyone actually get to see it?

AMARO

The Meeting

AND THIS IS WHERE things *really* started to go wrong. David, the "Distributor", you will remember, had told us that he needed a Trailer and at least one episode to take off to MIPCOM, the TV market in Cannes. We duly obliged, preparing a nice tidy version of Episode One, and a 3 minute taster to show to him at his office in London. On the appointed day Peter and I left James hard at work in the edit suite and traveled up to London with the program on a hard disk. We were supposed to be meeting David at his facilities house, where there were lots of high-end edit suites which would provide the ideal environment for looking at the fruits of our labor. We were proud of what we had achieved, and were excited about seeing it in a professional environment.

When we arrived we were shown into a small waiting area and given a cup of coffee. "David will be with you in a moment", we were told by a charming and friendly receptionist. So far, so good. But then David arrived with a sorry tale. It seemed that all the edit suites were busy, and he didn't have anywhere to screen the program. We offered to wait, but our "Distributor" was a busy man. MIPCOM was just a couple of days away and he had appointments for the rest of the day.

"Do you have a laptop with you?" he asked.

We did. He suggested we all go round the corner to a local cafe where we'd be able to watch on the laptop. We were a bit crestfallen by the idea that this man, who was going to get behind our series and promote it in the biggest and most competitive TV market in Europe, would be seeing our work on a laptop with tinny little speakers instead of on a big screen with professional audio. But at least this cafe (in the heart of TV land, in Soho, by the way) must be somewhere well-suited

251

to this sort of thing. It wasn't. We finally got to display our wares in a crowded workmen's cafe, sharing a table with someone eating an egg and chip lunch, while a TV blared MTV in the background. Even *I* wasn't much impressed with how the program looked in these less-than-ideal circumstances. This was a bad start to a relationship that would get slowly and inexorably worse over the next two years. Why do I say two years? Because in our haste to get signed up with a distributor before MIPCOM we had already signed an agreement assigning the rights to this man for two years. It is a decision we would live to regret.

There's a concept I came to know about called "sign and forget". I can't say that this is 100% true, but when the idea was explained to me a year or so after these events, it suddenly made sense of the way our "Distributor" had behaved. It goes like this... There are only so many series you can sell in any one genre. There's not an infinite number of slots for (as an example) cookery shows. Distributors are going to make their money through promoting a small number of highly-saleable, and lucrative, shows. Generally from big-name broadcasters like the BBC where the name alone is taken to be a guarantee of quality and success. It's the TV equivalent of the old computer business aphorism, "No-one ever got fired for buying IBM". The theory of "sign and forget" is that if you have one or two of these to sell you will concentrate on that. If you can sign up any other (lesser) program for (let's say) two years you can give it no promotion at all, but because you have the exclusive rights no-one else will be out there trying to use it to undercut your big sellers. Is it real? I have no idea, but it certainly seemed to fit with how our distributor dealt with *Cookucina*. Having said that, there was one sale that slipped through the net. For a brief couple of months Lia, Tam and *Cookucina* were household names in Croatia, the one place our "Distributor" managed to sell the series.

Am I bitter? Am I being unfair? Is the series, in fact, a stinker? Maybe. And maybe I am too close to it all. But I have been making TV programs for many years - enough to know a good one from a bad one (and I've been associated with one or two bad ones over the years). This is a good one. But maybe it's just not stylistically what everyone wants these days. The woman at Sky told me she loved it, but it was too relaxed for the frenetic world of Sky. And perhaps I am being unfair to the "Distributor". But I doubt it, because I am pleased to say that round about the time the two years was up his company went bankrupt. None of us, I have to say, shed a tear at the news. And as to the quality of the program, well time has moved on and we have decided to distribute it in a totally different way, and I hope by now you will have seen enough of it to know for yourself how good it is. And whether the "Distributor" was a charlatan, or yes, I *am* just bitter and twisted.

PBS

By now more than two years had passed since that manic summer. The exhausting days spent hurtling round the countryside filming trout fisheries and dark basements full of dangling salamis were long gone. So too the sauna that was Lia's kitchen. And the joyful creativity of the edit suite with its impromptu green-screen "studio" and endless accordion music. Hard work though it was, the whole process had been so enjoyable that I had allowed myself to believe that this was really going to work. That somehow, we were going to break all the unwritten rules of television and make a global success out of a series knocked up in our kitchen. A bit like the TV equivalent of *Fifty Shades of Grey*. But without the bondage. (Maybe *that's* where we went wrong.)

But it hadn't worked. So far, all that hard work had been seen only by a handful of Croatian housewives. I decided to look back at all the reasons I gave Lia right back at the beginning about why this was *never* going to work.

"TV is a complicated business," I had told her, "You need money, equipment, people, a studio to shoot in... and a TV channel for it to run on". I had tried to explain the complexities of the 21st century broadcast environment - its cartels, restrictive practices, and almost total lack of moral compass. It would be a costly folly that would lead nowhere, I told her. She had just smiled and laughed it off. Why on earth hadn't I listened to myself?

Now, two and a half years on, we had recovered the rights, but none of the money we had spent editing the series. We had even had to spend yet more money to extract the broadcast-quality footage from the "Distributor". But what about the sale to Croatia? Swallowed up in the "Distributor's" expenses I am afraid. Difficult to see where we could go from here, and to be honest, it was hard to summon up the enthusiasm to start all over again. But then a ray of sunlight appeared over the horizon. In the form of a slightly larger-than-life American woman called Linda.

Linda and Dan arrived in Sarnano a couple of years back. She is (or was) a high-powered lawyer, and he's an engineer. They married late in life and they are (I think even they would agree) a slightly unlikely couple. She loves Italy, and Sarnano in particular, because she's an Italian-American by birth. In lots of ways she fits the stereotype, she's highly-strung, emotional, artistic. She no longer ploughs the spiritually unrewarding furrow of the American legal system. Instead she gives lectures about the history of Italian art on cruise ships in the Mediterranean. And every five minutes she seems to produce a little artistic something-or-other - a novel, or a bijou little book of pen and ink drawings of Sarnano.

Dan, on the other hand, rides a Harley Davidson and shoots things. Just about the first thing Dan did when he arrived in Sarnano was to seek out the local firing range. He shoots targets there with a Magnum .357. The targets are those ones that look like a man who's trying to do something nasty to you. I think he pretends they're Democrats when he's pulling the trigger. Dan likes to make things out of metal. When he's in Sarnano he has withdrawal symptoms from his workshop in Florida. I think of Dan as my polar opposite, but we get on famously. He makes a living making and repairing brake systems for vintage aircraft. He's about the only person on the planet who can do it.

Linda loved *Cookucina*. She was wildly enthusiastic about it from the very start, and couldn't understand why it wasn't already showing on TV. Until I explained the way the TV business works. It comes to something when a fugitive from the US legal system thinks *your* line of business is dysfunctional. One day Linda had a brainwave.

"*Cookucina* is just perfect for PBS" she told me.

PBS (for those of you outside the United States) is America's Public Broadcasting Service. A bit like the BBC but (this is the USA) without any public funding. It's a complex network of local stations all across North America and its staple diet is History and How-To programming, which includes cookery, of course.

"Why don't you try the PBS station in Rhode Island," said Linda, "there's a big Italian community there and *Cookucina* would go down a storm."

So I did. I called the woman who runs Rhode Island's PBS station and told her all about the series. She even watched an episode I sent her online. She loved it. And she told me I had to get in touch with an outfit called American Public Television who supply How-To type programming to all the several hundred PBS stations across the US. And she gave me the name of the man to talk to.

So I called him. And he watched the show. He liked it too.

"This could work really well for us" he said.

He started to tell me how the PBS system works, and it was nothing like the TV world I had been used to in the UK. I had (foolishly) asked him how much APT/PBS would normally pay for a series like ours. We don't pay anything at all, he told me. In fact *we* would have to pay *them*. We would need to stump up about $3000 an episode to prepare our finished series for transmission in America. They use a different TV standard to the rest of the world. It's called NTSC, which bearded and be-sandalled TV technicians in the UK will tell you stands for Never Twice the Same color. Our series was shot in High-Definition PAL, so it seemed to me we were going to have to pay $18000 to make it worse.

"And," he said, "you'll want to employ a Station Relations Manager, which will cost you another 5 or 6 thousand."

Her job, it seems, was to make sure that all the bigger, more important stations, with which she had long-standing relationships, took the series. *Cookucina* was going to be offered (provided we said "yes" to all this, and came up with the initial investment) to all these stations as part of a six-monthly offers round. We would be one series amongst many on offer. The SRM's job was to make ours stand out in all the right places. But here's the rub. There were no guarantees. The best that you could hope for was that quite a lot of these stations said they would (probably) broadcast the series. But they wouldn't be saying when, or how many times. And we were going to be handing over the rights, again. This time for three or four years.

I can hear you thinking now, how on earth are these guys going to make any money out of this. Well the answer is sponsorship. Or "underwriting" as the American euphemism has it. We would get the chance to sell the program to sponsors, whose name would be attached to the series each and every time it went out on any PBS station in America for three or four years. Which could, in the most lucrative TV market of all, be (literally) hundreds of thousands of outings. Or none at all. And therein lies the difficulty. How to persuade potential sponsors to stump up money in advance when there is no guarantee *whatsoever* that the series will get picked up by anybody at all. And, talking of euphemisms, they told us there were a few rules about the sort of sponsorship that would not be permitted on American Public Television. One of the exclusions was "waist to knee products". I don't even like to think about that, especially in the context of a cookery series.

Nevertheless Tam and I were enthused. Transmission on PBS seemed a genuine prospect to begin with. And there was the dangled carrot of being able to promote our own ancillary products - maybe a cookbook, a Youtube channel of quick one-off recipes (I even did a pilot, at **https://youtu.be/FN47AGYGWFk**), even *this* book. Yes, this could have been the start of something big. The main problem was none of us were prepared to risk our own money Peter and I had already stumped up a few thousand dollars each for the editing, and were reluctant to dip into our pockets for more. To get any further down the road with PBS we had to guarantee the $3000 a show costs that APT would need to get it into the offers round. And it seemed highly likely that we would not find *any* sponsor prepared to advance that sort of money without a guarantee that their advert would get shown. We found ourselves in a Catch-22 situation, and after a great deal of effort trying to persuade potential sponsors to put up the proverbial something for nothing, we had to graciously withdraw the program from APT's offers round.

Once again we had hit a brick wall in trying to make TV by ourselves. PBS take a lot of BBC programs - and I guess the BBC, with all its resources, would be quite happy to guarantee the costs up front. And even if you are an independent TV producer trying to sell the North American rights of something you have already made for your local broadcaster, then the PBS system will, probably, work for you, because you've already been paid for making the program in the first place. But we couldn't find any way round the problem and once again had to concede defeat. But we did have one last card up our sleeve. Tourism.

Tourism to the rescue?

Cookucina is a cookery show, of course. But it's also a bit of a travelogue. We deliberately set out to showcase Le Marche, the region in which Sarnano and all the other places we filmed, are to be found. So we decided to try to see if we could get some sponsorship, or even just some help in finding a sponsor, from the Regional Tourist Board. First of all there's research to do. We found out the name of the relevant woman at the Board. And discovered she was giving a talk to local hotel and restaurant owners in a nearby town. So we booked ourselves in to see what she, and the Tourist Board, were like. The answer was not encouraging. We had gone along with a friend, Damien, who runs *Villa San Raffaello* a small holiday villa near us. You will remember Damien. He's the guy who came to dinner when Tam made her onion soup and gave it a somewhat improbable 8 out of 10. He's a veteran of these sort of meetings. But this one, he said, was worse than usual. The Italians are not very good at meetings. There will be 5 or 6 people on the stage and every one of them has to speak. Not just a few words either. It's as though they have to justify their position, their reason for being there. At length, with lots of thanks to mayors, and community leaders and everyone else on the stage. Then it's time for the main speaker (there were three of them on this occasion) who will have a completely incomprehensible Powerpoint presentation which is so minutely detailed that 90% of it is completely illegible. And despite Italian being the most mellifluous of languages, they generally manage to deliver it all in a dreary monotone. I know Carlo Conti is not like this, but after about an hour and a half of it, I could see the attraction of four girls in identical dresses jiggling about to loud music for about a minute and a half. It would break the monotony, for sure.

Damien is used to these sort of meetings, but he's also a bit hyperactive, with a short attention span. It was all we could do to keep him in his seat. I think it was only the fact that he would have had to climb over people that stopped him leaving. Finally, though, we were approaching the end. All Italian meetings seem to end in the same way - with everyone talking over everyone else. It was a bit of a scrum, but we managed to make an appointment to see her to discuss *Cookucina* and American TV. Perhaps there was light at the end of the tunnel.

Winter and Presepi

Back in the balmy days at the beginning of all this we had a Grand Plan. This series of six programs was to be the first of four. Shooting during Sergio and Lia's summer break from *Piatto Ricco* meant we were filming smack in the middle of August - a fact which was hard to ignore at the time. The produce we were cooking with was very much the food of summer. The countryside, too, was rich with the plump grasses and heavily laden trees of a Marchigiana summer. It would very different in the spring, when the hillsides are covered with emerging wild-flowers, or the Autumn which gives an excellent impression of Fall in New England with its extravagantly colored trees. In winter, of course, the countryside takes on an altogether different aspect, often gleaming white with fresh snowfall. And as you can imagine in a place that prides itself on the freshness of its produce, the food of each season varies accordingly. Four seasons, four series. A kitchen year in Le Marche. That was the plan - and it would not have been a bad one had we pulled it off.

Winter was to be next. And the centerpiece was going to be Sarnano's *Presepi Viventi. Presepi* are cribs and *Presepi Viventi* means living cribs. Each Christmas the narrow streets of the medieval *centro storico* of Sarnano are turned into a winding candle-lit path along which houses and *cantinas* open up to reveal biblical scenes from the Christmas story featuring children dressed in medieval clothing, with real donkeys, sheep, and cattle. Sometimes the manger itself will contain a real baby. It is a magical scene - especially when, as happened a couple of years back, the snow arrives. I like to think that Sarnano does it best, but it's a tradition in towns throughout Le Marche, and one that goes back a very long way.

About a two hour drive across the mountains from Sarnano will bring you to one of Italy's most sacred and wonderful places - the Basilica of Assisi. In the days shortly before the foundation of Sarnano itself, St. Francis came here often on his travels around Italy. The most celebrated account of his life was written by Ugolino Brunforte, the son of the feudal lord of the area round Sarnano. It was St Francis who created the first living crib just outside Assisi in 1223. It was he who decided to bring the traditional, painted, images of the Christmas story to life using real livestock. And that tradition has been kept alive in places like Sarnano for almost eight hundred years. We saw it as a spectacular climax to our second, winter, series of *Cookucina*. The American audience would have loved it. Or so Linda tells me.

I spoke to a Station Relations Manager once. While PBS still looked like a workable option. We had a useful chat, but she asked me the same question several times. One that the man from APT had also asked. They wanted to know if we had plans for another series. Yes we did, I told them. Maybe three more. But after I had put the phone down a light went on in my head because of something else the SRM had said. She was very keen to hear about the timescale for production of the next series *because it would be a lot easier to sell thirteen than six* (my italics). So that's why they were all so keen to know about our next round of shooting. They wanted to offer the stations thirteen episodes not six. That's because most of American TV is scheduled in 13 week segments. Offer them only 6 and they might be inclined to pass, since they would have to find a different series to fill the remaining seven weeks. I realized that if we were to have had any chance of take-up by the PBS stations we would have needed to promise them thirteen episodes not six. And, in the absence of any sponsors coming on board for the first six, who was going to pay for the next lot? We were already well out of pocket, and doing it all again in the winter, doubling the debt just on the off-chance the series would sell appealed to none of us. Perhaps we were well off out of *this* deal too.

Take a Message to Marta

We did eventually meet Marta, the woman in charge of tourism for the Le Marche Region. But not before the appointment had been shifted a couple of times in ways which did not seem particularly encouraging. We had convinced ourselves that she would have lots of money to spend, largely because a few years back they had hired Dustin Hoffman to make a video promoting the region. And he cannot have come cheap! You can see what they did at...

https://youtu.be/srHStR8HW_w

...nice as far as it goes, but weird that it's in Italian. Surely an ad with Dustin Hoffman is supposed to bring in *foreign* tourists? We were wrong about that. And about the money. All this year's money had been spent, they were expecting cutbacks soon and nothing could be done until after an upcoming election. Then there would be the summer holidays. And - Italian bureaucracy being what it is - the only way she would be able to help us at all, would be with EU money which we would have to spend first and invoice for later. But none of that could be *guaranteed* anyway. Maybe they had spent all the money on Mr Hoffman.

As we drove away, contemplating the fact that yet another door had closed, the penny finally dropped. It was time to do something else for a living!

Writing the Article

But what would that be? And it seemed a shame to let all that hard work, the fun, the mistakes, the sweltering kitchen, the hours spent locked in an edit suite with a hunter/killer, go to waste. What could we possibly do to make it all seem worthwhile?

"What about a book?" said Tam one day, after listening to my litany of wasted effort for the umpteenth time. "You've written enough television scripts, surely you could write a book."

I pointed out that books are complex things calling for a brain that can weave together multiple strands over hundreds of pages, while TV scripts.... come in short bursts... often... not even making.... grammatical sense.

"I haven't got the patience. Or the talent."

She was not impressed.

"You wrote that article, didn't you? You enjoyed that."

It's true. When David the "Distributor" was heading off to MIPCOM I naively thought we would be making news in the trade press in no time at all. So I wrote an article for **Broadcast**, the biggest TV trade paper in the UK. At least that's who I thought I was writing it for. After the sales started to pour in in Cannes I would be ready. I would have the article all done, finely honed and ready to go when the inevitable phone call came asking me to write a piece about how we made top-quality television on a shoestring. That was all eons ago, of course, and I hadn't looked at it in a long time. So I dug it out to see if it was still funny. I forgot to tell you that it was meant to be funny, and thought I had better warn you in advance, because now you can judge for yourself. Oh, and you'll recognize a couple of the stories you've come across in this book, because the article was where it all started. Here it is:

COOKUCINA
making TV in an oven

I gave it up ten years ago. Television, I mean. Well, strictly speaking I gave up making it and settled for the cosier option of telling other people what to do (and what they had done wrong, of course). But, like a moth to a flame, when the opportunity came to set up a small team to film an Italian cookery series in the medieval Italian hilltown that I now call home, I just couldn't resist.

Foolish man!

In the three weeks it took us to film COOKUCINA it all came flooding back — all the reasons I'd given it up in the first place. But this time in spades. To start with we'd decided to bypass the usual channels and make it ourselves with a view to selling via a distributor at MIPCOM. Fabulous I thought, no more compromises trying to satisfy the ever-changing demands of a commissioning editor desperately struggling to second-guess her (or his) boss. Yes, but the upside is that they tend to give you some money to actually make the thing, instead of which we were embarking on a let's-do-the-show-right-here-in-the-barn sort of journey.

262

Which is how I came to find myself being Producer, Sound Recordist, Translator, Lighting Technician, Hair and Make-Up Artist and Dog-Wrangler all at the same time. Not a happy mix, which became apparent on Day One as the cameraman (a.k.a driver, set designer and continuity "girl") started to move to follow the shot.

"Don't pull me," he barked/whispered. "You're pulling my cable."

"It's not me," I whispered/barked, aware that I should be telling myself to shush at the same time. "It's not me, it's the dog".

Somehow the spaghetti of audio cable that I had not yet learned how to master had become tangled up with the dog's lead, while the dog had set off in the other direction hopeful of eating some of the props. Suddenly I had become much more appreciative of the multi-tasking capabilities of the modern media studies graduate.

Oh and I forgot to mention that we were crammed into the corner of a small kitchen under lights which were never quite under my control, with the oven on full blast, water boiling on the hob and the outside temperature pushing 40 degrees. Trust me, when your time comes to have a go at a speculative cookery series – try to avoid doing it in a Mediterranean heatwave that has even the nut-brown locals searching their memories for a previous summer quite this hot. And here's another tip – don't try to work in two languages. One of our presenters spoke English (allegedly), the other only Italian. So everything had to be explained in two languages – which can sometimes lead to confusion. (NOTE: if insistent on making a bi-lingual show, try to be fluent in both languages) And when choosing your cameraman make sure he's got at least smattering of the language being spoken by the cook – editing can be oddly difficult when the camera is always pointing at the wrong thing.

But hey, that's just a minor part of the editing challenge, because not content with doing a cookery show on minimal resources in two languages, we thought we'd make it a language primer too. Just as well, because when the (Italian) cook got carried away none of us was entirely sure what she was talking about. The general idea was that our number one (English) presenter, who's being taught to cook by number two (Italian) would sort of translate "on the fly". The difficulty was that as soon as we got going it quickly became apparent that some of the Italian was a bit beyond her, and the translations were sometimes a bit, what shall we say... loose. And once the balsamic vinegar has gone into the marinaded wild boar and baby onions there's no way back. So it's very helpful in the edit to able to offer a few on-screen translations, and maybe correct a few minor errors. Otherwise there's a real danger that you might get two entirely different dishes depending which version of the instructions you were trying to follow.

The other thing about self-financing is, of course, that you'll be trying to cram too much into every day (instead of spinning it all out for as long as you can which is what all commissioning editors think all independent producers try to do all the time). And when you're handling continuity as well as lights and audio things can get a bit tricky. "No, no, this shot's in the orange dress, not the designer jeans!" And "No, you haven't got time to change – we've got to be at the fish farm by four".

Which is why one of our cooking sequences contains a shot of the star in a beautiful orange dress with her trousers round her ankles. But hey, this is television, and the trousers won't be in shot, so who's to know. At least I hope they won't be – we haven't started editing yet

Actually that was the least of our problems with Presenter Number One. She was new to TV. A real find I thought (I foolishly ignored the fact that she came with a dog). The schtick of the thing is that she can't cook and Presenter Number Two was going to teach her. But I had no idea just how completely useless she was in the kitchen. She seemed surprised that the vegetables were fresh. And that onions had layers. Then there was a panic when the tap only produced cold water – "turn the handle to the left", Presenter Number Two helpfully offered. Separating eggs was a disaster, when she plopped her yolk straight into Presenter Number Two's bowl of pristine whites. Sugar, on the other hand, missed the bowl altogether, and the idea of cleaning an anchovy made her physically sick (see Episode Two). But that wasn't the worst of it, because while she may have been useless in the kitchen, she simply lurrrvved food. Which became apparent early on when we began to notice the props disappearing. You see, if you're going to go to all the effort of making **torta di cioccolato fondente***, filming each stage of the process two or three times as you go along, it helps to have a nice complete tart at the end of it for your lovely packshot. When you pop out of the kitchen for a well-earned breath of fresh air and come back to find only three-quarters of a tart it can be a bit of a challenge for the cameraman.*

Mind you, that wasn't the only way the cameraman was challenged. Like me he's not in the first flush of youth – and we were working him very hard indeed, but after a while things seemed to be getting on top of him a bit. There was the pull-focus that turned out to be a bit of a TV first... a "pull-audio", because his hand had been on the wrong knob. I'm not complaining mind, the lack of sleep was mostly caused by his insistence on getting dawn shots as often as he could (though he never managed to convince me how they might get into a cookery show). But it's just as well that we were shooting the final sequence when he eventually managed to fall asleep on his camera while filming a firework display noisy enough to wake the dead. Fortunately the explosions, and a bit of local music track, should drown out the snoring.

Well, those are just the highlights, of course. There were all the usual difficulties – two walkie-talkies that always seemed to be in the same place, lights that just had to be two inches shorter than the sound recordist (that's me!) who was constantly banging his head, and a Number One Presenter who just didn't listen (Me: "Now, I'd like you to ask Damien, Francesca and Iolanda in that order, what they made of the soup. And... Action!" Presenter Number One: "Iolanda, what did you think of the soup?"). And, of course, the bells. There are seven churches in our little town and they must surely be holding a competition to see who can find the most inappropriate time to start clanging away for no apparent reason. Or maybe it's just a desperate rearguard action by Jamie Oliver, who's realizing his time is nearly up! I'm sure he's behind it – and the medieval drummers.

So I know what you want to ask now. Would you do it all again? Of course I would. We ate fabulous food all day every day for over a fortnight, even if sometimes at rather strange hours. We did it all just how we wanted, and when and where we wanted. We were shooting in one of the most beautiful places I have ever seen. We got to meet some truly wonderful people, and had a lot of fun while we were doing it. And who knows, we may just have found a new genre and be super-successful. I'll tell you what, though... the next series is going to be winter food — that's for sure.

Dead Horses and Nutella

Of course, the phone call never came. I never did get my double-page spread in Broadcast. And you'll have realized that by the end of the experience I wasn't *quite* so keen to embark on a second series. Let alone a third and fourth.

The article never saw the light of day - until now. If you get this far, I guess you'll know if it was funny or not. I hadn't read it for two years, so it felt like reading someone else's work. I laughed, and that's what gave me the inspiration to to try to work it up into a full length book. I'm still trying to figure out how to bind the two things together, though - TV and book - and turn it all into a multi-media entertainment center. But by the time you are reading this I must have solved it, at least to some extent.

I hope you've enjoyed the story of our attempt to overturn the Laws of Television Physics. We set out with hopes of creating a new Jamie Oliver-style empire, but looking back on it we were more of a challenge to Mr Bean. Nevertheless you'll have learned a bit about life here in rural Italy, and it may even have amused you with any luck. It will certainly have introduced you to some simple yet interesting new recipes.

Talking of recipes, I realize that there's still one I haven't shared with you. It's a *dolce,* and curiously it's a quintessentially Italian dish. Its posh (i.e. Italian) name is *semi-freddo alla crema di nocciola*, but I know it better as Nutella Ice-Cream Cake. Here in Italy they are simply nuts about Nutella (you see how easily these witty asides fall from my pen?). It wasn't until a very rich man called Michele Ferrero died in 2015 that I realized Nutella was an Italian product. Signor Ferrero's dad dreamed it up in the 1950s when he adapted a local *Piedmontese* recipe for a hazelnut/chocolate mix, making it spreadable by adding palm oil. It quickly became a firm favorite with Italian families.

By the 1960s its appeal had spread throughout Europe and the USA (you see, I did it again there!). So successful, in fact, is this single product that Ferrero's production accounts for 25% of the global production of hazelnuts. On 14 May 2014, the Italian Post Office issued a 50th anniversary Nutella commemorative stamp featuring a jar of Nutella on a golden background. There's even a World Nutella Day on February 5. When he died Signor Ferrero was officially the richest person in Italy, with a personal wealth of $26bn making him even richer than the arch manipulator, Silvio Berlusconi. In May 2014, as Signor Ferrero celebrated 50 years of Nutella, the Bloomberg Billionaires Index listed him as the 20th richest person in the world. I'd say all of that makes Nutella a pretty successful product.

A while back we invited an Italian friend, Adriano, over for the evening. He arrived, of course, with a gift of food. Often it's a tart, or some *cantuccini alla mandorla*, or something like that. But Adriano thinks big. And he likes Nutella. He arrived, courtesy of his son's girlfriend's mother who runs a *pasticceria* (this is all *so* Italian, isn't it?), with a **giant** *cornetto*, a croissant literally about a foot across. It was filled with Nutella - about a kilo of the stuff. It took us about 3 days to eat it, and both of us came out in spots.

So you can see that are big on Nutella in these parts, and it came as no surprise when Lia offered this up for Episode 5:

SEMI-FREDDO ALLA CREMA DI NOCCIOLA

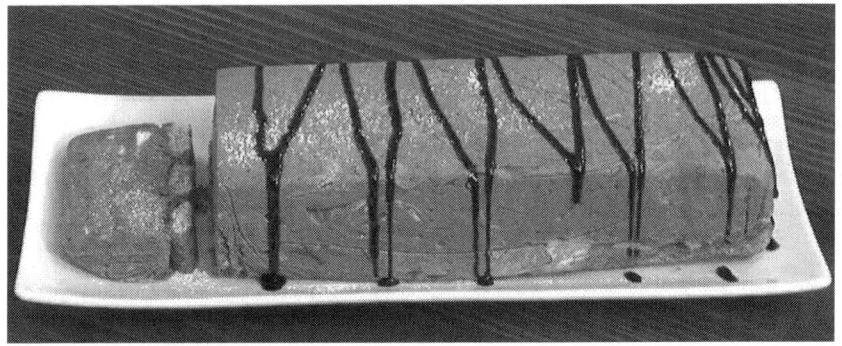

- 400g. Nutella
- 400g. whipped cream
- 4 savoy biscuits
- a cup of strong black coffee

Gently mix together the whipped cream and the hazelnut cream. Line a deep mold with clingfilm. Pour the mixture into the mold and smooth flat. Dip the biscuits briefly into the coffee, and cover the mixture with a single layer of biscuits. Place in the freezer for a minimum of 40 mins.

There's a lesson in all this somewhere. After Signor Ferrero dying with $26bn in the bank, after all our own ups and downs trying to make television on a virtually non-existent budget, the one thing that survives intact, is the food. It will outlast us all.

I'm off to the kitchen now. The summer sun is about to disappear behind the mountains, so I shall throw open the kitchen shutters to gaze out at the gentle pink glow settling on the rolling countryside. I might even enhance the experience with a glass of *prosecco,* or a crisp white *Verdicchio di Matelica.* And then I shall cook... well, what will it be tonight? *Tagliolini* with truffles? *Pasta Sibillini?* Or maybe Chicken with that delicious Route 77 beer. Rounding it all off with the *semi-freddo alla crema di nocciola?* Or maybe the Apple Cake with *Vino Cotto... Chissa?*

THE LAST WORD

A FINAL WORD on earthquakes. Since we shot Cookucina, and since I wrote this story, the earthquakes which struck the region in 2016 have changed the face of Le Marche somewhat. Sarnano itself suffered little damage, though our house has been ruled *inagibile* which means it's not safe to live in. Two of the local schools have been closed for the same reason. One of them has already been torn down and re-building started.

Gualdo, the nearest hilltop town (the one to which they were building a new road when they discovered the San Giacomo spring), fared much worse. Many houses collapsed and lessons in its only school now take place in a tent. Closer to the epicenter of the earthquakes, Norcia made international news because of the damage to its Basilica. Smaller towns like Visso, and Castelluccio (of lentils and *La Fioritura*) have suffered severe damage and may never be re-built. They are both in the *Valnerina*, the valley of the river Nera, along which runs the fault-line that causes these quakes. Caldarola, which featured in the story of the partigiani, has been evacuated and is now something of a ghost town. It sells itself as *terra dei castelli*, the land of castles. Goodness only knows what damage has been done to this exquisite heritage of more than a thousand years.

A ten minute drive from Sarnano, on the road up towards the mountains, a narrow road drops away to the left, winding down into a beautiful secluded valley overlooked by heavily-wooded mountains. At the end of the road there's a small meadow surrounded by woods. At the bottom of a small gorge hidden in the wood you can just make out the sound of a rushing stream. Ten centuries ago, this spot was chosen by Benedictine monks as the site of a new Abbey, the *Abbadia di San*

271

Biagio. For a thousand years it stood here, a place of peace and pilgrimage. At the end of October 2016, when the third earthquake struck, the Abbey's campanile, its bell tower, collapsed onto the nave. If this were the ONLY damage caused by the earthquakes the reconstruction and restoration would be a five-year project, with specialist architects and builders brought in from across Europe, and strenuous efforts made to find exactly the right materials to faithfully reconstruct the fallen tower. Art historians would be brought in, and expert conservators, to carry out the restoration of the damaged frescoes that adorn the abbey's interior. Infinite pains would be taken to ensure the abbey was restored as faithfully as possible. Books and magazine articles would probably be written chronicling the techniques and painstaking work for posterity.

Yet this is NOT the only building damaged. This extraordinary region has many thousands of such buildings. Not all are as old, or as sacred, of course, but the number of damaged abbeys and churches alone will run into hundreds. Of castles and palaces there are many, many more. Even the houses in the old medieval hill-towns are, many of them, precious historical jewels. Our own house, once home to nuns attached to the Abbey, has spectacular vaulted brick ceilings that are on the point of collapse. These earthquakes struck at the confluence of four different regions - Lazio, Abruzzo, Umbria and Le Marche. In Le Marche alone there are 90,000 buildings judged to have been damaged in some way. As I write, eight months have passed since the last of the big tremors, yet I do not believe that, even now, anyone has a true idea of the scale of work needed to put this area back together.

Seismologists will tell you that earthquakes never killed anybody. It's buildings that kill people. The land that shook so terribly in those dreadful few minutes last year is still there, 60 centimeters lower we are told, but still there. It's a strange feeling to be walking in the countryside looking at the spectacular Sibillini mountains and realizing that that whole vast mountain range moved and shook on that extraordinary day. Yet it is, of course, just as beautiful as ever. "Will you leave?" we are often asked. Not a chance. This breathtaking beauty is there *because* of the seismic activity of the whole Italian peninsular, not in spite of it. I am prepared to take the rough with the smooth - I wouldn't give up this lovely region for the world.

And neither should you. We're a little more battered than we were here in Le Marche, but there's more than enough beauty to go round in the built environment as well as the natural surroundings. Such is the wealth of architecture here that there are plenty of churches, museums, galleries, restaurants, even homes that remain untouched and waiting to be discovered. And the mountains, lakes, woods and rivers are eternal, shrugging off the *terremoti* like an irritating fly. Come and see for yourself, and help this lovely region to recover, help us to get back on our feet and to preserve this little-known Italian gem for visitors for a thousand years to come.

Stephen Phelps, Le Marche, Italy

June 2017

COOKUCINA TV SERIES

The TV series that accompanies this book is available online through Amazon Video Direct, Google Play and iTunes.

Amazon   http://amzn.eu/19rlEnz

Google Play   http://bit.ly/2sOlKme

iTunes   http://apple.co/2s5RAgo

Other Books By
STEPHEN PHELPS

The Tizard Mission: The Top-Secret Operation That Changed the Course of World War II

August 1940. Britain's finest hour, yet also the moment of her greatest vulnerability. After Dunkirk, and France had fallen, a Nazi invasion looked inevitable. Britain stood alone. Yet even as Britain reeled under the onslaught of the Battle of Britain, a secret mission designed to turn the tide of the war was getting underway. Led by scientist, airman and academic, Sir Henry Tizard, a team of scientists and engineers boarded a transatlantic liner carrying a box containing Britain's most valuable technological secrets. They were going to the United States. To give them away. **The Tizard Mission** tells the story of the giveaway that helped shape the modern world.

> *One of this book's many attractions is its emphasis on the importance of inter-relationships among social, political, and technical worlds in bringing ideas to reality.* [The Wall Street Journal]

> *An erudite, literate, and thoroughly absorbing piece of WWII history.* [American Library Association's Booklist]

Link: http://amzn.com/1594161631

Before I Forget: One Man's Radar War

A richly readable account of a young RAF serviceman's life during WW II.

> *This memoir is a very interesting account of World War II life, beautifully written by George Phelps and lovingly presented by his son, author Stephen Phelps. I particularly appreciated the absence of fluff and drama. Written as an account, a diary of sorts, it should be quite interesting reading for veterans and historians of World War II and those interested in the development of radar.* [Linda Ferreri]

Link: http://a.co/e4ABBdi

22924619R00160

Printed in Great Britain
by Amazon